PORTFOLIO/PENGUIN

Think BIG, Act SMALL

Jason Jennings is the bestselling author of four highly acclaimed leadership and management books—*Hit the Ground Running; Think Big, Act Small; Less Is More;* and *It's Not the Big That Eat the Small . . . It's the Fast That Eat the Slow. USA Today* called him one of the three most in-demand business speakers in the world. He and his family divide their time between Tiburon, California, and Timber Rock Shore in Michigan's northern peninsula.

Visit www.jason-jennings.com

Think BIG, Act

SMALL

How America's Best Performing Companies
Keep the Start-Up Spirit Alive

Jason Jennings

PORTFOLIO/PENGUIN

PORTFOLIO/PENGUIN
Published by the Penguin Group
Penguin Group (USA) Inc., 375 Hudson Street, New York, New York 10014, U.S.A.
Penguin Group (Canada), 90 Eglinton Avenue East, Suite 700, Toronto, Ontario, Canada
M4P 2Y3 (a division of Pearson Penguin Canada Inc.)
Penguin Books Ltd, 80 Strand, London WC2R 0RL, England
Penguin Ireland, 25 St Stephen's Green, Dublin 2, Ireland
(a division of Penguin Books Ltd)
Penguin Group (Australia), 250 Camberwell Road, Camberwell, Victoria 3124,
Australia (a division of Pearson Australia Group Pty Ltd)
Penguin Books India Pvt Ltd, 11 Community Centre, Panchsheel Park,
New Delhi – 110 017, India
Penguin Group (NZ), 67 Apollo Drive, Rosedale, Auckland 0632,
New Zealand (a division of Pearson New Zealand Ltd)
Penguin Books (South Africa) (Pty) Ltd, 24 Sturdee Avenue,
Rosebank, Johannesburg 2196, South Africa

Penguin Books Ltd, Registered Offices: 80 Strand, London WC2R 0RL, England

First published in the United States of America by Portfolio,
a member of Penguin Group (USA) Inc. 2005
This paperback edition with a new preface and chapter updates published 2012

3   5   7   9   10   8   6   4   2

Copyright © Jason Jennings, 2005, 2012
Preface copyright © Jason Jennings, 2012
All rights reserved

LIBRARY OF CONGRESS CATALOGING-IN-PUBLICATION DATA
Jennings, Jason.
Think big, act small : how America's best performing companies keep the start-up spirit
alive / Jason Jennings. — Rev. pbk. ed.
p. cm.
Includes index.
ISBN 978-1-59184-393-1
1. Success in business—United States. 2. Creative ability in business—United States.
3. Executive ability—United States. 4. Corporate culture—United States.
5. Organizational effectiveness. I. Title.
HF5386.J46 2012
658.4—dc23   2012010464

Printed in the United States of America
Designed by Helene Berinski

This book is dedicated to my mother and father,
Bill and Beverly Jennings,
for being great parents and wonderful friends.

CONTENTS

PREFACE TO THE PAPERBACK EDITION

In April 2010, I met with my publisher to discuss an idea I had for a book about reinvention. I had my fingers crossed, hoping he'd give it a green light.

We'd only been talking for a few minutes when he said, "I love it; let's do it." (It's titled *The Reinventors* and was published in 2012.) "But," he added, "there's something else we need to do, too. *Think BIG, Act Small* came out five years ago but still sells strongly online and in stores. How would you feel about updating and rereleasing it?"

I felt an immediate pump of adrenaline.

In 2003, my researchers and I set out on a two-year study to identify all the companies we could find who'd grown both revenues and profits organically by double digits every year for ten years without a miss. In the process, we uncovered breakthrough findings. The financial performance of the companies we identified placed them in the top one hundredth of a percent of all companies. Those companies were profiled in the 2005 hardcover edition of *Think BIG, Act Small*.

"What would you change about the book and how would you approach it?" he asked.

My mind started racing.

"I'd go back to all the original companies," I replied without missing a beat, "and dig for any changes that had taken place in the last five years and figure out if they'd managed to continue their growth."

As those words left my mouth, an anxious voice popped in to my head and warned, "You better look before you leap."

After twenty years of tracking high performing companies, I've become very aware that every success has an expiration date. High flyers can fall so fast it surprises everyone, and above average companies routinely slip to average or below in months instead of years. I've interviewed nearly five thousand entrepreneurs and executives during these last six chaotic years. The one message that I heard repeated over and over was how uncertain everyone has become. Ninety-eight percent of CEOs feel the clock is ticking and think that future success could elude them. Was I going to discover that my original *Think BIG, Act Small* heroes had stumbled and stalled?

If the companies we'd originally identified and written about had managed to keep their double-digit-growth streak alive through the Great Recession they would be—without question—the world's best at consistently growing revenues. Each would have achieved an unparalleled record of fifteen years of nonstop growth and weathered two recessions that had caused millions of other businesses to close their doors.

If the companies had continued their growth streaks, the book would become a must-read for every person in business. The findings would come close to constituting the Holy Grail for growth. But first, there were loads of questions to answer:

- Had the companies done the almost impossible and maintained their double-digit growth?
- There had been key personnel changes at some of the companies. When new people took charge, did things go off the rails?
- Had some of the companies fallen victim to the financial devastation that began in 2008?

You're about to learn what we discovered when we went back—five years later—and plotted the progress of those companies we'd previously identified as being the world's best at achieving continuous organic growth.

Initially, I intended to leave the original chapters intact and add a several-page update at the end of each. What seemed like a good idea turned out to be quite awkward; readers would have read only ancient history and the tales of business leaders who aren't around any longer before getting to the updated material. So, in the end, my head of research and chief thinker, Laurence Haughton, and I revisited all the chapters. You're reading a fully revised and updated book.

Study the lessons carefully and note their findings; make them your own and implement them in your company. I promise that you will experience revenue growth in your business like you could have previously only imagined.

Jason Jennings
Tiburon, California
October 2011

INTRODUCTION

The Holy Grail for Growth

You're about to learn the identities of a handful of companies whose consistent revenues and profit growth places them among the top one-hundredth of 1 percent of all American companies. Each organically increased revenues and profits by 10 percent or more for ten consecutive years between 1995 and 2005. At the time, they were among the best and most successful companies in the world. Here's why what these companies do is vitally important . . . to *you*.

Raising Revenues and Profits Isn't an Option

The bottom-line need of every business is constantly higher revenues and profits. Ambitious workers want to improve their lot in life and expect raises. Competitive spirits demand runs on the scoreboard. And investors and shareholders have insatiable appetites for constantly higher returns. Companies that aren't going forward are going backward!

Executives and managers who fail to consistently increase revenues and profits end up with their heads on a stick, and business owners who don't grow revenues end up with empty storefronts, deserted factories, and haunting memories of what could have been. Historically, business managers and owners have had three choices for constantly improving the financial performance of their business.

Increase Revenues

It's easy to increase revenues when the economy is in terrific shape, the competition isn't paying attention, and people are knocking down your door to buy what you sell. Unfortunately, those days are over. Economies everywhere are fragile. Everyone has more and better competition than ever before (and that won't change) and nobody absolutely needs anybody; everyone has plenty of alternatives. Today business managers and owners are forced to constantly increase revenues in the most challenging environment that has ever existed. The problem is that the tactics used by most owners and managers to grow revenues are tired reruns of old conventional wisdom.

"Haul the sales staff in here!" bellows the boss. "I'll give them the 'Come-to-Jesus' routine and fire them up."

Regrettably, the result of rallying the troops is always short-lived.

Enter the recent MBA graduate, bursting with ideas. "Maybe increasing sales commissions for brand-new businesses and lowering them for existing customers is the answer," he muses. "In one case we studied during my semester abroad, a Mongolian company did that and increased its sales of yak jackets by twenty percent."

Unsurprisingly, changing incentives and playing with people's paychecks and livelihoods seldom have a positive effect on morale.

"I have an idea," pipes up an assistant brand manager. "Let's add some jalapeño flavoring to our Super Crunchy Rice Flakes, call them Olé! Olé! Olé and have the sales staff introduce the product wearing sombreros!"

Sorry to be the bearer of bad news, but 96 percent of brand extensions fail—and the failure rate is probably higher for last-gasp measures.

"What we really need," laments the old-timer who has been around the block more times than a septuagenarian streetwalker, "is to find some low-hanging fruit, some real easy business." Hoping against hope, he adds a wistful, "It's got to be out there in some place we've never looked before."

Alas, competition is tougher than it's ever been. What to do when all the low-hanging fruit has been picked?

Invariably, the same old tactics for increasing revenues bring the same old results. More often than not, companies end up failing to achieve their revenue growth objectives and so resort to quick fixes to demonstrate short-term profit growth.

Cut Costs

A second way to improve a company's financial performance is usually the most unpopular option for your employees: cut costs. Cut cut cut. Layoffs, shutdowns, contractions, and asset sales are employed in order to improve short-term profits. All of these moves, of course, come back to bite these companies on their backsides. Reducing, snipping, and nonstop rounds of cutting do nothing to jump-start or grow revenues. Downsizings and layoffs frequently become as addictive as street drugs, and the companies that abuse them end up emaciated shadows of their former selves.

Or, Cook the Books

When companies fail to increase their sales and find their bag of cost-cutting tricks empty, many resort to playing loose with the truth. Of the 1,200 publicly traded companies forced to restate their operating results for 2003 under the Sarbanes-Oxley Act, *every single company* had to adjust their revenues and/or profits downward. They had all claimed that their revenues or profits were higher than they actually were. Not a single company had *understated* revenues or profits.

What We Found

So what do you do if the three common ways of posting financial health are close to defunct? We went on a hunt for answers. My team of researchers and I evaluated and studied every publicly traded company (about twenty thousand of them) in the world as well as more than fifty thousand of the largest privately owned companies in the United States in order to find the companies that do the best job of consistently increasing revenues and profits. (You'll find a narrative describing our complete research methodology in Section 5.) We reasoned quite simply that if we could identify the companies that do the world's best job of consistently increasing revenues and profits, there'd be valuable lessons to learn. So we traveled the nation; got inside every company we'd identified; and interviewed, studied, observed in action, and got to know the people who lead America's best performing companies. We were hardly disappointed.

We discovered that none of these top companies embrace tired old tactics for growing revenues, cutting costs, and exaggerating their operating results. Instead, they have figured out how to consistently increase revenues and profits without using manipulation or gimmickry. They don't recycle the same old stuff that has a history of either being marginally effective or simply not working. In the process, each of these top performing companies has turned conventional wisdom upside down.

America's Best-Performing Companies

Here they are, the companies we identified as having increased revenues and profits by 10 percent or more each year for ten years or longer. Their identities may surprise you. Their CEOs may surprise you. Their locations may surprise you. Even where they're *not* located may surprise you. We think this group of companies is on to something that may change the very face of how companies drive revenue and profit.

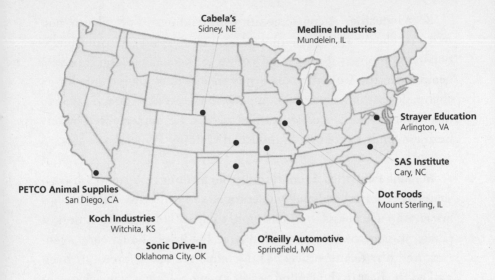

Cabela's Headquartered in a small town of a few thousand people on the western plains of Nebraska, Cabela's has built a sporting and outdoor goods empire that mails out more than 120 million catalogs annually, making it the largest direct marketer in the United States. By tossing out the traditional retail rulebook, its large-format destination retail stores, filled with waterfalls, mountains, aquariums, and exotic-game trophies, are among the top tourist attractions in its states. Cabela's has institutionalized doing something that most companies can't or won't do, and it's the thing that prevents most businesses from ever achieving their full economic potential.

Dot Foods Who could have guessed that a young couple with twelve children would mortgage the house, ramble around Illinois and Missouri delivering dry dairy goods out of the back of their family station wagon, and that their children would invent a brand-new business that would revolutionize the way food is distributed, eventually becoming the largest food service redistributor in the United States? The same things Dot Foods did to revolutionize the food distribution business can be applied to hosts of other industry categories.

Koch Industries A conglomerate with holdings in petroleum, natural gas, chemicals, fibers, minerals, ranching, and securities might not sound too sexy. But when it comes to the second-largest private company in the United States, which has created more value for its shareholders than any other company in the world, you'd do well to take notice. Koch's secrets in this task can be implemented by any business ready to commit to the Koch Guiding Principles.

Medline Industries From humble beginnings as a small Chicago shop where a husband-and-wife team sewed uniforms, Medline has grown into a business that sells more than 100,000 products to hospitals, surgery centers, extended-care facilities, home-care agencies, and physicians' offices. This company's sales force has been ranked the best in the United States and you'll know why when you learn how it operates and how it compensates.

O'Reilly Automotive Most seventy-two-year-old businessmen sent out to pasture at the directive of a know-it-all young consultant would hang it up. Instead, Charles F. O'Reilly and his son "Chub" O'Reilly decided that the best way to even the score was to open a competing store selling aftermarket automotive tools, professional service equipment, and accessories. Today the company's 3,600 stores generate almost $7 billion in annual sales and for the past decade they've achieved average operating income growth of more than 30 percent a year.

PETCO Animal Supplies By picking its competitors wisely, PETCO has become the leading specialty retailer of premium pet food, supplies, and services, and sells more than ten thousand high quality pet products in its stores and online. Besides selling pet supplies, PETCO offers grooming, obedience training, vaccination clinics, and even sponsors an online pet adoption center.

SAS Institute The world's largest privately held software company achieved a string of twenty-five years of more than 10 percent annual revenue growth. The company is frequently lauded in surveys of the best places to work in America. The leaders at SAS do something most CEOs and managers refuse to do—and it's why they grow during good times and bad.

Sonic Drive-In Want chocolate syrup on your fries? You got it says Sonic, America's largest chain of quick-service drive-ins (more than three thousand five hundred restaurants in forty-four states) where every order is completely customizable, completely *your own*. The company has grown from a single root beer stand in Shawnee, Oklahoma, and differentiates itself by using a model whereby virtually every employee, including the carhops, has a financial stake in the success of the business.

Strayer Education Founded in 1892, Strayer educates more than sixty thousand working adults on its thirty campuses and through Strayer Online. It purposely chose to grow slowly, in order to preserve the highest educational quality and protect its brand, yet the company's consistent financial performance is still stellar and has become the model for education-oriented companies.

A Common Thread

One day as I was nearing completion of my research, I was conducting a follow-up interview with Pattye Moore, former president of Sonic Drive-In. The interview was almost over but I had one final question.

"What's the magic," I asked, "that's allowed Sonic to raise its revenues and profits by double digits every year?"

"That's an easy one," she answered without hesitation. "We think *big* but we act small. When big companies start *acting big*, they get in trouble."

Those few words absolutely nailed what we'd found inside every company in this book. Each one thinks *big* but acts small.

Right after talking with Pattye Moore, my researchers and I

sent e-mails out to all the companies we were writing about. We
told them that we finally had a title for the book. Then something
surprising happened. Most of the companies began e-mailing us
with copies of old company memos, speeches, and articles. As I
read them it was hard not to smile. The leaders of almost all the
companies in the book had been using the phrase "think *big*—act
small" for years. And so we had a title for our new book.

What's Here for You

Our findings genuinely surprised us. We didn't discover any
mind-bending tactics or top-secret methods that enabled these companies to grow their revenues consistently. Instead, because each
has nailed the *fundamentals* better than all other companies, their
dramatic and consistent growth occurs naturally, even organically.

In the following pages, you'll learn the ten Building Blocks
these companies use to grow their revenues and profits every year
and distinguish themselves as being America's very best.

Each Building Block reveals one of the truths we discovered,
introduces one of the companies, briefly tells its story and shows
how the Building Block is applied at the other companies we researched. The Building Blocks we present would be no less valid
if they weren't practiced by every company, but surprisingly, in
almost every instance, everything we found is a way of life at all
the companies.

Just Common Sense?

At some point during your reading you might be tempted to say to
yourself, "Well, that's only simple common sense." When so tempted,
I'd urge you to recall a few unforgettable words shared with me several years ago in Asia.

I had just finished giving a speech in Hong Kong when I was
approached by an elderly Chinese lady. "I enjoyed your speech very
much," she said to me. "The things you said were really just simple
common sense."

I took it as a backhanded compliment, if a compliment at all. Seeing the crestfallen look on my face, she looked up, smiled, and quietly added, "Remember, the most common thing about common sense is how uncommon it is."

If you're ready to learn the ten Building Blocks that promise to help you increase your company's revenues and profits every year, it's time to start reading—and discovering.

SECTION ONE

Think Big

In the Beginning

Imagine what a dismal place the planet would be if no one had ever had a big idea. We'd still be naked savages communicating with grunts and groans, seeking shelter under upended tree roots and scavenging for scraps of food.

Thankfully, one of our ancestors thought big and wrapped himself in animal skins to ward off the elements; another thought big and constructed a primitive shelter; still another thought big and decided to stay put and cultivate a crop rather than roam and forage with the seasons.

Millions of years later Ralph Lauren thought big, stitched a logo on those animal skins, and founded Polo, a fashion empire with $6 billion in annual reveneus. William Levitt thought big, founded Levittown (inventing the suburb in the process), eventually building 35,000 small, detached, single-family shelters and netting a $60-million fortune (when $60 million meant something). And way back in 1867, Alva Kinney thought big and began selling the bounties of the field in the form of bags of flour, and ConAgra, a company with $12 billion in annual revenues today, was born.

Thinking big has been responsible for every advance, every development, and every successful business known to man. There were big thinkers behind rocket ships, skyscrapers, computers, assembly lines, fast-food hamburgers, and every leap forward in medical science. Along the way, the marketplace has handsomely rewarded many big thinkers. Bill Gates, Warren Buffett, and Sam Walton all defied conventional wisdom, thought big, significantly changed the world, and amassed fortunes worth tens of billions of dollars in the process.

No Shortage of Big Thinking

Each year millions of businesses are founded worldwide. Sometimes it's an individual going solo in a home office. In other instances it's friends and partners pooling resources to pursue a dream. And other times it's the launch of a manufacturing or service facility designed to employ thousands. In the case of every new business there are two certainties: there was some big thinking behind the decision to make the leap, and not a single business was created with the intention of failing. Unfortunately, judging from business mortality rates, just thinking big does little to ensure a business's success.

A Conundrum

Each year the United States records more than sixty thousand business bankruptcies. Each year the dreams of hundreds of thousands of sole proprietors are dashed. In the past decade more than one thousand big companies, famous titans that had seemingly withstood the test of time—with names like United Airlines, Kmart, WorldCom, Enron, PG&E, Conseco, Lehman Brothers, Washington Mutual, and CIT Group—ended up in bankruptcy court. Many widely quoted studies conclude that four of every five new businesses fail within the first five years of their existence. A recent University of Texas study argues that 98 percent of small companies disintegrate within eleven years. Is seriously flawed big thinking responsible for such miserable performances and track records or is there another missing ingredient?

Four Types of Thinking and Acting

Evidence of thinking big is present in every successful human enterprise. But big thinking without proper execution inevitably results in failure. There are four types of thinking and acting (executing) available to every leader and company. We found that companies that excel at achieving consistent, long-term financial performance all fall into only *one* of these four possible categories.

Think Small, Act Small The enterprises that fall into this category are either small mom-and-pop businesses, companies where the sole ambition is to provide a living wage to the owner(s), or enterprises desperately trying to hold on to a vestige of a better past. They're unwilling to invest in their businesses, and either because of necessity or a basic character flaw, they're notoriously cheap.

Unless their market niche requires an unusually high degree of skill, or there's a dearth of competition, these operators disappear when the management retires or dies or when customers abandon them in favor of enterprises with more compelling offerings.

The sole exception to the previous description is people who have intentionally chosen to think small and act small because they believe that all business is inherently evil. These people typically opt to reside deep in the woods in cabins without utilities where they weave macramé, string brightly colored beads, and cast candles in sand molds for sale at art fairs and protest festivals.

People who think and act small are generally not dangerous to anything but their own enterprises.

Think Small, Act Big Because they infrequently have original ideas, this type contents itself with exaggerating past accomplishments and providing unsolicited opinions to others about how to run their businesses.

You'll find them pontificating on the evils of Wal-Mart and how it destroyed Main Street every time there's a breakfast meeting of the chamber of commerce featuring free Krispy Kremes. Even though their own businesses never achieve their full economic potential, that doesn't get in the way of their overinflated views of their accomplishments.

Unless their advice is taken seriously, people who think small and act big generally aren't serious competitors in any given marketplace, but their nonstop bravado can be tiring.

Think Big, Act Big Everyone is familiar with this type, whether it's located in Clinton, Mississippi, or on Madison Avenue. Armed with a delicious big idea, they start out on a promising track—and then something happens that sends them over to the dark side.

First there are the sizzling suites of offices filled with snappy young execs, phalanxes of kowtowing assistants, and an increasingly bloated hierarchy. There's more swagger than walk, and eventually strategy is trumped by arrogance. Later it's almost always discovered that revenues had been artificially pumped up, profits overstated, share prices manipulated, and treasuries looted.

People who think big and act big are dangerous to workers (they'll probably lose their jobs when the big cheese begins announcing layoffs designed to protect his backside), vendors (who may not get paid without the approval of bankruptcy court), and shareholders (whose investments may very well disappear in smoke).

Think Big, Act Small (Sigh of relief.) These are the people and companies who *get it right*. Their consistent long-term financial performance distinguishes them. Their big thinking is based on authentic big ideas, genuinely solving customers' problems, making something better, or creating value.

These people don't use the company as their personal exchequer. Rather than allowing success to go to their heads, they remain humble. They continue to work closely with customers and understand that the organization won't have a long-term future unless short-term objectives are achieved.

They're ready to let go of what is no longer working; get everyone to think and act like owners; and constantly invent new businesses, providing customers with win-win solutions. They carefully select their competition, work tirelessly to build communities of raving fans, and their biggest thrill is identifying and helping build future leaders.

People and companies who think big and act small are good for workers; vendors and suppliers; and shareholders and community.

Go Ahead . . . Think Big

Go ahead and think *big!* But when it comes to executing your ideas, follow the principles of thinking big and acting small as practiced by the companies who grow their customer count and satisfaction, revenues, and profits, year after year in good times and bad.

The Building Blocks

Down to Earth

The people who lead the American companies that do the best job of consistently growing revenues aren't celebrities and don't seek fame. In fact, much like the first time you heard your recorded voice played back and wondered why it sounded so strange, most of these people will find it awkward to see their names in print.

By the time we'd whittled our list of companies from seventy-two thousand candidates to the nine most consistently profitable businesses we'd be studying and writing about, we were convinced that each CEO and company would be rightfully proud they'd been chosen and more than pleased to cooperate with us. Instead, as you can read in more detail in the research section, getting inside each of these companies was like pulling teeth . . . only worse.

As someone who is constantly besieged by CEOs and PR people asking, "How can I get my company in one of your books," I scratched my head and wondered, "Why wouldn't companies that had accomplished so much want their achievements known?"

Eventually, as we spent time with and got to know the leaders of this remarkable group of companies, the answer became unmistakably clear. There's little doubt that part of their reluctance to open themselves and their companies to us was their desire to remain secretive, but it wasn't their primary reason for not wanting to meet with us. None of these company's leaders has any interest in being portrayed as a celebrity CEO. The very thought is anathema to them.

You won't find a single slick, overconfident, swashbuckling sales type leading any of the companies that do the best job of consistently increasing revenues. In fact, you'll find just the opposite: very humble people leading and managing equally humble enterprises.

Just a Regular Guy (Gal)

As we crisscrossed the nation, meeting and interviewing the people who lead the companies we'd eventually write about, we were continually struck by the down-to-earth nature of every one of them. As we'd complete each daylong CEO interview we'd invariably wait until we were out of sight and earshot, then grin and say, "Can you believe it . . . no pretense . . . just another regular person?" Each of the leaders we encountered was more modest than the previous. Because of the humble nature of these people, they had been keeping their compelling stories much to themselves for years. What we found was a treasure trove.

Even after we'd spent hours getting to know each other and discussing his company, the moment the discussion turned to him as an individual, each CEO became noticeably uncomfortable. Typical of our interviews is the following exchange taken verbatim from our interview transcript with Robert Silberman, CEO of Strayer Education.

> **JASON JENNINGS:** Finally, talk to me about you. Tell us your story, just so I—
> **ROBERT SILBERMAN:** It's not really that important, frankly—
> **JJ:** I know, but just take us through it. "I was born in—"
> **RS:** Well, most important, for me, this really ought to be about the business model—
> **JJ:** And it will be—

RS: And what we're trying to accomplish—

JJ: I just need a little bit of background stuff—

RS: Because most of what I see in this kind of journalism really is bullshit. And I think—

JJ: I agree. But I also happen to know that you read my last book and used it and didn't think it was BS.

RS: That's true.

JJ: So, a little about you please—

RS: It's just that I find that the focus on CEOs is—

JJ: Listen, you have my commitment; the book's not about you, I just need a little flavor. I need to let the readers know that somehow we touched the souls of the people we're writing about—

RS: OK, I was briefly a naval officer . . .

Nobody was anxious to share their personal story because no one believed there was a story to be told. They maintained that the real story was the company and that their personal contribution(s) in founding or leading it was of little importance.

We kept waiting to bump into our first larger-than-life, perfectly coiffed, *trumped* up caricature of a CEO ready to captivate us with tales of his personal and professional conquests. It never happened and we constantly found ourselves searching for new words to describe the absolute genuineness and self-effacing personalities of the people we encountered.

After each interview, we'd end up discussing the same subject: what was the magic that allowed these companies to be the top revenue performers in the nation? And we always ended up with the same conclusion: the unassuming nature of the people who head these companies is central to the enterprise's ability to consistently grow revenues. Egos are just not relevant at these companies. The people who lead the businesses get a strong psychic reward from the success of their enterprises and their contributions in guiding them in ways that less successful, less humble, CEOs can only envy.

Humble People Build Humble Cultures

The first requirement of effective leadership is making a realistic assessment of the people and resources being led and determining an agenda for the group. When an enterprise is headed by a cocky, publicity-seeking egoist, the agenda has already been determined, and eventually the company will come to resemble the leader and take on his psychological and physical traits. But when an organization is headed by someone who does not have the need to constantly trumpet his own importance and is of modest pretensions and dimensions, the organization and its agenda will come to look a lot like him.

Each of these organizations takes on its own characteristics and culture, reflective but also independent of the founder/CEO/leader; the culture becomes bigger than any one individual. In our research and interviews, we found that every company that does the best job of consistently growing revenues is at its core a humble organization.

Seven Attributes

During our research we identified seven traits shared by the leaders and the organizations they'd built or led that we deemed noteworthy. Here's our take on the seven main attributes of humbleness we found at the companies profiled.

```
Stewardship
Transparency
Accessibility
Low-Key Demeanor
Work Ethic
Stand for Something
No Superficial Distinctions
```

1. Stewardship

In CEO Robert Silberman's 2003 letter to Strayer's shareholders, we found something that best describes the attitudes shared by each of the CEOs toward the enterprise they lead. "I would be remiss," he wrote "if I didn't express, on behalf of the entire Strayer management team, how fortunate we consider ourselves. We are truly grateful for the opportunity to be the *stewards* of your capital in an enterprise which creates so much value, opportunity, and unalloyed joy for our students."

Each of the people leading the companies we wrote about here sees her role not as a swashbuckling soldier whipping the corporate steed on to new conquests, but as a steward entrusted with the responsibility of carefully and judiciously shepherding and guiding the organization. It's a responsibility she takes very seriously, much like a religious vow.

When we asked David O'Reilly, former CEO of O'Reilly Automotive, a publicly traded company with more than three thousand six hundred locations, why he has stayed with the company for his entire career, he provided further insight into the minds of these leaders. "First, it's about responsibility," he said. "I always feel responsible for the company and everyone in it."

Good stewards share an attitude about personal wealth and money that is often surprising to people who are cynical about anything having to do with business: it's simply not about the accumulation of vast personal wealth for the people who head these enterprises.

"It was never about the money," O'Reilly contends. "Of course we all wanted to earn a good living and take care of our families; that's simply a result of hard work, but it's certainly not why we built the company." He continued the discussion by saying, "My dad, my sister and brothers, and I are very competitive and we wanted to accomplish building an enduring enterprise. We really wanted to make our mark and achieve something. We were driven to be bigger and better than we were the day or year before."

Another steward of a company who saw money as a secondary

benefit was Ron Bailey, former professor and eventual president of Strayer University. When Bailey sold his shares in the university for $200 million, he paid his taxes and began the Bailey Family Foundation, funded with the remaining $150 million. Bailey's foundation, not surprisingly, is in the business of granting scholarships. As Bailey says, "What the heck else was I going to do with the money? I'd made it in education. The obvious thing to do was give it back."

Less than 250 miles from the Missouri offices of O'Reilly Automotive are the Illinois headquarters of Dot Foods, the nation's largest privately owned food redistribution business. Founded by Bob and Dorothy Tracy, using the family station wagon to deliver dried milk products to ice cream factories, the company was headed by CEO Pat Tracy, one of eight children of the founders working for the company during our initial research. A story Tracy told us speaks loudly to the institutional humility of the company.

"Mom and Dad always lived in a small brick house where they raised all their twelve kids," he says, "and right next door to their house is a modest building we call The Country Store." Tracy explains that the store sells products nearing their shelf life expiration and those that have been dented or whose outer casing has been damaged. "One day," he says, "my mother told me, 'Pat, I used to go next door and buy those half chickens that are perfect for your father and me, but the price has gone up so far that I don't buy them anymore.' And she wanted to know why there'd been a price increase." Tracy explained to her that she owned the store and could well afford to pay the small increase, to which she responded, "Oh no, I couldn't possibly do that."

Collectively the leaders and owners of these companies are worth billions of dollars. But we couldn't find one palatial estate (we went looking); we didn't witness a single instance of conspicuous consumption; and never saw personal wealth flaunted.

The people who founded and/or now lead these nine companies want the same things everyone wants: a nice home, a good living, financial security for their families, and the opportunity to be in charge of their own destinies and make the world a better place. In the truest sense, they are stewards.

2. Transparency

While we were in San Diego with PETCO chairman[*] Brian Devine, he brought up the subject of transparency when he told us, "You have to tell the horror stories to everyone. Everyone must know the bad stuff so it doesn't happen again.

"Twenty-seven years ago," he recalled, "I lost a key ally due to a miscommunication and promised myself there'd never be a miscommunication again. Until an organization is transparent, where it's all out there for everyone to see, miscommunications are inevitable."

As we stood by the bank of elevators waiting to leave Sonic Drive-In's home office in Oklahoma City, my lead researcher turned to me and said, "Check out the CEO's office space." I turned and looked at Cliff Hudson's office area and the small, walled-in, glass-paneled conference area behind it that we'd used for our interview. Brian said, "Even this guy's private meeting area is transparent—everything's out in the open."

As we continued our study of each of our top nine companies, it appeared that all were just as transparent as Cliff Hudson's office and Brian Devine's steadfast belief.

The takeaway here is remarkable. We have found business societies where all the knowledge and information (the currency) is available to everyone. In these companies, because there's zero personal profit or gain to be achieved in hoarding, trading, or trying to passionately protect knowledge, everyone in the company has access to the same knowledge and information. The people in these firms are free to spend all their working time advancing and achieving the collective goals of the organization instead of worrying about engaging in commerce with their currency, trying to bolster their personal survival and advancement.

---

[*] In March 2004 Jim Myers became CEO and Brian Devine remains an executive management member and executive chairman of the board of directors.

It is truly a measure of one's humility and selflessness to be able to offer up all the lucre with a generous, "Here it is for everyone to use and share." Only when the hoarding of knowledge and information is stopped and everyone can see clearly through the organization will genuine collegiality commence. Humble leaders have sufficient confidence in themselves and the value they bring their organizations that they see the benefit of having the complete organization be transparent.

3. Accessibility

Collectively, the people who lead these companies generate almost $150 billion in annual sales and employ more than 250,000 people. Running enterprises that large entails a lot of responsibility. Conventional wisdom suggests these are very busy people whose time is extremely valuable and must be parceled out parsimoniously. In fact, it turns out that another testament to the humility of the people running these organizations is their accessibility. We concluded our research having rejected the cynical hypothesis that their accessibility is merely a good business tactic; concluding instead that it's part of their DNA. When people don't believe that they or the work they do are more special or important than everyone else in the company, the need to hide out in a corner office protected by layers of assistants is unnecessary.

Once we'd settled into the hotel where we'd be staying in Mount Sterling, Illinois, while conducting interviews at Dot Foods, I began leafing through the local telephone directory. By accident I quickly located the listed home telephone number for then-company CEO, Pat Tracy. How many CEOs of almost $4-billion enterprises do you know with a listed telephone number? If you agree that having a listed home telephone number is a fair metaphor for accessibility, then we'd stumbled on to an accessible bunch of leaders; it turns out that most of these people have listed home telephone numbers. They aren't afraid that a worker or customer might disturb them at home. Compare their conduct with the decision of most executives to build impenetrable walls to separate and protect themselves from workers, customers, and stakeholders.

Although Robert Silberman runs an educational institution with almost sixty thousand students, he continues to teach management studies. He didn't understand our surprise and maintained that it's simply common sense. "How else could I better stay in touch with my students and faculty than teaching and being close to them?" he wondered aloud.

The home offices of SAS, located in Cary, North Carolina, look more like a bucolic university campus than any commercial enterprise you'll ever see. When strolling the grounds you pass manicured athletic fields, physical fitness facilities, a health-care center, a high school, day-care facilities, stunning buildings, sculptures, and the university president's house. Oops, you almost forget you're not on a university campus in front of the president's house, you're standing in front of CEO Jim Goodnight's home. A stone's throw away is the residence of Goodnight's cofounder, John Sall. The men who founded and built an enterprise that experienced double-digit growth for twenty-five consecutive years are so accessible they've chosen to live in full view of the six thousand people who work at SAS headquarters. How many billionaire CEOs do you know who've chosen to live on the factory grounds?

During our company visits, one of our standard requests was for a walking tour of the facilities. To prevent any possibility—there's the cynic again—of these events' being staged or orchestrated we always made our request at the last minute. Walking the hallways, factory floors, and company lunchrooms with these leaders was always interesting. Warm, affectionate, first-name greetings, often accompanied by gentle ribbing and teasing, were the norm. We could have been the IRS, a couple of software salesmen, or prospective customers and it wouldn't have mattered. Workers had no hesitation to approach the boss and say, "Hey, Pat, gotta tell you that new equipment is a piece of junk. It keeps breaking down all the time. Save yourself some money and us some aggravation next time." It was always hard to suppress a smile and imagine such an interchange taking place between traditional and imperious CEOs and their workers. It either wouldn't happen or the worker would have signed his own death warrant.

4. Low-Key Demeanor

Perhaps the best way to describe the outward bearing of the leaders is to relate a story about the frequent frustration of the people responsible for transcribing this project's interviews.

Having experienced firsthand the utter frustration of discovering, after an interview, that there'd been a technical glitch and a tape was blank, I decided we'd always use two digital recorders for the project. Hoping that redundancy would prevent encountering any problems, we were surprised that the people transcribing the tapes were still running into problems. The beginnings of sentences were being lost.

It took some time, but eventually we discovered the source of the problem. Both devices were voice activated, and several of the CEO's spoke so gently, taking frequent and lengthy pauses to consider their words before they spoke, that both machines would shut themselves off and require a few seconds to begin recording after they started speaking again. There wasn't a fast-talking motor-mouth in the bunch. These were just your regular, unassuming, soccer-coaching, church-going, have-a-beer-at-the-golf-course kind of folks.

Even the physical movements of these leaders were fascinating to observe. While one would expect that navy veteran Robert Silberman, CEO of Strayer University, would have the carriage of a former military officer, all the CEOs shared the same posture—erect and determined yet natural. Each moved easily and gracefully but in a way that wholeheartedly hinted at their confidence and certainty.

Many CEOs and executives surround themselves with "yes-folk" who defer to their every whim and opinion, but that isn't what we observed during our scores of visits to the companies we studied. There's a big difference between deference and genuine respect;

what we witnessed was a warm spirit of collegiality, with everyone on a first-name basis and an atmosphere that spoke more of trust for the leader than misplaced deference.

5. Work Ethic

Charles Koch of Koch Industries is one of the world's twenty wealthiest individuals. With his $25 billion fortune he can do whatever he wants to do. And he does. Koch and his wife live in Wichita, Kansas. He has a long workday, eats lunch every day in the company cafeteria, and says he can't imagine doing anything else.

"I love what I do," says Koch. "It turns me on and makes me happy."

When we asked for further explanation, Koch says, "It's hard for me even to answer that, because it's a given. I get to work with great people, see them grow and develop, see the company create value, and get to reward people who contribute to our success. Instead of asking why I do what I do, the question should be why *not*?"

The more we questioned Koch—a man who could theoretically spend $1 billion annually on himself for the rest of his life, without ever touching the principal—about his motivation for continuing to work long, hard, challenging days to build the company, the more fervent he became. "If you spend your life striving to profit by creating real value for customers and society, you are in fact making people's lives better, and when we do that it makes the world a better place." Koch concluded by adding, "We've built a win-win enterprise. What would I want to do with my life, if not that?"

6. Stand for Something

In recent years, many businesses have clamored to create a published set of corporate values of guiding principles. In fact, it became a management fad to do so. In many instances the guiding principles are the result of a weekend team-building exercise held at a lakeside cabin with cases of beer and box wine as lubricants for the words.

Once completed, the document is posted on a few walls, published in the employee handbook, and referenced by the boss during the annual employee recognition dinner. For most firms, other than those occasional uses, the document doesn't mean squat. A good case in point is Enron's "code of ethics," which decreed the moral and honest manner in which the company would conduct its business. Ken Lay's document, from July 2000, is now collecting dust in the Smithsonian.

In stark contrast, each of the individuals who head these companies possesses a fundamental set of truths and laws by which he leads his life and which in turn becomes the basis of reasoning and action within the organization he leads. It's only when a set of beliefs is practiced by everyone from the top to the bottom of the organization that it has any meaning.

We found one of the most effective, institutionalized uses of a set of guiding principles at Koch Industries. The principles by which Charles Koch leads the organization come from his view of the world and the way he thinks it ought to be. If you want to work for Koch Industries and be part of helping him change the world, you must agree with and believe the following:

1. **Integrity**—All business affairs will be conducted lawfully and with integrity.
2. **Compliance**—Strive for 10,000 percent compliance: 100 percent of us fully complying 100 percent of the time.
3. **Value Creation**—Create long-term value by economic means. Understand, develop, and apply Market Based Management® to get superior results. Eliminate waste.
4. **Entrepreneurship**—Demonstrate the sense of urgency; discipline; accountability; judgment; initiative; economic and critical thinking skills; and risk-taking mentality necessary to generate the greatest contribution to the company.
5. **Customer Focus**—Understand and build relationships with customers to profitably anticipate and satisfy their needs.
6. **Knowledge**—Seek and use the best knowledge in decisions and proactively share your knowledge while embracing a *challenge process.*

7. **Change**—Embrace change and envision what could be, challenge the status quo, and drive creative destruction.

8. **Humility**—Practice humility and intellectual honesty. Constantly seek to understand and constructively deal with reality to create real value and achieve personal improvement.

9. **Respect**—Treat others with dignity, respect, honesty, and sensitivity and encourage and practice teamwork.

10. **Fulfillment**—Create value and produce results in order to realize our full potential and find true enjoyment in our work.

In many enterprises where the published set of principles is merely a piece of paper, people can survive while snickering at, being disdainful of, or treating the principles of the company lightly. That wouldn't happen at any of these nine companies. You either agree with and adhere to the values held by each of these enterprises and their leaders or you'll promptly be shown the door. Each of the people who lead them stands for something. There's nothing wishy-washy about the principles, beliefs, or code of conduct at any of these companies.

The cultures of these companies are so strong that each self-selects the team members who will become successful. If someone fits the culture, they're in. If they don't fit the culture, they're out *fast*.

7. No Superficial Distinctions

As we set off on our first research trip to San Diego to interview PETCO's CEO Brian Devine, we were dressed for an important mission. I wore a standard dark blue suit, crisply starched white shirt, burgundy tie, and shiny lace-up shoes. The moment we stepped into Devine's office we all realized we were way overdressed. Devine and his colleagues looked like they were dressed for playing a round of golf or watching NASCAR in chinos and casual shirts.

The meeting began with the PETCO folks lined up on one side

of the table and us, the researchers, resembling Mormon missionaries without name tags, on the other. Realizing it could turn out to be an agonizingly stiff meeting unless something happened fast, I asked, "Do you mind if we lose these ties and jackets?" They nodded permission, and within minutes the meeting was relaxed and headed in the right direction.

Not wanting to make the same mistake again, we began e-mailing ahead and asking what the appropriate dress was for our meetings with the CEOs. With only one exception we were told the same thing, "It's khakis and polo shirts all the time in our offices, except on Friday's when it's *real* casual dress."

The fact that we encountered casual dress to be the standard at all the companies is not superficial: it's *important*. They have neither the time nor the inclination for pretense. When clothing is allowed to convey class status within an organization, a hierarchical structure built on rank and position is perpetuated.

Leaders who by their own example make it clear that clothing doesn't convey rank send a loud message to the organization: we're all equals and this is about collegiality and collaborating for the achievement of our agreed objectives.

This lack of pretension extends to other facets of appearance as well. When you visit the Oklahoma City offices of Sonic Drive-In, it's hard not to be impressed. Located across the street from a brand-new old-time baseball stadium in an area known as Bricktown, the company's headquarters have been built to match the look and feel of the once abandoned warehouses that now teem with restaurants, nightclubs, and shops. It's impossible not to smile when you enter the building and confront the fun and whimsy that have made this fifty-year-old fast-food chain one of the nation's best businesses. But the biggest surprise comes when you get off the elevator on the third floor on your way to visit CEO Cliff Hudson.

The first thing we saw was a big, curved reception desk with light-filled hallways heading off in many directions. A male administrative assistant in his midforties stood up from behind the reception desk to greet us.

"Hello, we're here to see Cliff Hudson," I said, handing him my business card.

"So you're the author. Nice to meet you," he said.

"It's great being here," I offered. "Will you please let Mr. Hudson's assistant know we're here?" I asked.

He smiled and said, "We'll, actually, I'm Mr. Hudson, but you can call me Cliff, and this," he said as he surveyed the reception area, "*is* my office."

Cliff Hudson's office is the third-floor reception area. It's where he works, takes his phone calls, answers his e-mail, and holds meetings. "Being out here in the open," Hudson says, "is one of the best decisions I've ever made. It makes me accessible, lets me interact with everyone, and lets me keep my finger on the pulse of the company."

The offices of all the CEOs reveal their feelings about space and the egalitarian cultures of the companies they've built.

The office of Charles Koch, who leads the nation's second-biggest privately held company, with revenues exceeding $100 billion, resembles a small reading room in a library. Every inch of wall space is lined with floor-to-ceiling bookcases filled with thousands of books. The books aren't for show. In response to nearly every question posed to him, Koch stands, moves down the walls of books, pulls one out, and says, "I don't necessarily have the answer, but this author did when he wrote this," and proceeds to answer our questions by reading a paragraph from both obscure and classic texts.

Our first meeting with Jim Goodnight was held in a conference room. At the end of a long session, Goodnight looked at me and asked, "Would you like to see the dashboard?" "Sure," I said and he led the way down the hall to his private office. (Goodnight's dashboard is a single-screen real-time summation of every aspect of the business from customer counts to cash balances, client renewal rates to customer support response times and employee satisfaction survey data, and so on.)

Anyone expecting Goodnight's office to be grand would be sorely disappointed. The offices of most administrative assistants are far larger. His space is perhaps 140 square feet and has a plain desk and well-worn credenza. When I commented on the modest nature of his furniture, his only comment was, "Yes, it's pretty old. It's the same stuff that was here when I moved in years ago and I've just never gotten around to changing it."

In dramatic contrast to a business world populated by managers and executives who measure their self-worth on the size and trappings of their offices, the people who lead the nine best-performing enterprises in America have the most modest of digs. They don't have a need to waste valuable resources trying to prove their importance to anyone.

The Conclusions

While studying the nine companies that do a better job of growing revenues than all other companies, we were constantly reminded that each has taken on the modest and humble personality of its leadership. These are truly inspired, collegial, group endeavors where the momentary accomplishments of individuals are overshadowed by the consistent, long-term achievement of a team that's gently and deftly kept on course by a humble leader.

Cabela's, Dot Foods, Koch, Medline, O'Reilly, PETCO, SAS, Sonic, and Strayer are among the top one-tenth of 1 percent of all U.S. companies in terms of consistent revenue growth—and the most basic trait shared by each is *a heritage of authentically humble leadership.*

Does humility really set these organizations up to win the revenue and growth game? The answer is an incontrovertible y-e-s! If these organizations had been incapable of holding on to their humble values, each would have become as distracted as the hundreds of thousands of companies that perish annually by spending time on the wrong priorities.

The Building Blocks that follow reveal the guiding principles employed by these companies to achieve their consistently outstanding increases in revenue. Each principle, taken alone, can have a powerful impact on an enterprise. The impact of each is magnified many times when it's initiated and implemented by humble leaders and humble teams.

Think BIG, Act SMALL
DOWN TO EARTH

- Be a steward.
- Make information available to everyone.
- Be accessible.
- Praise others.
- Love what you do and lead by example.
- Stand for something good and noble.
- Erase superficial distinctions.
- Stay humble.

2

Keep Your Hands Dirty

SAS INSTITUTE

Sometimes I'll put together a small team of programmers and we'll code a rudimentary version 1.0 of a new product idea.

DR. JIM GOODNIGHT, CEO of SAS Institute

One of the most important lessons observed during our research is that in the companies that consistently grow revenues, everyone in the organization keeps their hands dirty.

SAS Institute

There's no better poster boy for keeping your hands dirty than Jim Goodnight and the story of the company he founded and runs— SAS (whose initials, which no longer mean anything, are always pronounced as a word).

SAS Institute is the world's largest privately owned software company and creates and sells business intelligence software that helps its clients make the right decisions. The firm's software is used by 93 percent of the top one hundred companies in the 2011 *Fortune* 500 list in more than fifty thousand installations in 126 countries worldwide.

One example of its work is the services it provides to Staples, the nation's leading office-supply chain. Staples does $30 billion in 1,500 retail stores as well as through a very busy online business and a catalog channel. Collectively the three channels have more than 35 million customer records. It's the job of Staples' marketing department—aided by SAS software—to collect and analyze the data on all 35 million customers and hundreds of millions of transactions, and then predict what and how many products future customers will buy, how customers will find out about these products and when they'll buy them, and even where new retail stores should be located. The pioneering business intelligence software made by SAS in effect allows its clients to keep its hands dirty in the sense of keeping in closer contact with emerging consumer trends.

Eureka!

Jim Goodnight, the founder of SAS, was raised in Wilmington, North Carolina, where during junior high and high school he worked in his father's hardware store. Although he excelled in science and math, he admits he barely squeaked through high school, earning a D in his senior-year English class.

During his freshman year at the University of North Carolina someone told him about a new class being offered on computers and he signed up. "I didn't even know what a computer was," he says, "and for the first few weeks I was bewildered. But one day I just figured it out." He figured it out so well that by the time he started his sophomore year, a professor enlisted him to *teach* his lab, and Goodnight's life calling had been found.

Goodnight was so intrigued with computers that before long, he'd managed to snag two half-time programming jobs: one at the University of North Carolina and another at North Carolina State. "Heck, I was just a programmer," he says, "and I loved it." "Programming," he contends, "is fascinating because it's like working a puzzle all day long. You get to write instructions, make a computer do what you want it to do, and create results that help other people do their jobs better. It's extremely rewarding."

By 1968 Goodnight had earned his master's and he and his friend Jim Barr were working for NC State University programming and analyzing data for the university's research stations. Eventually thirteen other colleges in the Southeast began using the duo's computer programs rather than writing their own. The other universities didn't have to pay anything for the software because Goodnight's work was being underwritten by a federal grant.

When Richard Nixon became president, he decreed that only universities with hospitals could continue receiving the type of grant money that Goodnight had been getting. That decision was a blessing in disguise for Goodnight because the university officials said, "If you fellows want to keep playing with your computers, you'd better figure out how to make enough money to pay your salaries."

Founding SAS Institute

Goodnight and Barr went to the thirteen other universities and asked each to kick in $5,000 annually and they all agreed. Additionally, the duo received permission to begin licensing their software to other organizations and quickly signed several pharmaceutical companies as clients. By 1976 Jim Goodnight had been awarded his doctorate and was an assistant professor at the university, and SAS had 120 clients. That same year someone at Abbott Laboratories decided to host an SAS users conference and 300 people showed up. Goodnight recalls his surprise. "I remember thinking, 'Wow, this is pretty good stuff, we've got three hundred people using our software who want to get together and talk about it.'"

But there was a problem back at the university. Goodnight and Barr needed more space for SAS to grow and there wasn't any room on campus. SAS was finally born as a private enterprise on July 1, 1976, when the duo agreed to move SAS off campus, let the university keep all the money it earned that year (about $150,000), and further agreed to locate near the campus so they could continue to analyze data for the statistics department. They took two colleagues along with them: John Sall, a graduate student, and Jane Helwig, the group's technical writer.

Goodnight doesn't remember putting up any money. "Hell, we didn't have any," he says. "As I recall we sold shares for a dollar apiece to each other and didn't take a salary for a month or two until we'd sold a few licenses and had some money." During its first year the firm generated $138,000 in revenue and began an uninterrupted twenty-five-year string of double-digit revenue and profit growth.

By 2010 SAS had grown to $2.43 billion in annual revenue. The company employs more than twelve thousand workers in close to three hundred offices worldwide. Worthy of mention is that SAS spends about one quarter of its total annual revenue on research and development—a number that dwarfs the amount spent by its competitors.

For the three decades of the company's existence Jim Goodnight has continued to do what he learned in his freshman computer class: listen to customers, discern a need, and help write the code that creates the software to solve the problem.

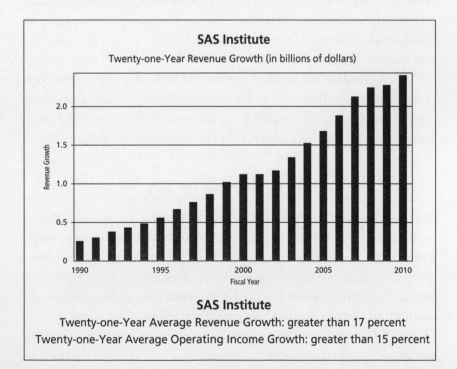

SAS Institute

Twenty-one-Year Revenue Growth (in billions of dollars)

SAS Institute
Twenty-one-Year Average Revenue Growth: greater than 17 percent
Twenty-one-Year Average Operating Income Growth: greater than 15 percent

Keeping His Hands Dirty

We found that keeping your hands dirty was a recurrent theme at SAS and, in fact, has become a vital part of the culture at a company that has consistently been named among the best places to work by a multitude of rating organizations and business magazines. A senior executive we spoke with said, "Sometimes, with my team, I'll find somebody putting up a barrier as if to say, 'Hey, that's not my job,' and I'll say that as long as Jim Goodnight still codes, you'll still pick up boxes and so will I. Nobody has a job description here. We do what needs to be done."

Keith Collins has been with SAS for twenty-seven years and serves as the company's senior VP and chief technology officer. "You wouldn't believe some of the things he does," says Collins. "At least sometimes he's polite enough to call me and tell me to cough up a few good developers, without letting me replace them, but other times, he comes over here like a thief in the night and steals away a handful of my best people and puts them to work on a new project."

Collins continued, "It's just one of the things you come to accept when you work for SAS. We look for innovation wherever we can and Jim's a great innovator."

When Goodnight is pressed on whether he'll stop writing code one day, he responds, "We want to be the single most valued competitive weapon in business decision making. When we fully realize our dream, maybe then I'll stop." He adds wryly, "But then again, maybe not."

Lots of Companies Try But . . .

The predecessor to the reality show *Undercover Boss* was 2004's new reality television program *Now Who's Boss?* Both were designed to show the heads of companies performing work on the front lines alongside workers. The premiere episode of *Now Who's Boss?* featured the chairman and CEO of a big hotel chain changing beds, working in the kitchen, and serving as a bellman.

The CEO spent five days working in one of his hotels while taping the show. "It got me closer to the people," he said in an interview with

Hotel Magazine. "I learned that housekeeping is physically demanding, uniforms are polyester and uncomfortable, and that many people don't tip the housekeepers." But his biggest surprise occurred when he got stiffed while serving as a bellman. He carried fifteen bags for one customer and received no tip!

This person, who has been chairman and CEO of the hotel chain for fifteen years, says he was so inspired by his experience that he made a decision to implement an *annual* event for hotel general managers and executive committee members to spend *one day* doing line-level jobs.

One day a year? *Whoosh* . . . whatever he learned went right over his head.

From time to time, many executives and companies eventually come up with equally well-intended initiatives designed to move their executives and management closer to the real work of the organization. The phrase that best describes such undertakings would be "getting our hands dirty once a year."

There's no need for getting-your-hands-dirty initiatives at the companies we studied because *keeping* their hands dirty is the very essence of who these leaders and organizations are. We uncovered three ways that these companies consistently grow revenues by thinking big and acting small.

Companies That Consistently Grow Revenues Keep Their Hands Dirty by Being in Frequent Contact and Involved with:

- Customers
- Workers
- Vendors and Suppliers

Keeping Your Hands Dirty—With Customers

When I began revealing and discussing the companies that had qualified for inclusion in *Think Big, Act Small*, we were frequently surprised by the reaction that the name of one of the businesses generated. When I mentioned Cabela's someone would interrupt me and say, "Now there is one incredible company," and either pull a Cabela's credit card out of his wallet or proceed to talk about his personal experiences with the company. We joked internally that'd we'd finally found a company that didn't have customers but apostles.

Once inside Cabela's, we quickly found one of the reasons the company has created such an incredibly loyal customer base and proven itself capable of consistently growing revenues.

Each morning when Jim Cabela, director and vice chairman of the company, walks into his office at world headquarters in Sidney, Nebraska, there's a tall stack of eight-by-five sheets of white paper awaiting him. Each sheet contains a customer comment, compliment, or complaint from the previous day, the customer's name and contact information, and the Cabela's representative who took the comment.

Cabela spends his mornings reading each of them, noting his comments, and separating the complaints into smaller piles. Then before heading home for lunch, he walks around the company and personally delivers the small stacks to the responsible parties for their immediate action and follow-up. Jim Cabela, who refers to his company's employees as partners, exists to keep his hands dirty.

How many chairmen of multibillion-dollar firms do you think spend several hours each day reviewing all the previous day's client comments and complaints and personally directing an immediate follow-up? A jealous competitor might cynically mutter, "What the heck else is there to do in Sidney, Nebraska?" At Cabela's, with a string of forty years of consistent revenue growth, Jim Cabela's response would be a benign smile and a question, "What could be more important than listening and responding to customers and doing whatever else you have to do to make and keep them happy?"

Chief marketing officer and senior SAS vice president Jim Davis says, "We don't undertake any new product development until we understand the issues and pains of the customer. When we created our markdown optimization solution we did it hand in hand with a retail client. Same for our software that makes a utility company's energy grid smarter and a bank's risk management less risky." SAS starts with a conversation in order to understand what it can do to solve a problem or take advantage of an opportunity, how it can pay off (like the 137 percent internal rate of return achieved at Staples), and then it works hard getting constant feedback during each step in the software development process to craft a solution that exceeds expectations. "We're not the norm in the software industry," Davis says. "What we do can only be accomplished by constantly keeping your hands dirty."

I reviewed the relevant research and Davis is right. SAS is not the norm. Studies show half or more of all enterprise software projects fail to deliver the expected benefits, leaving clients disappointed and more likely to jump ship to the competition. One surprising study of supply-chain software clients showed 33 percent of customers did worse than companies who did nothing. Keeping your hands dirty with customers is clearly the best weapon to avoid customer disappointment and fight high rates of turnover. (By the way, leaving lots of clients disappointed is a pandemic in business, with rates of 33 to 66 percent common across all industries.)

One Swamp Water to Go, Please . . .

One thing you won't find at Sonic Drive-In's headquarters is a big stainless steel test kitchen with executive chefs whizzing up trendy new recipes for the group's three thousand six hundred locations. "No way," says an adamant Pattye Moore, former company president. Company executives spend as much as half of their time visiting stores and in the kitchens.

"We'll never have a company test kitchen where we create recipes and foods and force them onto our franchisees," says Moore. "Our product ideas come from studying what our customers are ordering, listening to our vendor partners, and watching what our crew members cook for themselves."

One of Sonic Drive-In's competitive advantages is that nothing is prepared in advance. There's not a microwave in any of its restaurants.

Only after a customer presses a red button and places an order is the food cooked to order. As long as the restaurant has the ingredients on hand, customers can order whatever they'd like. "Last year," Moore says, "we launched a successful new drink called Orange Cool Breeze. That idea came from a store manager who had a customer drive in everyday and order a combination of Sprite with orange, pineapple, and cherry."

Another recent successful menu addition at Sonic came about because of a chance meeting Moore had while visiting one of the drive-ins. "I was talking to the crew members about breakfast items," she recalls, "and as we were talking, I saw one of the crew cutting up a piece of grilled chicken and rolling it up in a tortilla with ranch dressing, lettuce, and tomatoes. I asked her what she was making, and she told me that ever since we'd brought in tortillas she'd been making herself a grilled chicken wrap for lunch each day." Soon after, grilled chicken wraps hit the menu and became an immediate hit.

Many teenage customers at Sonic frequently order a drink called Swamp Water which isn't on the menu but is available chain-wide. Moore explains that Swamp Water is a combination of all the various slush flavors; when added together they turn a dark khaki green. "One day," Moore says, "my ten-year-old daughter came home from school and said she wanted to go to Sonic and have a Swamp Water. I asked her how she knew about Swamp Water and she said her friends at school had learned about it from their older brothers and sisters. That's how menu items get done at Sonic," Moore says. "The customer decides."

One of our interviews with Moore took place while she was in San Francisco with then-company CFO (now president) Scott McLain, taking part in a conference of financial analysts. "What do the two of you enjoy more," I teased, "visiting restaurants in towns like Pearl, Mississippi, or being an important part of the show at a sophisticated financial event in a big city?"

"Presenting at analysts' conferences and keeping them informed of what we're doing is important," answers McLain, "but the work we love happens in our restaurants," he says. "That's where our success really takes place."

If Pattye Moore and others at Sonic didn't spend time getting their hands dirty by visiting restaurants, going into the kitchens, and keeping a close eye on changing customer desires, it's unlikely that many of their recent hits would have ever been noticed by Sonic managers, who have the ability to roll out these new ideas systemwide.

Leaders Get in the Trenches—And Stay There

In the previous chapter we wrote about Robert Silberman, chairman and CEO of Strayer Education, also teaching a course at Strayer University in business administration. What's most surprising is that he never mentions that he's the CEO to his students. "Maybe a few of them know," Silberman says, "but I'd never mention it. It's just who we are and what we're about. There's no better way for me to get the pulse of what my students need in order to make this a beneficial experience than being in the classroom. Staying close to our students is simply the essence of what we're about."

We found the same commitment by the company's top executives to being closely involved with customers in Mundelein, Illinois, at Medline Industries. Almost any item you might find in a U.S. hospital or nursing home could have been sold to them by Medline's nine-hundred-member sales force. "We're essentially a sales organization that coincidentally happens to manufacture much of what we sell," says CEO Charlie Mills. "How can we run a large sales organization without being closely involved with sales and our customers?" Mills says that he and the other two top officers of the company are on the road almost every week calling on and working with customers, and each of them has a number of accounts he still handles personally. Mills even met his future wife while both were working as sales reps for the company.

Charles Koch has spent more than forty years with Koch businesses, holding positions from ranch hand to CEO, but he still keeps his hands dirty with customers and vendor partners. "It's imperative we develop trust with our key customers and truly understand them and what they value," he says. "The only way I can do that is to spend both work and leisure time with them. If we behave in the right way consistently, and really listen, they understand we're dedicated to trying to create value for them. With vendors and suppliers, our philosophy is to treat them the same way we treat customers. I stay focused on those who are critical to our company's performance, and participate directly in our efforts to build trust and understanding."

After graduating from college, Missouri native David O'Reilly, CEO of O'Reilly Automotive, quickly headed home to Springfield and joined the family auto parts store that had been founded by his father and grandfather. At the time he started, there were four locations.

"I'd spent all my teenage years working in the stores during summers and vacation," he says, "but when I joined the company full-time, I started working at the counter, taking and filling orders." The next stop for O'Reilly was the phone desk where he'd field calls from auto parts dealers in small surrounding towns. Eventually he became the firm's sales manager and spent his weeks traveling the state with the company's four salespeople lining up and servicing accounts.

"My years running sales were a great time," O'Reilly remembers. "I was able to see and learn the challenges and dilemmas of being a small business owner firsthand. Some of the most important lessons I learned were from seeing the stores that failed."

For O'Reilly, staying close to customers was fundamental to the eventual success of the company. By keeping their hands dirty with customers, O'Reilly says the company gained a significant competitive advantage. "Learning from our customers gave us and continues to give us a tremendous understanding of the basics of the business that some of our competitors don't have. They view things from a retail perspective while we see them from the customer's point of view.

"You can't get your hands dirty," says O'Reilly, "without being truly plugged in. In my opinion, you're either plugged in all the way or you're not and there's no substitute for exposing yourself to your customers, your team members, and your vendors. There are no shortcuts. When it comes to attending operational meetings, being present at company and customer functions, meeting with key vendors, there's no substitute . . . for being there. It all falls into the category of 'management by walking around,' which is something far too many executives don't do. If it doesn't start at the top of the organization," he warns, "you can bet it's not being practiced elsewhere in the company."

Keeping Your Hands Dirty—With Workers

The real workers in a franchise organization are the staff members and managers of the franchises who actually deliver the goods to a paying public. Sonic's Cliff Hudson says, "One thing you'll hear about franchisors, generally, is that they exist to drive up the sales at their franchisees in order to make more money for themselves, without caring whether or not the franchisees are profitable. I don't need to name who," he adds, "but you could look at some of the big franchisors in this country who've spent years trying to buy market share. In the process, they drove down the average store profitability of their own franchisees. We can't ever imagine doing that."

One of the ways Sonic keeps its hands dirty with the real workers is its unique Franchise Advisory Council. Hudson says, "We don't and won't pursue a single significant initiative, marketing or product development [company], or building design without running it through that group and gaining their approval and endorsement."

Keeping Your Hands Dirty—With Vendors and Suppliers

On a search for fast and easy answers, many companies have concluded that the only way to become successful is to out–Wal-Mart

Wal-Mart and they've taken to wielding tire irons and donning sets of iron knuckles when negotiating with vendors and suppliers. Unfortunately, the life expectancy of companies whose success is dependent on beating up vendors and suppliers is notoriously short. As soon as those vendors and suppliers can find a way to do business without you, or with your competitor, they will. We found just the opposite at all the companies we identified and re-searched.

Here's their prevailing view: we need to make a profit to exist, grow, and nurture our people, and our suppliers need to do the same thing. Each company has forged working partnerships with its vendors and suppliers which ensure that both parties are able to realize their full economic potential. One of the ways they accom-plish these unique partnerships is by staying close to and being actively involved in each other's business.

To stay close to their vendors and suppliers, PETCO hosts a monthly event, Open Wednesday. Any prospective vendor or sup-plier can simply show up; no appointments are required and the company's doors are wide open. Many start-up companies with lit-tle more than a good idea have gone on to become valued suppliers because of Open Wednesday.

But according to Chairman Brian Devine, the company's open-ness and accessibility to suppliers doesn't end there. "In most com-panies," he says, "when a buyer decides to take a pass and not purchase an item from a supplier that's the end of the road. But that's not the way we do things here."

Each year PETCO has a trade show and flies in all their store managers from around the nation. All the company's vendors (eight hundred to one thousand of them) attend the show. But Devine has added an unusual twist. "Every vendor that our buyers have passed on throughout the year, but would still like to do business with us, is invited to exhibit at the show," he says. "Then our store managers get to pick twenty-five items that the national support center hasn't purchased for their stores." Store managers nominate products they'd like to have added to their inventory and vote on electronic handheld machines with the tallies illuminated on large screens for everyone to see.

One of the company's biggest hits ever—Greenies, a dental chew treat for pets—got into the PETCO stores by way of the annual trade show. PETCO's buyers had repeatedly said no to the Greenies product line but store managers, closer to the dog and cat public, gave it an overwhelming thumbs-up.

At Sonic, Cliff Hudson and his team take the concept of keeping their hands dirty to the extreme. No one at Sonic's home office ever uses the words "vendor" or "supplier." All the companies they work with are always referred to as partners. But again, unlike the disingenuous efforts some companies make to occasionally refer to their suppliers and vendors as partners, when the folks at Sonic use the "p" word, it has a ring of authenticity.

In dollar terms, Coca-Cola is one of Sonic's largest suppliers, but Hudson says the interaction it has with its partners at Coke is vastly different from the relationships most fast-food enterprises have with their major soft drink suppliers.

"If you're going to call someone a partner," Hudson says, "then you have to treat them and they have to treat you as genuine partners, looking out for the interests of one another. When we have a strategic planning retreat, our partners from Coke are there as full participants. They know where we are, where we want to go, and how we plan to get there. By being that revealing with our partners, they're able to move beyond being transactional salespeople selling us syrup into full fledged win-win partners."

One of the most striking things about the massive merchandising and catalog complex that houses Cabela's in Sidney, Nebraska, is that everyone who works there looks like they're right off the pages of one of the company's catalogs. In one way or another, they are.

Because the company inventories more than 250,000 SKUs and offers an iron-clad, no-questions-asked, money-back guarantee on everything it sells, voluminous amounts of product testing are required. In order to involve the entire company with its suppliers and vendors, all team members are routinely asked to sign out clothing, shoes, hats, and sporting gear and are encouraged to actively use them for a full year while simultaneously being engaged in a dialogue about the product's quality. At the end of twelve months, the items are returned, taken apart, and analyzed.

By closely involving all team members in the evaluation and selection of all the products featured in its catalogs and stores, Cabela's has moved collegiality beyond the confines of the company and into the ranks of its suppliers and vendors. After all, the receptionist, assistant buyer, or bookkeeping clerk just might happen to be the person testing and evaluating your firm's product.

When leaders and companies keep their hands dirty, they're better able to spot trends; learn and act on what customers really want; and better earn the respect and trust of customers, employees, and suppliers. For something that's such a no-brainer it's amazing that more leaders and companies aren't prepared to keep their hands dirty and build the kinds of companies they'd want to shop at.

By keeping their hands dirty, the senior executives are, in a sense, relinquishing some of their power to the common employee, vendor, or customer. They are favoring a bottom-up management approach as opposed to a top-down one. A bottom-up approach imbues the team with a sense of ownership, which translates into its taking responsibility and contributing to the bottom line because it wants to, not because it *has* to. This is important because it also speaks to the leaders' humbleness and self-confidence. At most other companies, you don't find the senior executives actively and genuinely seeking advice from throughout the organization.

Think BIG, Act SMALL
KEEP YOUR HANDS DIRTY

- Never become too important for customer contact.
- Turn workers into valued team members—not employees.
- Turn suppliers into partners.
- Be available to people who want to do business with you.
- Give all team members a voice in the decision-making process.
- Be prepared to be evaluated and graded.
- Respond to every customer communication.

3

Make Short-Term Goals and Long-Term Horizons

SONIC DRIVE-IN

"We're not capital constrained and could grow faster, but our long-term vision for expansion is irrelevant if we lose focus of doing things right every day."

CLIFF HUDSON, CEO of Sonic Drive-In

The remarkable and consistent revenue growth achieved by the companies we identified, researched, and wrote about did not occur because they had five-year plans carved in stone. In fact, one of the primary reasons these companies are able to consistently grow their revenues by double digits every year is thanks to an absence of an inflexible long-term plan. While continually casting their collective eyes toward the long-term horizon, each company understands that locked-in long-term plans are a waste of time unless short-term plans are properly executed and achieved.

Serious consequences occur when organizations bind themselves to rigid long-term plans.

- **Resource Allocation** The manager or executive who believes that her company will be many times larger in the future is likely to allocate resources for functions, facilities, and people that may never be needed. Years after the dot-com bust, thousands of companies were still trying to lease or sublease millions of square feet of office space they'd built or leased in accordance with faulty long-term plans.

- **Future Talk** When companies adopt long-term plans, they often become preoccupied with the achievement of the plan and stop paying attention to the vital day-to-day details of business. In many instances their *plan* becomes more important than their customers.

- **Greed Takes Over** When managers and executives start dreaming about the coastal homes, private jets, and yachts they're going to buy when they cash-out at the end of the plan, they're concentrating on the wrong things.

- **Mismanaged Expectations** When the tomorrows don't take place as promised, workers often experience a crisis of confidence in the people who sold them the long-term plan and become cynical or leave.

- **Investors Lose Confidence** When a business presents a long-term plan to outside investors and lenders, the plan becomes the de facto bible by which the enterprise will be judged. Any deviation is seen as an indication of managerial malfeasance.

- **It's Tough to Change Course** When people are herded up and sent off in one direction, it's almost impossible to get them to change course.

- **It Can Blind You to Reality** When companies are locked into a plan, they frequently become unwilling to envision anything that doesn't fit their plan. They become less nimble and lose the ability to zig and zag as required by market circumstances.

Each of the companies we studied patiently concentrates on profitably executing and achieving its short-term objectives, knowing that each step brings it closer to the achievement of its full economic potential.

The Sonic Story

There's no better example of a company where execution takes precedence than Sonic Drive-In, with three thousand six hundred locations in forty-four states and the highest customer frequency rate in the fast-food industry. (And the most fun company one could ever research.)

When customers drive into a colorful Sonic Drive-In, park beneath the large canopy covering customers' cars, and ask for cooked-to-order hamburgers, extra-long cheese coneys, deep-fried tater tots, and thousands of drink combinations including cream pie shakes, it's hard to imagine the company as anything other than a classic all-American rags-to-riches success story.

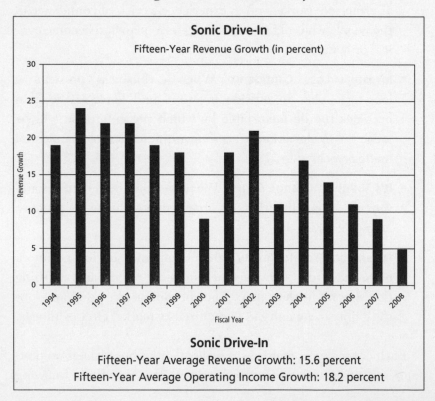

Sonic Drive-In
Fifteen-Year Revenue Growth (in percent)

Sonic Drive-In
Fifteen-Year Average Revenue Growth: 15.6 percent
Fifteen-Year Average Operating Income Growth: 18.2 percent

But the story of Sonic's first forty years is one of a company that faced the same troubles and intrigue that simmer beneath the surface at millions of companies and prevents most from ever achieving their full economic potential. A great idea and innovation almost got lost because of growth that was too rapid. There were scores of grandiose plans and more time was spent dreaming about the pay-offs of tomorrow than the details of today. Rampant infighting and maneuvering for power threatened to upend the company. A lack of systems and process resulted in a brand that lacked a definitive identity. Silos got built and were zealously protected, and almost all the players had their own hidden agendas.

The Early Years

The company's humble beginnings read almost like a fairy tale. Following military service in World War II, Troy Smith, the founder of Sonic, returned home to Shawnee, Oklahoma, and went into the restaurant business. Before long he noticed that a root beer stand on the edge of town was busier and apparently making more money than his restaurant. So in 1953 he bought the drive-in and renamed it Top Hat.

Before long, Smith was approached by an eager salesman named Charlie Pappe, a man whose very name, according to those who knew him, conjures up apt images of his demeanor. Described as "wearing a pork pie hat and possessing a moving-down-the-road deportment," and with a flourishing pitch typical of the times, he told Smith, "I love your deal and by the way, together, we can have fifty of these some day!" With a handshake, a new partnership was promptly formed.

Together the partners began implementing a string of innovations, including a novel way of taking orders. Reasoning that car-hops wouldn't have to write down orders and run them back to the kitchen, they installed both a microphone and loudspeakers at each parking place. Smith says that as soon as the loudspeakers were installed and music started playing, "Business exploded!"

By 1959 the partners had opened additional locations and as they approached number five decided it was time to begin franchising. Disappointingly, they discovered that their name had already been copyrighted and they needed a new one. With the recent installation of the loudspeakers complete, Smith went to the dictionary and looked up the word "sound." One of the words listed under sound was "sonic" and without a penny ever being spent on brand research, he'd found a name and slogan that epitomized the time: Sonic—*with the speed of sound.*

In order to keeps things administratively simple, rather than charge prospective franchisees a big upfront fee, the partners collected their money in an innovative way: through a *bag royalty.* Each restaurant was required to buy all their wrappers from a single paper company and each month the paper company sent Smith and Pappe a check representing one penny per bag. Even today, old-timers in the Sonic system fondly recall the bag royalty because it never felt like it was coming out of their pockets.

The Trouble Begins

By the 1970s Pappe had died and a group of a dozen young enterprising subfranchisors and franchisees had swelled the number of restaurants to 250—and they wanted to grow even faster. They went to Smith and asked him to fold his company into a new one with all their restaurants. Instead of agreeing, Smith challenged them, "Form your company, continue building restaurants and if you prove that you all can work together, I'll put my company in later." Two years later, with the group apparently working well together, Smith merged his part of the company into theirs. The company took off, adding more than one thousand franchisees in only six years. Troy Smith was still receiving his bag royalty, but the new group began charging a $15,000 fee to join the system and a 3 percent royalty on sales.

When so many strong-willed people get together, inevitably there's dissension and trouble. Sonic was no exception. By the mid-1980s several partners had been kicked out of the company; marketing had ground to a stop; there was no common centralized purchasing; everyone was fighting with everyone else; and the operations support from headquarters was almost nonexistent. As one company insider says, "We had what amounted to a very weak franchisor with sub-franchisors, who were beginning to wonder why they were paying a three-percent royalty and getting nothing in return, busy building their own feifdoms." Eventually almost four hundred restaurants left Sonic's fold or were closed. Acrimony reigned.

By the mid-1980s, after a number of false starts, the remaining board members and owners decided to give one more shot at turning things around and brought in a new CEO. Several months later he brought in a young attorney to fill in for the firm's corporate counsel, who was on maternity leave. That young attorney, Cliff Hudson, was about to receive a baptism by fire that eventually led him to the position of CEO, a job he still holds today.

Hudson took up what he thought might be a short-term assignment and found a company in disarray. He says there were three dynamics going on that threatened any chance of reversing the company's backward slide. "First," he says, "the new CEO really wanted to buy the company himself. You had the attempted turnaround itself, which was hard because you had ten board members constantly fighting and bickering with one another. And then, there were license renegotiations going on that had the potential to tank the company."

One particularly difficult franchisee and board member (who owned thirty restaurants) had already succeeded in changing the company's royalty agreements. Instead of being paid a flat 3 percent royalty from franchisees, the new royalty started at 1 percent and grew based on how well the home office drove individual unit sales. Goaded by his success, the dissident franchisee went to Smith and said, "Next, I'm going to acquire fifty-one percent of your company and take it apart."

Smith, sensing the urgency, arranged for his management team to be granted an option for control of the company as a preventative measure. To the surprise of everyone, the management scrambled and in 1986 was successful at finding $10 million in financing and actually exercised the option for 51 percent control. Hudson, at age thirty, was the youngest member of the team and says, "None of us had any money. We arranged more than nine million in loans and people mortgaged their homes, pawned their wives' wedding rings and scraped up whatever they could for the balance," recalling that his own equity contribution (excluding personal bank loans) was a personal check for $1,250.

As franchisees began modestly dressing up their restaurants and the new owners' fledgling marketing and advertising efforts gained some traction, revenues started growing and many locations were witnessing annual same-store sales increases of 10 to 15 percent. In 1991 Sonic went public and the company that had been valued at $10 million a few years before was suddenly worth $100 million and eventually enjoyed a market capitalization of more than $1.5 billion. Hudson, who became CFO when the company went public, was named COO in 1993 and then CEO in 1995 (and still serves in that capacity).

A New Beginning

"When I became COO I knew I had to change the culture," Hudson says. "Although most of our franchisees' revenues were growing, the home office was horrible. The entire company had developed into a group of independent silos and nobody was working with anyone else. We had a marketing group that didn't use our operators' guide to test new marketing ideas; we had a purchasing department that acted like the marketing department, and we couldn't execute. In trying to change the culture, what I found was that no one was interested in working together."

Finally, Hudson had enough. "One day," he recalls, "I simply said that anyone who can't buy the fact that the days of the silos are over should leave. Everyone is going to work together or there isn't a place for you at Sonic." When Hudson didn't relent, every member of the senior management staff, except one, finally left. Pattye Moore, the one who remained, was eventually named president of the company.

While working to change the culture of the home office, Hudson was confronted with another dilemma. Half of the franchisees asked for a new contract that would extend the terms of their franchises for twenty years and give them greater protection on trade radiuses around their stores. Hudson was prepared to comply with their request but wanted concessions in return. He wanted authority.

"You have to understand," says Hudson, "that this was a forty-year-old company without a consistent menu or look across the chain and without the authority to require it." He gave the franchisees what they wanted and in return the company received the authority to determine the menu and make participation in purchasing and marketing cooperatives mandatory, and an agreement that all stores would be retrofitted every seven years. Along with this came an increased royalty stream.

Hudson and Moore knew the company had to stand for something and crafted four core values to guide them on their journey of change.

The Sonic Road Rules

To offer special items that surprise and delight our customers
To promote respect for everyone touched by our brand
To emphasize the importance of relationships as a way of life
To reflect an entrepreneurial spirit and the power of the individual

---

After years of having had the subfranchisors and franchisees calling the shots, many executives might have been tempted to use their new powers in an autocratic or dictatorial fashion. To have done so would have violated Hudson and Moore's road rules and instead they chose to involve and listen to the subfranchisors and franchisees regarding menus, retrofits, and advertising.

"There was no way we were going to use our new power and shove anything down their throats," says Hudson of the franchisee organization. "We engaged everyone in the turnaround process but with the knowledge that when we reached the finish line, everybody was going to have to step to the line."

Hudson and Moore's listening paid off. "One of our subfranchisors in the Carolinas was distraught at the prospect of a consistent menu," says Hudson, "and was afraid we might get rid of ice cream. When he told us that his top store did 30 percent of its revenues in ice cream, instead of shutting him down, we decided we'd better listen to him. As a direct result, in 1996 we introduced fountain and frozen favorites and began promoting it.

"Sales," Hudson reports, "absolutely went through the roof. We'd never seen anything like it in our history. Afternoons, evenings, weekends were jammed." Because of the high margins gathered on ice cream sales, the restaurants were suddenly making more money than ever before and went along with Hudson and Moore's plans.

Hudson credits the changed culture at the home office to a consistent menu chainwide, the retrofit of all the stores, and a marketing budget that now exceeds $200 million annually and closely involves the franchisees in every decision with building a chain of drive-ins where the average store generates $1.1 million in revenue and $150,000 in annual profit. Considering that some owners have as many as thirty to two hundred locations, the economics are very attractive.

Today, as demonstrated by their financial performance during the past ten years, Sonic is a model of culture, creativity, and efficiency.

When we began pressing Hudson as to why Sonic isn't in every state of the union and why it doesn't have ten thousand restaurants instead of almost thirty-six hundred, his responses said almost everything we needed to know about the company and what it has become. As Hudson responded to our intense questioning, he chuckled and we learned some of the magic that's allowed him to create a company that wows customers and, unlike Wendy's or

Burger King, consistenly grows its revenues by double digits every year.

"We're just not that greedy," he said. "We're not capital constrained and could grow faster, but geography and store count just aren't that important to us. We can grow by a couple of hundred locations each year without even expanding geographically out of the thirty states we're in. More important to us is growing profitably, making certain all our partners do well, being very respectful of our brand, making certain we grow the right kind of team members so we can continue to expand, and growing judiciously where it makes the most sense."

Rather than relying on magical tactics or locking themselves into a timetable for how many restaurants they'd have in five years, Hudson and Moore executed on the basics: having all restaurants purchase together to ensure significant cost savings and quality control, implementing marketing cooperatives with financial muscle for media advertising, consistently upgrading the appearances of all locations, and offering a standard menu chainwide.

Hudson and Moore know that by growing same-store sales every year, patiently adding restaurants at the rate of a couple of hundred per year, ensuring that every vendor and supplier becomes a valuable partner, making certain that a silo never rises again, and by consistently and steadfastly executing and achieving their short-term goals, the company will be around to achieve its full economic potential.

Then in 2008, Sonic's terrific momentum stalled. Like every other business in America, it ran headlong into the banking crisis, nationwide recession, and an epic level of unemployment that left many Americans fearing the worst. "It [the last four years] has definitely been the most difficult time in my twenty-five-plus years in this business," says Hudson. Franchisees saw shocking losses in their sales and profits, new stores didn't reach the high levels of frequent visits that the core stores achieved, and expensive promotions drove new traffic but not loyal customers. Hudson had to face the music—success had opened the door to complacency, a condition

Hudson says made the bad times worse. "The recession is tough for everybody, but had we been more on our toes, the downturn would have been less painful. The last five years have really been a serious juggling act. Sustained success can always leave you complacent. We took a number of things for granted. I realized that many of the aspects of our business model that had served us so well needed to change." It was like a whack on the side of the head.

Sonic Takes Its Medicine

Creativity experts recommend a whack on the side of the head as an almost magical prescription for more innovative thinking. "It jolts us out of our routines," writes Roger von Oech in the aptly named book, *A Whack on the Side of the Head*. "It forces us to look for fresh approaches." I believe von Oech, and Hudson does too. Still, we would all like to avoid that whack if we can. To spare you the pain, Hudson has generously explained what he learned.

1. Customer Feedback Systems Were Good but Not Good Enough

Sonic was renowned for getting its executives into the stores, talking to customers and listening to their feedback, but after growing to almost thirty-six hundred locations, executive visits weren't enough.

"The scale needed to grow," Hudson explained. "Individual perceptions weren't enough to inform a forty-four-state chain. We needed methods that used technology to get our eyes and ears into each store and across every daypart so that we could have a richer, more comprehensive snapshot of what our customers were thinking about us. We started this in o-eight, just as the recession was hitting.

"We started acting on that feedback—focusing on service, recruiting new talent, delivering new tools to the franchisees, stepping up and changing specs in some of the fundamental parts of our menu—like real ice cream in the soft serve instead of ice milk. Then we started driving hard to find the right pricing components so we would get the customers saying 'the value is better than it was a year ago.' We're achieving that now.

"The biggest thing is to hear what the actual customers are saying—to have the accurate feedback—to figure out what it would take to delight them right now and how we can engage them to come back frequently." Hudson concluded, "The customer focus was not as keen as it needed to be."

2. Help People at Every Level Get Laser Focused

As Hudson saw, the scale of Sonic's operations in 2008 had gotten bigger than his customer feedback systems could measure. If this was happening at the national level, the same thing had to be happening to his franchisees, he reasoned.

"I don't mean to say our operators weren't focused on the customer. They were and are very focused. But ten years ago many of them were running a five-million-dollar enterprise and now it's more like twenty million dollars or more," Hudson stated. "How are they going to manage the critical differences? How are we helping them? What does the customer think today versus fifteen years ago? These were the big questions. We needed to have all our teammates getting customer feedback to imagine and execute the initiatives that could separate Sonic from the competition."

Hudson shifted the accountability measures from internal numbers to customer satisfaction. He made sure his team checked and double-checked that food quality, service, and value was meeting and exceeding customer expectations. "We're hearing customers say 'You've really stepped up' over the last two years," Hudson said with pride.

3. Maintain Urgency

It's clear that Sonic has taken their whack, learned from it, and let it help them find the new improved path for getting even better. Hudson is uncommonly frank in sharing what he learned during Sonic's economic downturn.

"You've got to have accountability to ensure that you're moving upward and forward at all times," Hudson declares. "You have to have the talent on board to drive your business. You can't focus on internal numbers. You have to focus on the customer. You have to be mindful of the complacency that success can bring. You need to stay keen, on your toes, in tune with the market, and running as hard as you can.

"Coming though this recession," Hudson says, "has been about staying focused on the basics, staying more keen, and scaling our four rules of the road to the new realities: even more demanding customers, a bigger, more complex business model, and the urgency to always be better than we were.

"There's a lot of opportunity for us," Hudson says with real enthusiasm. "We're on the path now and have a better future ahead."

Everywhere we looked we saw that these remarkable companies, whose consistent revenue growth places them in the top one hundredth of a percent of American companies, are able to grow revenues because they aren't burdened with delivering on a five-year plan. They're free to execute the basics instead of constantly playing catch-up, kissing the banker or analyst's bottom, or trying to explain away variances in their plan. And even a terrible recession, banking crisis, and epic problem of unemployment (and dysfunction in Washington) couldn't derail them.

Imagine It and Then . . . Get Back to Business

In 1982 Dot Foods held its first national sales conference, attended by six people in a meeting room at the Knights of Columbus hall in Mount Sterling, Illinois. "We didn't even have a conference room," says CEO Pat Tracy, "so there was nowhere else to hold it. At the beginning of the meeting," he recalls, "I wrote the number one hundred million dollars on a flip chart and never mentioned the number during the meeting. Finally, at the end of the meeting, someone asked, 'What's that number mean?' and I told everyone that if we paid attention to business and executed well, that some-day we'd hit that number."

Within six years Dot Foods broke the $100 million number, and everyone asked Tracy which number came next, and he shared another number: $1 billion. The company achieved that goal twelve years later, and when we first interviewed them in 2004, Dot Foods was well on its way to the $2 billion mark. "Sure there are other big numbers we'd like to hit," Tracy says, "and if we stick to our knitting and execute well we'll achieve them someday. But we've never really said that the target is this number or that number." He saves his important comment on the subject for last: "Volume is vanity and profit is sanity and we're far more interested in being sane than we are in being vain."

You'd never catch Tracy and his siblings allocating resources to handle revenues they might hit someday. They'd wait until they were closing on the next hurdle and operating at maximum efficiency before committing to facilities designed to handle a sales volume that might never happen. Dot Foods is committed to profitable growth and won't undertake any initiative that might endanger its long-term profitability.

You Need to See the Target

Charlie Mills, CEO at Medline Industries, another company based in the nation's heartland, shares the same feelings about getting locked into long-term plans and achieving big elusive numbers. "Look," he says, "every one of our five thousand team members wants to do well financially. By accepting the obligation to allow our workers' paychecks to grow, we're locked into improving sales every year. And we have to do that in an ultracompetitive industry that actually faces deflation every year."

When quizzed as to whether Medline, at the time doing $2 billion in annual revenues, could one day achieve $10 billion in annual sales, Mills takes on an incredulous look. "Jason, you need to be able to see the target," he admonishes. "If we continue to execute well, remain debt free, and provide team members and customers a better future, then we'll continue to do better year after year. If we do those things, we can envision a company doing four billion in sales." He concludes his thoughts on the subject with, "but let's hit that number before we think about a bigger one." For the record, five years later, Medline's annual sales far exceed $4 billion.

Keep Doing What's Working

O'Reilly CEO David O'Reilly recalls how, at a family get-together nearly twenty years ago, his brother said, "Someday we'll have one hundred stores!" O'Reilly says that everyone laughed and his brother protested and offered up, "Yes, we're going to have one hundred stores someday and when we do, we'll go to Hawaii together." At the time the chain had twenty-five stores, and O'Reilly says, "No one could possibly imagine ever having one hundred stores."

The company did grow to one hundred stores within seven years (they never did take the Hawaii trip together) but O'Reilly says that hitting a big number and having a locked-in five-year plan wasn't in the cards. "We never, and I want to emphasize the word 'never,' had a plan to hit two hundred, four hundred, eight hundred, or a thousand stores. Instead, we all agreed that we'd never have some faraway target we couldn't see but just keep doing what we were doing and growing consistently, steadily, and profitably. Wherever that took us was just fine."

Don't Chase Numbers

According to Robert Silberman, CEO of Strayer Education, his mission is to build a nationwide university for working adults that makes getting a college degree possible for people who would otherwise not get one. While the consistent revenue and operating profit growth of Strayer has been nothing short of remarkable, Silberman insists, "We simply aren't focused on revenue or operating profit growth."

For several years Strayer added three additional campuses annually and in the past two years has opened five new campuses each year. "We'd like to continue adding five campuses each year," says Silberman, "but it's easy to chase numbers and we won't do that. We'll only expand by that number if we have sufficient internal personnel to offer an extremely high-quality education."

Silberman won't grow for the sake of growing in order to hit some big magical number. "I actually worry more about overgrowth than anything else and I spend a lot of time with my board and with investors cautioning them not to invest with us if they want us to quickly chase numbers. In any trade-off between growth and quality, we're going to choose quality because in the long run, that's how we'll succeed in building a nationwide university."

The short-term objective that matters most to Silberman is quality and he's unwilling to consider allowing that commitment to be endangered.

"What about analysts and investors," I wondered. "When they see the compelling rates of return that additional campuses can generate, don't they push you to expand faster?"

"For the most part," Silberman says, "analysts and investors want to know what we're doing, and why and when they do, they appreciate our candor and the honesty." Silberman's final take on the subject of being pressured by investors to grow faster was an especially telling one. "I believe," he said, "that over the long run a company gets the investors they deserve, and we're real happy with ours."

Don't Let Plans Weigh You Down

Keith Collins, senior vice president and chief technology officer at SAS, says, "The greatest thing about Jim Goodnight and SAS is that when everyone told him he needed this big grandiose five-year plan, it simply never made sense to him and he didn't do it. We don't have five-year plans at SAS because we don't want to get wedded to them or have them weighing us down like anchors."

Goodnight says, "In the technology industry everything changes so quickly. If you stuck to a five-year plan your product would be irrelevant by the time you got to the end of it. Imagine ignoring the early stages of the Internet or wireless technology in our business. It would be suicidal."

Another SAS executive echoes the sentiment, saying, "One of the reasons this company works so well is that we're not locked in to a plan but instead stick to our knitting and do what we do best. We never try to go wild or do things that would be unnatural for us in order to gain market share. We take care of our core business," he says, "and then slowly explore other areas." Agreeing with Collins, he added, "If we were tied down to achieving a specific five-year plan, we'd lose our sense of innovation, commitment to our customers, and our competitive advantage."

Companies that think big and act small can achieve remarkable revenue growth by staying focused on the execution of their important short-term objectives while constantly maintaining a watchful eye on the long-term horizon.

Think BIG, Act SMALL
TIME HORIZONS

- Don't get locked into long-term plans based on fairy tale numbers.
- Don't become preoccupied with tomorrow. Take care of customers today.
- Don't let greed cloud your vision.
- Don't obsess on the big something you're trying to achieve. Take it in bite-sized pieces.
- Set targets that people can see and believe.
- Keep doing what's worked in the past.
- Don't chase big numbers for the sake of the big numbers.
- Don't let long-term plans become anchors.

Let Go

CABELA'S

"If something isn't working, fix it, and if it can't be fixed, then get rid of it."

DENNIS HIGHBY, CEO of Cabela's

It's not so much the things they do that allow the nation's best revenue-producing companies to grow their revenues by double digits every year. It's the things they *don't* do.

Companies waste so much time trying to resuscitate yesterday's breadwinners, defending past decisions, assuaging executive egos, and tinkering with broken processes that they don't have time to concentrate on the important things, like adding customers and growing revenues. They always have a crisis to deal with or a fire to put out.

- GE Capital spent years pouring hundreds of millions of dollars (by some estimates more than $1.4 billion over many years) into Montgomery Ward even though the company had had a tag on its toe for generations. It couldn't admit it had made a mistake, cut its losses, and move on.
- General Motors tried to foist a dead brand on the American

public by quadrupling the advertising budget of Oldsmobile to almost $400 million with their disastrous "It's not your father's Oldsmobile" campaign when everyone already knew it wasn't your father's Oldsmobile . . . it was Granddad's.

- Blockbuster, the movie-rental giant, once boasted a $7 billion market capitalization and employed 60,000 workers at its 2,000 stores in eighteen countries but watched it all evaporate because it couldn't let go of its retail model of forcing customers into their storefronts in less than desirable neighborhoods. Each time they attempted to move into online distribution, a new CEO would come on board and squash the plans. By the time Netflix and Red Box were finished with them, Blockbuster was bankrupt and a billion dollars in debt.

When confronted with problems, most companies try to make

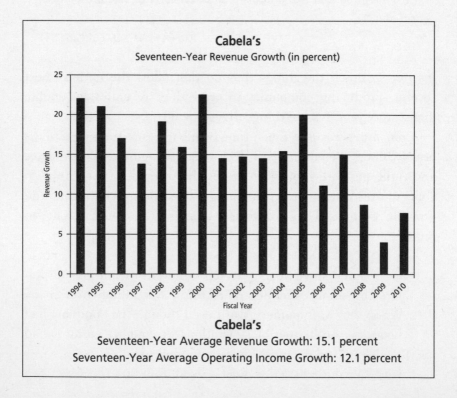

Cabela's
Seventeen-Year Revenue Growth (in percent)

Cabela's
Seventeen-Year Average Revenue Growth: 15.1 percent
Seventeen-Year Average Operating Income Growth: 12.1 percent

small changes or Band-Aid fixes and hope things get better or that the problem goes away. This approach doesn't work and ensures that they'll waste vast amounts of time and energy. In stark contrast, when the companies we researched confront a challenge, the problem child may get a second chance; otherwise they quickly invent a new way of doing things, jettison the old way, and get on with the important business at hand—finding customers and growing revenues.

One of the characteristics of our top nine companies is that each proves the proposition of thinking big and acting small by mastering the art of abandoning products, services, and processes whose time is past.

In having mastered the art of letting go and challenging the way things have always been done, Cabela's has built one of the most successful business and retail organizations in U.S. history.

The Cabela's Story

In 1961 Dick Cabela, an avid outdoorsman from Chappell, Nebraska, found himself at an outdoors and sporting goods show in Chicago. Walking up and down the aisles, he saw an item that intrigued him: fishing flies for only pennies apiece.

Dick bought a bunch of them, and when he returned home ran a classified ad in a Casper, Wyoming, newspaper offering "12 hand-tied flies for $1.00." The ad generated only one response. He mulled it over, abandoned his original plan and decided to run a small classified ad in a national sporting goods magazine. The new ad read "Free Introductory offer! 5 hand-tied flies . . . 25¢ Postage . . . Handling." Orders started pouring in.

Each evening, Dick and his wife, Mary, sat at the kitchen table filling that day's orders and inserting a simple mimeographed catalog of other outdoor items for sale. Their first warehouse, built the next year, was a small shed in their backyard. Dick recruited his brother Jim to join the fledgling enterprise in 1963. None of the three took any money out of the company for years, spending it instead on equipment and inventory. By 1964 the new business moved into its first headquarters; the basement of their father's furniture store.

Today, Cabela's produces more than 7,000 catalog pages annually and sends out more than 120 million catalogs each year; its mammoth outdoor stores-cum-museums are the top tourist attractions in nearly every state where they're located; the world headquarters in Sidney, Nebraska, is the size of six football fields; and more than 1.5 million customers carrying a Cabela's Visa card issued by their own bank will spend $13 billion in 2011.

The Difference Between Merchants and Retailers

One of the big reasons for Cabela's continued success is that the company is made up of authentic merchants. According to Dennis Highby, who joined the firm in 1976 and was Cabela's CEO until 2009, "A good merchant is a person who is an end user, someone who goes out in the field with a product, uses it, and gets sweaty and dirty with it."

Highby says that most retailers have become so burdened with regulations regarding samples that they've ceased being merchants. "At most companies," he says, "if a salesperson came in and offered a buyer a rod and reel and said, 'Go ahead and use it,' he wouldn't be allowed. And if the salesman asked you to join him in Alaska for a week and try out his gear, that'd be totally off limits. We have our rules, but our merchandisers really enjoy trying new gear, seeing what does and doesn't work, and being out in the field." Highby says it gives the merchandisers at Cabela's a distinct competitive advantage.

To walk the halls of Cabela's headquarters is to witness the pages of their catalogs come alive. Almost all 1,200 people who work there in merchandising, catalog design, production, and other departments become product testers when they're asked to wear a pair of shoes, outerwear, or casual clothing for a year. "Some people love the program," Highby says with a grin, "while others hate it. Our merchandisers ask people to sign something out to wear or use for a full year, and just when those nice new shoes, waders, or coat are getting broken in, they have to bring them back in, give them up and we rip them apart and dissect them."

One third of Cabela's products carry the company's own label and have been designed and patented in house. Highby says, "We have lots of people here who have patents, including myself. There isn't any way you can invent something and get it patented unless you're an avid user and see a need for modification or improvement."

There's more to the magic of the Cabela's experience than simply being able to purchase the same innovative and high-quality merchandise that's used (and often designed) by the merchants themselves. Since the day Dick and Jim Cabela started the business, they've shared a nearly religious zeal for exceeding every customer's expectations. That commitment to satisfying customers has become the unifying ethos of the organization.

Dennis Highby says, "Lots of companies say they're committed to the customer, and in many instances it's simply not true. Whether it's a pair of shoes that haven't fit quite right for the year a customer has owned them, or merchandise returned six months after the purchase, our answer is always the same," Highby says, "Yes, we'll take it back and exchange it or give the customer his money back."

Such an unflinching committment to treating customers right doesn't extend only to shoes and outerwear. "Just yesterday," Highby relates, "I heard a story about one of our customers who was on an eight-thousand-dollar hunting trip through our travel and adventure agency. We pride ourselves on sending people only on great trips. However, on this particular trip the customer didn't really have a chance to hunt because he was kept busy helping the outfitter set up camps for the next guy coming in. We want this customer to be happy and tell his friends that Cabela's treated him right so we wrote a refund check for the full eight thousand dollars, apologized, and fixed the problem so it won't happen again."

Cabela's unwavering commitment to its customers is what

convinced Tommy Millner, Highby's successor as CEO, to leave family, friends and the dream home he and his wife built in the Carolinas to live in Nebraska. "You can't buffalo the customer because they often know just as much as or more than you do," Millner points out. "When I lined up all the universe of retailers, big and small, that I knew as the CEO of Remington, the one place where the people lived, ate, slept, and never tried to buffalo a customer was right here in Sydney, Nebraska.

"I don't care how damn big you are, it's all about the customer. So when they asked me to join them in March 2009, I thought 'this would be my dream job,' and it is. It's the greatest move of my life."

Millner is just as excited about the culture of continuous improvement that is at the core of Cabela's. "Adaptation is critical. You've got to adapt. No matter how successful you are, the minute you can't do what you've done, you've got to let it go. If you don't continuously improve, you die."

Abandoning a Logo

Contrary to that wholesome value of "stick-to-it-tiveness" that people in America's Midwest pride themselves on having, Cabela's has proven itself remarkably adept at letting go of merchandise, products, and processes that might stand in the way of its growth.

Highby recalls attending a seminar in Chicago on the subject of making company catalogs more effective. The expert conducting the workshop had collected catalogs from the companies in attendance and was using them in his presentation, citing what was right and wrong with each. Highby recalls being dutifully proud of the current Cabela's catalog, especially in light of the fact that the company had recently passed the $100-million mark in revenue. Finally, the expert held up a Cabela's catalog and began criticizing it, saying, "One of the things wrong with this catalog is that on the bottom of the cover page it says, 'quality, service, price, and satisfaction guaranteed.'" In Highby's version of the story the teacher continued his lecture by pointing out, "the problem with talking about quality, service, price, and satisfaction being guaranteed is that everybody says it and nobody believes it."

Highby and the Cabela brothers could have returned home to Sidney and thumbed their noses at the instructor's advice. After all, they were the real success story; already doing more than $100 million in annual revenue. But instead, in Highby's words, "We spent nearly a month stewing on the subject and considering if we should change the front of our catalog." Having spent time with Highby and the Cabela's team, his use of the word "stewing" is appropriate. Soon after meeting them, it was clear that once they get hold of an idea, someone would have more success wrestling a bone away from a rabid dog than getting them to give it up until they were finished with it.

In dollar terms, Cabela's was already the largest outdoor sporting goods company and a trip to Europe confirmed that no company there was larger. "We traveled all over," says Highby. "Amsterdam, Munich, London, and found all these little dinky stores and holes in the wall and finally realized that indeed we were the biggest. Off the masthead and catalog came the too-familiar "quality, service, price, and satisfaction guaranteed" that had been used on catalogs sent to hundreds of thousands of customers over the years. It was replaced with the newly trademarked "World's Foremost Outfitter." Later came "World's Foremost Bank," "World's Foremost Hunting and Fishing Consultants" (the Outdoor Adventures division), and the "World's Foremost Outfitter" retail locations.

Letting Go of Merchandise

Cabela's has spent forty years cracking the code on how to economically produce compelling, jam-packed, full-color catalogs. The 130 million catalogs that Cabela's mails out each year include hosts of titles addressing scores of outdoor, hunting, and fishing interests including those directed at fly fishers, saltwater fishermen, camping and backpacking devotees, turkey hunters, salmon fishermen, clothing for hunting, outdoor footwear, cabin owners, all-terrain–vehicle enthusiasts, and boat and gun owners. Customers fortunate enough to be given one of the company's Special Limited Edition catalogs receive a full-color, hard-bound collection of all the company's specialty catalogs containing nearly 1,500 pages and more than 100,000 items. The catalog items aren't chosen randomly or because a Cabela's team member personally likes the item—there is a highly orchestrated reason behind every item choice. They've turned catalog sales into a finite science and can predict within a percentage point precisely the total sales that each catalog will generate.

"Let me show you an example of how we work," says Highby, grabbing and randomly opening a catalog. "See this?" he asks. "It's page 684. We know exactly what it costs to prepare, produce, and mail this single page and we know exactly what the items on the page [the page he was pointing at featured turkey frying kits, food oil filter pumps, and cajun marinade kits] have to generate in gross profit to make it back into a catalog again."

"What would happen," I wonder, "if an item generated sales but failed to return the anticipated gross profit?"

"First," he answered, "there'd be a lot of questions for the merchandiser who selected the item. If the merchandiser had a solid defense, such as a bad picture or botched copy, the item might be given one more chance. But it wouldn't happen twice. Our business is built on knowing precisely how many calls, hits, faxes, and mail orders we're going to receive, when we'll receive them, and the dollars they'll generate."

We pushed him further and wondered what would happen to a merchandiser who consistently made bad choices for inclusion in the catalog. "If you're asking if they'd be fired," he responded, "the answer is no. We need lots of good people here for all the work we have to do and we'd find them a job that was better suited to their skill set."

Each year the company abandons approximately 15 percent of the items carried in previous catalogs that failed to achieve the company's required gross profit. Each year the company also reinvests a significant portion of its operating profits into new specialty catalogs and the expansion of their mailing list. Being experts at forecasting the revenues and profits that each catalog will generate provides the company a unique competitive advantage.

But even this immensely successful catalog strategy is itself open to change. "Our old catalog format is being reinvented," Millner said. "We still mail about 130 million copies, but now we are making them smaller and more focused on 'what to do with the product' lifestyle issues rather than the dense product and price assortment. And our new format prompts you to go visit our Web site." Catalog and Web site business continue to grow and now bring in about $1 billion annually, 38 percent of Cabela's total sales.

Abandoning the Traditional Approach to Retail Stores

When Dennis Highby arrived at Cabela's in the mid-1970s the company was already active in retail with a small store in Sidney, Nebraska, that had "one store manager, a single employee, and a single game trophy hanging on the wall." Retail was decidedly second string to the catalog business, which was growing 20 to 40 percent each year.

Eventually, the team decided to open its first large store—three hours outside Sidney on Interstate 80—in Kearney, Nebraska. It was a surprise hit and led to the decision in 1991 to open Cabela's 89,000-square-foot flagship store in Sidney, Nebraska. At this point, opening retail stores was still not part of any grand strategy—the Sidney store was built to showcase the catalog offerings. However, it was another surprise hit. According to Mike Callahan, senior vice president of retail operations and marketing, the flagship store, located next door to the company's world headquarters "in a town of six thousand, a county of ten thousand and hours away from the nearest metropolitan area, draws more than one million people and rings up sales of more than forty million dollars each year."

Before joining the company, Callahan had been the merchandising manager for a chain of forty sporting goods stores in Utah and, upon arrival at Cabela's, he says he was horrified by what he found. "I was mentored under some tough sporting goods businessmen," he says, "who'd come out of the war surplus business where every last inch of floor space was devoted to selling merchandise and visual display was nonexistent." Callahan soon discovered that Jim and Dick Cabela and Dennis Highby were abandoning the traditional rulebook about retail stores.

"I couldn't believe," he says, "the amount of nonselling space being built into the Sidney store. Everywhere you looked there were going to be mountains packed with wildlife, larger-than-life bronze statuary, and aquariums teeming with fish. The leadership had the vision," he says admiringly, "to abandon tradition and say, 'this is who we are, this is what we're about, and this is what we stand for.'"

Based on the success of the flagship store, Cabela's had developed a strategy to place stores in the right locations based on a number of factors including a critical mass of hunters, fishermen, and outdoor enthusiasts. The company soon began planning their next store and, again bucking conventional wisdom that dictates stores must be located in dense urban areas, they selected another rural location: Owatonna, Minnesota, population 35,000. The only change in the Minnesota store was to double the new store's square footage to more than 150,000 square feet (more than three times the size of a football field). It quickly became Minnesota's second most popular tourist attraction, trailing only the world's largest mall—the Mall of America—in popularity.

In short order there were other retail outlets in East Grand Forks, Minnesota; Prairie du Chien, Wisconsin; Mitchell, South Dakota; and Dundee, Michigan, where the store is more than 225,000 square feet and does more than $400 per square foot in sales in an industry where one third of that is considered a solid performance. In 2004 Cabela's opened its first East Coast store in Hamburg, Pennsylvania. The Pennsylvania store is nearly 250,000 square feet and is expected to draw 7 million visitors and customers during its first year of operation. In 2004 Cabela's also opened a 176,000-square-foot store in Wheeling, West Virginia, adjacent to a 595,000-square-foot distribution center. The company announced it would build two stores in Texas—one in Fort Worth and one in Buda—as well as one in Utah. In 2009, seeing the end of easy access to capital and a severe slowdown in new real estate development, Cabela's let go of the "monster store" concept that had worked so well for them. They started imagining the "Next Generation" storefront. "These new designs," Millner explained, "range from 80,000 to 125,000 square feet [half the size of the previous model]. They are also often repurposed [using a structure created for some now-defunct Mervyn's department stores, for example] and located where people already shop instead of in new, but more remote locations. It's all a big departure from a strategy a lot of people would cling to as 'what made Cabela's great.'"

But Cabela's knows why you need to let go. Designing and refining the Next Generation storefronts has paid off big. "Currently our Next Generation stores are outperforming Cabela's best-in-the-industry company averages for sales per square foot," says Millner. "That's a big number!" he adds. "You see, a merchant has to be right on the peg when you've got so much less space, or the customer will be disappointed. So we've gotten even better, even sharper at merchandising the stores. The Next Generation stores are teaching us to use all our product expertise, local knowledge, intensive training for store associates, and our big box efficiencies to adapt to the world of 2011 and continue to wow the Cabela's customer."

Necessity can be the mother of incredible reinvention if you can let go of what's always worked in the past.

Letting Go of Pay Plans

There are few places that executives fear to tread more than the area of changing pay plans. The belief that people are fiercely protective of their paychecks and don't want management tinkering with and changing them has been proven time and again to anyone who's ever tried changing a pay structure.

For twelve years between 1994 and 2006, Dave Roehr was Cabela's go-to guy, serving as executive vice president, CFO, president, and head of Cabela's World's Foremost Bank, the issuer of the company's Visa cards. According to Dennis Highby, "He previously served as VP and CFO of the company before we started formalizing titles."

Roehr says one of the most important things Cabela's ever abandoned was its former compensation plan in favor of a company-wide, performance-based structure that he was charged with moving throughout the company. Roehr, who was a partner in the international accounting firm Grant Thornton prior to joining Cabela's, says that the previous plan looked just like the compensation plans at most companies. "It was real hodgepodge," he says. "People generally got the same bonuses each year simply because they'd gotten one the year before. We really didn't have a comprehensive program. It had been cobbled together over the years as the company had grown and in most cases it rewarded revenue growth instead of profitable revenue growth."

We wondered if it was difficult selling the new plan inside the company. Roehr says, "Pick the words you want to use to describe the reactions: fear, trepidation, anger, frustration. We had it all. It was a big sales job. But as soon as the first year's bonus checks were paid out, the culture absolutely changed and our real dramatic profit growth began."

In addition to equity-based compensation being available to workers, under the changed plan, which has no caps, the company sets aside 15 percent of its profits each year for distribution to all exempt employees. Then the top executives analyze the company's performance and allocate a percentage of the pool to various departments based on their contribution to the company's overall performance.

Next, the manager of each department awards bonus payments to individuals based on their performance and contributions to the company that year. It's a generous program, and in many instances the bonus exceeds an employee's annual salary. By 2011, more than

40 percent of Cabela's employees had become stockholders, which is significant in that nearly half of its labor force is part-time, given the seasonal nature of its sales.

Roehr says the benefits of the performance-based compensation plan are well worth the effort of selling it to the company. "It's forced everyone to work together as a team," he says. "Interdivisional rivalries were eliminated. There's no sense in being a lone ranger. Company politics were eliminated and people let go of their little territories." Because the program is so generous and there's no upper limit to how much an individual can earn, Roehr says that there's been a huge unintended benefit as well.

"We suspected that the program would provide us extremely low turnover," he says, "and it's accomplished that because no one wants to leave such a generous compensation program behind. The unintended benefit occurs when we're recruiting people to join us. People who want the specific dollar amounts of their individual compensation program agreed to in advance," he says, "probably aren't right for Cabela's. This is a company where you come on board, join a team, pitch in and do whatever needs to be done and are generously rewarded for your efforts."

Let Go of Rules

Millner is very explicit in spelling out his attitude about rules. "There are two ways to run a big company: by rules or by values," he says. "As we grew so rapidly over three decades, the way leaders maintained order and avoided chaos was by writing a rule. After a while, there was a rule for everything. We had rules for vacation that were so tight that I got handed a request for thirty minutes of vacation from the CFO. I said, 'Roger . . . what the hell.' He said, 'It's a rule.' Another example was the rule about using a unique five-digit code when dialing on a company phone. I had to plug 12281 every time I made a call. It annoyed me and made me feel like big brother was watching.

"Ninety-nine percent of the 12,500 employees at Cabela's come to work every day and to do the right thing. We need to trust them,"

Millner continues. "The fact is everyone knows who's playing games and not pulling their weight. Managers need to deal with that. If someone abuses our trust, we coach them. If they do it too much, they don't work here anymore."

Millner says that Cabela's leadership has made changes to reflect the faith they have in their employees. "We've stopped tracking vacation at headquarters. We empower the associate with their manager to take the right amount of earned vacation. We trust them. We stopped demanding a five-digit code for every call. We trust them to make phone calls. Having rules at this point is totally counterproductive because it constrains the entrepreneurial spirit. Now our values keep us from chaos, and it has unleashed the organization to adapt and succeed."

Knowing When to Stick It Out

Even though Cabela's has become masterful at letting go of logos, merchandise, processes, conventional wisdom, and pay plans, Dennis Highby cautions against tossing the baby out with the bathwater. "We almost had a category failure a few years ago," he says, "with our Salt Water catalog. It was a small catalog, about one hundred and twenty pages, and it simply wasn't working. Our merchants were frustrated and beating themselves up and starting to think, 'We're in Nebraska, what do we know about saltwater?'"

Highby's suggestion to the merchant group was to add a hundred pages and nearly double the size of the catalog. He says, "They looked at me like I was crazy and asked, 'Why in the world would we do that?'"

Highby continues, "I told them that as good merchants we had to try something before killing it off. If something isn't working, fix it, and if it can't be fixed, then get rid of it." According to Highby, "They did it and it turned out to be a huge home run."

At Cabela's and all the other companies we studied, we observed what appeared to be an unspoken rule: if it was a good enough idea to try, then it deserved one dramatic reinvention before being tossed out.

Standing on Principle

Guiding principles are critical for companies and help them decide when they should stand like a rock and where they can free themselves to let go. Many agents of change don't fully appreciate the beauty of what exists and demand change for change's sake.

Cabela's stands like a rock with two guiding principles that it won't abandon under any circumstances:

1. Prudent but Impatient Growth

"The core reason for our success," Millner clarifies, "is this amazing culture Jim, Dick, and Dennis built. The retail landscape is littered with companies who grew too fast. . . . Circuit City, Wards, others. I mean they were once great retail companies but grew fast and beyond their ability to satisfy customers. I won't stand for that. We will grow, but it will be prudent, impatient growth, always at a measured pace, five or six stores next year."

2. Getting Customers to Say "Holy Smokes"

"We can never lose the feeling we create when dad or granddad brings a youngster into the store and the child says, 'Wow!' That's core DNA here," Millner said adamantly. "We have big boards that tell the customer what fish is biting on the lake and where the deer are running. We have mountains and aquariums and beams with a trophy bear crawling.

"We're doing trips now—pheasant hunting, fly fishing, bird safaris in Argentina, water fowl events, and more. We're pulling off an incredible trip for our loyal customers, something they always wanted to do but haven't. We want to deepen the loyalty bond and get them to say 'holy smokes' again."

Adapting to Public Ownership

When we identified Cabela's as a company that qualified for inclusion in the book, it was a privately held company. In 2004, with half of Cabela's stock still owned by the two founding brothers, the difficult decision to finally go public was made. Most often when companies go public it's for one of two reasons: either they need capital for growth or it's an estate planning tool for the founders.

"In the late nineties," says Highby, "we began asking what we were going to do with the company. We were asking the question because if one of the brothers suddenly wasn't around one day, we could have had a real big problem. We looked at selling but knew that anyone interested in buying it would probably think it's too hard to recruit people to Sidney, Nebraska, and use that as a reason to justify moving the company. Jim and Dick live here in town and wanted the company to stay here."

Highby says, "If the company had been sold to another company there could have been a big mess: a strategic buyer probably wouldn't have paid what the company was worth, and a buyer from the financial community might have tried ramping up the company too quickly in order to do their own IPO. So in order to keep the company's culture intact a decision was made to go public."

When we initially interviewed Highby in 2004, we asked him if he thought going public would change the company. "I don't think so," said Highby. "We're in it for the long haul and have promised continued annual growth in the sixteen- to seventeen-percent range. As long as we do that," he said, "long-term investors should see an increase in their share value each year."

The company went public in 2005, and since then it has increased its annual revenues from $1.3 billion to nearly $3 billion. Anyone who purchased shares when the company went public has been well rewarded.

If There's No Profit in It . . . Let It Go

We quickly discerned that the art of abandoning wasn't limited to Cabela's. One thing that separated all the top nine companies from their lesser performing rivals was that each has demonstrated the ability to let go of processes, profit centers, and even legacies when they risk distracting the company from the realization of continued revenue growth and the achievement of its full economic potential. Dot Foods was no exception.

In 1986, as the big warehouse clubs were taking off, Dot Foods began distributing to them. In only four years, that piece of business grew to more than 25 percent of the company's total and was very profitable. Then suddenly, the industry rapidly consolidated. There was intense downward pressure on already slim margins and as the supply chain changed, Dot Foods lost a major contract.

Instead of abandoning one quarter of their total annual revenues, most companies would have desperately tried to replace the supply contract and slashed their own costs even further to accommodate margins that were being continually compressed. According to Pat Tracy, Dot's former CEO, "We packed our bags and painfully left that business in order to apply our business capacity in other areas."

Dot Foods, which was founded as a distributor of dry milk solids to food manufacturers and ice cream manufacturing plants, is even considering leaving *that* business. Today, because that portion of the business requires more attention than its revenues and profits justify, Pat Tracy says the family may consider divesting itself of it.

Dot Foods has demonstrated its willingness to abandon unprofitable business units and is even prepared to let go of its legacy business for the greater good and future of the organization.

Letting Go of "What You've Always Been"

Medline is a company that has historically manufactured its own products. A big part of its sales pitch to existing and prospective customers has been, "Because we manufacture our own products, we can deliver them to you at a substantial savings."

However, according to John Marks, the company's director of corporate communications, in recent years many large hospitals and health-care systems have consolidated the number of vendors they work with in order to gain efficiency and cost savings.

To keep business it already had, Medline had to become a distributor of competitors' products as well as a manufacturer of its own. "There was risk involved," says Marks, "because we were entering an entirely different business." Medline demonstrated its ability to let go of egos, history, and the way things had always been done and as a result, according to Marks, the firm has gained significant and profitable business and has become one of the nation's four major distributors of health-care supplies in the nation. Medline proved its ability to let go of the "same old, same old" that said, "we're manufacturers" and grew to the next level.

Letting Go . . . at the Last Minute

At PETCO, Chairman Brian Devine prides himself on creating and nurturing a culture where workers and executives are encouraged to challenge the direction of the company or suggest new ways of doing business.

"Recently," according to Brian Shaw, the company's director of strategic development, "executives and designers at the company had spent more than a year developing a new store design to carry the retail chain into the future. The first test store was already open and everyone agreed that the new design represented the future PETCO store.

"Then," says Shaw, "one of the company's junior executives presented a daring new store design to senior management. He was surprised to find an open-minded audience." His suggestion, according to Shaw, "was to expand the aquatics department beyond anything the design team had imagined, and place an elaborate collection of tanks and displays smack in the middle of the store. The proposed new display included every type of aquarium imaginable from live reef tanks to koi ponds."

Shaw says, "The idea was a completely new one; customers would walk around the racetrack and, while being awed by the aquatics presentation, would be simultaneously exposed to all the other merchandise in the store, including dog, cat, bird, and small animal."

The proposed changes were dramatic considering that fish had always occupied just a small portion of a single wall in the typical PETCO store, and the merchandise had been a limited assortment for beginning and intermediate hobbyists. "Adopting the new design would mean the company would also have to significantly change its merchandising strategy to appeal to advanced hobbyists as well," Shaw says.

"Even though the executives being shown the new, last-minute proposal were all personally invested in and had signed off on the prototype," says Shaw, "everyone in the meeting got excited about the proposed change because the idea had the wow factor that all retailers constantly seek.

"Immediately," he recalls, "a team was created to plan for a test store. Within six months it was open and all new stores and remodels reflect the new design."

There's not a snowball's chance in hell that the scenario played out at PETCO would occur in most companies. In most businesses the junior executive wouldn't have gotten on the agenda, much less have found a receptive audience. Either the idea would have been deep-sixed by others with egos on the line or stolen away and presented at a later date as belonging to them. At PETCO, ideas that make you go wow are more important than defending past decisions and massaging executive egos.

A Word of Warning

Stunning execution is something that separates great companies from the mediocre. Occasionally execution takes a while. The art of letting go shouldn't be confused with either constantly coming up with new strategies or failing to properly execute a strategic plan already in place. A strategic plan should only be thrown out after it's been determined that the execution was as error free as possible.

Companies that consistently grow their revenues prove the

proposition of thinking big and acting small by not allowing yesterday's breadwinners, a same-old philosophy, and huge egos to get in the way of their biggest objective: finding, keeping, and growing the right customers.

Think BIG, Act SMALL
LETTING GO

- When it's DOA, bury it.
- Leave yesterday's breadwinners behind when they no longer make sense.
- If it was worth doing the first time, it probably deserves one reinvention.
- If reinventing it doesn't work—let it go.
- Don't defend the way things have always been done.
- Egos aren't a valid reason for continuing to do things the same way.
- Constantly search for "wow" in order to replace "okay."
- Traditional approaches seldom yield giant results.

Have Everyone Think and Act Like *the* Owner

KOCH INDUSTRIES

"In a market economy, the decision-making ability naturally flows to people who create value and away from those who don't, and thereby suffer losses."

CHARLES KOCH, chair and CEO of Koch Industries

Companies that consistently increase revenues prove the proposition of thinking BIG and acting small by mastering the art of creating and sustaining organizations where everyone thinks and acts like the owner.

Before I launch into our discoveries, look again at the top of the page. I italicized the word "the" in the title for a reason. There's a world of difference between *the* owner and just *an* owner.

Wall Street is an owner. They buy in and sell out quickly, focusing on immediate gains, and if they find none, then they put lipstick on the pigs and go looking for a greater fool. One senior financial services director laughed when he heard me say that six months was the average ownership tenure in mutual funds. "I thought you were going to say six minutes, not six months," he said. "Just before you called I asked one of my fund managers if we should make another move on a stock intraday. We've got a casino mentality where everyone constantly cashes in."

Many people in business act like a Wall Street owner. They look out for number one, are very political, do just enough to meet minimum expectations, and follow that casino mentality. Some of these are very high-profile people who have founded and built companies. You'd expect them to act like the owner, but they don't.

An owner puts money into a business; the owner invests a lot more than dollars and cents. An owner keeps his finger in the wind, ready to change direction; the owner has beliefs and boundaries that act like stakes deep in the ground. An owner will break his word if he can legally get away with it; the owner keeps commitments to stakeholders at every level and doesn't need threats from governments or lawyers to do what's right. Being an owner is a high-profile gig that's supposed to be fun and sexy with time for cocktail parties and exotic vacations. Being the owner is long hours, keeping one's hands dirty, constant learning, and facing your mistakes and fixing them—all without a lot of fanfare. Still, people who are the owners have no regrets. They love all they do.

Steve Jobs was the owner at Apple. He thought differently. Ingvar Kamprad is the owner of IKEA. He's not cashing in his chips. Dan DiMicco (Nucor), Michael O'Leary (Ryanair), and Jim Goodnight (SAS) are, along with score of others, cut from the same cloth.

One company I researched is not only led by people who think and act like the owners but has figured out how to get nearly all its 67,000 employees to embrace that same mind-set. Its story can be a game changer for your business.

Koch Industries

Since 1960 the stock market (using the S&P 500 and assuming the reinvestment of all dividends) has grown more than ninety-five-fold. Using this same assumption, GE, constantly heralded as the world's best example of a well-managed company, has grown more than six hundredfold. But during the same time and using the same

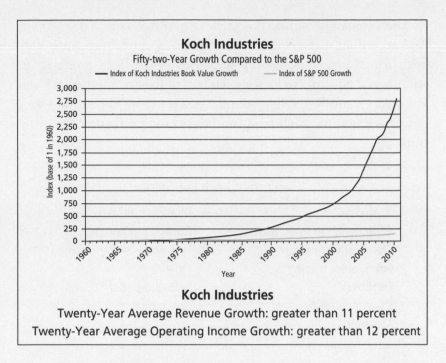

Koch Industries
Fifty-two-Year Growth Compared to the S&P 500

— Index of Koch Industries Book Value Growth   — Index of S&P 500 Growth

Koch Industries
Twenty-Year Average Revenue Growth: greater than 11 percent
Twenty-Year Average Operating Income Growth: greater than 12 percent

assumption, Koch Industries, based in Wichita, Kansas, has grown more than two thousandfold, or twenty times the rate of the S&P and three and a third times better than GE.

Koch Industries is one of the most efficient, consistent, productive, and profitable companies in the world. Its unparalleled forty-year track record is compelling evidence that it knows more about consistently increasing revenues and profits than any other company.

The lessons to be learned from Koch are better understood when the company's genesis and evolution are known.

The Early Years

Koch Industries' predecessor firm was cofounded by Fred C. Koch in 1940 with roots in the refining industry. Today the privately held company is led by his sons Charles and David and views itself not as a product-focused company but as "a collection of capabilities on a continuous search to create value."

The company's annual revenues currently exceed $100 billion. And according to *Forbes*, it's the nation's second-largest privately held firm. Current ownership activities range from ranching to refining and pipelines to plastics. The list of the areas in which Koch Industries is involved might sound like a portfolio of less-than-sexy businesses but, as you'll read, nothing could be further from the truth.

The Current Koch Portfolio

Asphalt	Municipal finance
Capital market investments	Natural gas liquids
Chemical technology	Petroleum and chemicals
Commodity trading	Pipelines
Fertilizers	Pulp and paper
Fibers and resins	Ranching
Minerals	

To the people at Koch, like the owners of any enterprise, their business is very stimulating and even sexy. "I was pretty damn excited when I took this job," said Koch's head of mergers and acquisitions, Ron Vaupel. "And I'm even more excited today!"

Vaupel is right to be excited. Koch Industries is one of the most efficient, consistent, productive, and profitable companies in the world. Koch's unparalleled forty-year track record is compelling evidence that it has acquired more knowledge about consistently increasing revenues and profits than any other company. More important, it has done something very rare: creating and sustaining a huge enterprise where everyone think and acts like the owner. This is not an accident. Charles Koch and his leadership team made up their minds to get new people and acquired companies to unleash an incredible potential. They looked into experience and history and decided success required a different mind-set to do incredibly well in a market-based environment, to think and act like the owner.

Koch's entire team openly shared with me their strategies and lessons learned. But for us to absorb it all, let's first take a look at the company's genesis and evolution.

Charles Koch's father put him to work at age six, pulling dandelions at the family's large Wichita property. "We had a quarter section," says Koch. "I could have pulled those weeds twenty-four hours a day and never gotten them all." Even though the family home was across the street from a country club, there'd be no golf or tennis for Charles. "By the time I was nine," he says, "my father decided I wasn't busy enough and put me to work baling hay, digging ditches, and working in the shop downtown."

At the age of eleven Charles was sent off to a series of boarding schools in Colorado, Texas, and Arizona. Finally, after being kicked out of a military academy in Indiana following an episode involving beer, his parents sent him to Texas to live with an uncle and to finish his senior year of high school. While there he scored a perfect one hundred on the math final and was razzed by his friends. "Why didn't you just finish enough problems to get a seventy and pass instead of a hundred?" they teased. But Koch's aptitude for math earned him entrance to MIT.

"I loved MIT," he says of the school where he earned a bachelor's degree and two masters in six years. What Koch enjoyed so much about MIT is reflected in the character of the company he leads. "I've always been a free spirit and a rebel," Koch confesses, "always bucking the system in boarding and military schools. But MIT was great. You didn't have to go to class, you didn't have to do anything other than complete your projects and pass the tests." Eventually, it turned out that completing projects and constantly being tested would become a big part of the Koch culture.

After Koch completed his studies at MIT, he joined a top consulting firm in Boston. Before long his father was imploring him to move back to Wichita. "He worked on me for more than a year," recalls Koch, "and finally told me he was in poor health and either I had to move back and run things or he was going to sell the company."

Koch, a strong-willed individual, had hesitations about going back to Wichita. "I'd seen other sons go to work for their fathers, and it was always a nightmare. They were never allowed to develop or grow." But according to Koch, his experience with his father was just the opposite.

The Son Rises

"The company my father owned," says Koch, "was a crude oil gathering company called Rock Island. But there was also a small company named Koch Engineering Company, selling a single product, that he'd put in the names of my three brothers and me. As soon as I walked in," says Koch, "my father told me to go and run that company." His father offered only two pieces of advice. The first was to head to Europe and figure out whether it made sense to build a factory in order to replace the inconsistent fabricators they'd been using, and the second was a wish: that his son's first deal would be a loser because otherwise "you'll think you're a lot smarter than you are."

Koch got a European factory up, running, and profitable and upon his return to Wichita, Charles arranged for Koch Engineering to begin offering allied products for refineries and chemical-processing plants. It wasn't long before the earnings of Koch Engineering were approaching what the total revenues had been when Koch took over. After that his father asked him to take over Rock Island as well.

In short order, Koch and Sterling Varner, his second in command at Rock Island, began plotting ways for the company to become more aggressive and grow more quickly. "One time," says Koch, "my father was leaving on a trip to Africa, would be unreachable for weeks, and knew we were contemplating two possible acquisitions." His father's stern warning to the duo was to agree on a single acquisition but under no circumstances to do them both.

"The moment he was on the airplane," he recalls fondly, "we

bought both companies and sent him a telegram, which was read aloud in front of his entire expedition." According to Koch his father was so angry that when he returned home and Charles picked him up at the airport, he wouldn't even speak to him. "Only later," Koch says with a smile, "after both purchases worked out well, would my father begrudgingly admit both made sense.

"It was about that time," he says, "that I became aware of how little I knew about business. The mathematical stuff had always come easy, and I had some idea that you had to have a competitive advantage, but beyond that all I knew was that we had an opportunity to grow and," in his words says, "I was too ignorant to know why we couldn't do things. I just tried. There were stumbles and mistakes," he adds, "but thankfully they were all small enough that they didn't kill us."

The Real Learning Begins

It was about that time that Charles Koch began reading *Philosophy of Science* (a journal committed to furthering study of and free discussion about the philosophy of science from diverse standpoints). "I'm not someone who can handle more than one bucket," he says. "I can't have a business bucket in one hand and a philosophy of science bucket in another so it was natural to begin integrating them." The more Koch read and learned, the more voracious his appetite became. "I developed two passions," he says. "One was to build a great company and the other was to understand the principles that lead to peace, prosperity, and social progress.

"I began studying hundreds of books," Koch says, "and had so many that my bookshelves were overflowing and there were so many on the floor I had to tunnel through them." Koch read everything he could get his hands on: economics, history, philosophy, psychology, and the hard sciences. Koch recalls that while reading a book titled *Why Wages Rise* by F. A. Harper, the founder of the Institute of Humane Studies (later chaired by Koch), he had his eureka moment. "I thought to myself, 'My God, if I keep reading and learning, I can figure out the way the world works!'"

One of the books that impressed Charles Koch was an arcane text titled *Eupsychian Management* by Abraham Maslow. ("Eupsychian" was coined by Maslow and comes from "eu" meaning good and "psyche" meaning soul . . . thus meaning having a good soul.)

"What Maslow did," says Koch, "was put one thousand people on an island and then go through a thought experiment on how they would organize themselves. Even though he was kind of a socialist," he says with a frown, "the way these people organized themselves and cooperated with one another led Maslow to conclude that people can only truly gain by making other people better off." This led Koch to conclude that a company can only achieve authentic success by creating value for others. Although the book had been long out of print, Koch had it reprinted and gave copies to company employees.

Each time Koch reads a worthwhile book and makes a discovery, he integrates his findings into the way the company conducts business. Many of these findings led to his belief that responsibility and accountability are intertwined with a sense of ownership. "Even the way we interview and hire people came about as a result of a book," he says. "Are you familiar with the former Freudian Karen Horney's book, *Neurosis and Human Growth: The Struggle Toward Self-Realization?*"

I admit that this is one that had never appeared on my radar screen, and Koch explains, "She came to the United States from Germany, repudiated Freudian philosophy, and wrote in this book about something she called vindictive glory and vindictive triumph. She said psychological health is being comfortable with and being able to face who you really are and deal with reality."

Koch says, "I'd always wondered why some people work to destroy any evidence of their shortcomings and wreak destruction on anyone who attempts to point them out. As a result of Horney's book, the way Koch Industries interviews people changed and questions were added to identify defensive people and learn whether they would be willing to admit when they'd made a mistake or would instead try to cover them up."

Market Based Management

By the time Koch's father died in 1967, Charles Koch was in charge and had begun systemizing the implementation of all the things he'd learned. The collection of everything Koch learned was eventually given a name: Market Based Management® (MBM).

Koch Industries MBM is essentially a nonbureaucratic, market-driven approach to management where the value that an employee creates determines his or her responsibilities and pay, not title and formal hierarchy. Steve Daley, one of the leaders of MBM system training explains, "You can have two employees who have exactly the same title, exactly the same experience—length of time at the company—but have radically different decision rights. Some are able to hire while others haven't proven themselves capable. Some have hundreds of thousands of dollars at their disposal; others have zero in terms of authorizing a capital expenditure. It doesn't mean they are precluded from being a manager. We just don't allow role to determine the authorities; competency and capability determine it. In fact," Daley adds, "You could find a subordinate who may have more authority for certain decisions than her supervisor. The supervisor would oversee and provide feedback but not have the authority himself to make a decision at that level."

Applying MBM and using its tools keeps the Koch organization flexible and fast instead of bureaucratic and slow. "It's a dynamic process," Daley explained. "We're constantly reviewing, analyzing, measuring, and making adjustments rather than waiting for some end date." MBM is passionately believed, constantly reinforced, and lived by the people who lead Koch Industries. While Charles Koch will tell you that much progress remains to be made toward full implementation throughout his very large organization of old and new Koch companies, MBM is designed to ensure that everyone acts like an entrepreneur and thinks like the owner.

That's another critical difference at Koch. "We allow time and space for people to grow," Daley said. "We will be very explicit about what we aspire to and what our culture is. We expect people to grapple with it, to ask 'What does this mean for me? Can I be effective? How do I feel? Am I comfortable? How am I doing?' It takes time. If we bought a new business, we would look at a five-year investment in changing the culture. It's not a one- or two-year journey."

Koch Industries Market Based Management®

Vision: Determining exactly where and how the business can create the greatest *long-term* value.

Virtue and Talent: Ensuring that people with the *right* values, skills, and capabilities are hired, retained, and developed.

Decision Rights: Ensuring that the right people are in the right roles with the right authority to make decisions and holding them accountable.

Knowledge Processes: Creating, acquiring, sharing, and applying relevant knowledge and measuring and tracking profitability.

Incentives: Rewarding people according to the value they create for the organization.

Vision A vision statement is the organization's view on how it plans to create a superior value for the firm and for society. Koch Industries vision is to apply MBM to identify and capture those opportunities for which their capabilities will create the greatest value and develop and implement strategies that will maximize value long-term. The core capabilities that currently represent Koch's greatest competitive advantages and enable it to create superior value are:

- Market Based Management®
- Continuous Innovation
- Operational Excellence
- Trading

- Transaction Excellence
- Public Sector Excellence

Each of these are described in great detail for all Koch employees. Vision must be clear to work. According to Steve Daley, "We believe in being explicit." They dislike what they call "pretty tie" directives. "That's when you are told you must wear a tie to the office and it must be a pretty tie," explains Ron Vaupel. The people who issue such vague rules never say what is or isn't a pretty tie, "but if some boss doesn't like your choice, you go home! How can anyone succeed in that environment? Vaupel is incredulous that there's so much vagueness in rules, regulations, directives, and strategies, and so few connect that fact with rampant dysfunction and missed goals in our world.

Virtue and Talent　In Chapter 1 we listed the ten guiding principles of Koch Industries as an example of a highly successful company's standing for something. Koch's guiding principles have teeth. "If we've made a mistake and hired someone who doesn't agree with principles one and two [total integrity and 10,000 percent compliance]," says an adamant Koch, "we have to get them out of the company immediately. We cannot take any risk with someone who will create legal or integrity issues for the company. People are the most productive and have passion for their work when they agree with the values of the company. Those who don't may still be good people, but would be happier somewhere else.

"A culture based on vision and virtue can only exist," Koch says, "when everyone in the company":

- knows and practices the principles;
- understands what the company is trying to accomplish;
- understands their specific role in the achievement of the objectives; and
- is prepared to have their recommendations and decisions challenged.

"It's not for everybody," Vaupel cautions. "In mergers and acquisitions it's common to get full of yourself, arrogant, to think you know more than you really know. That's how dealmakers—and managers at every level—get into trouble. We have a 'Transactional Excellence University' where leaders from across all our companies sit down two, three times every year." The goal is to get more humble and arrest the typical human fault of arrogance using a lesson-learned approach.

"There are decisions that are wildly successful," Vaupel explains, "but not for the reasons we anticipated. It's critical that you are able to dissect and understand that if you want to actually know what the hell you are doing.

"We go over the details, the key drivers, and our assumptions and then take the outcomes and look at where we missed, what we got right, and why. We try to learn from that. It's pretty humbling. It would be more fun to gloss over those details. But you need to learn to stay on top, and that means getting out of your comfort zone."

Decision Rights One of the ways Koch Industries tries to ensure that decisions are made in the company's long-term interest is by having the people with the best knowledge make them. Charles Koch says, "In a market economy, decision-making ability naturally flows to people who create value and away from those who don't, and thereby suffer losses. We strive to ensure the same thing happens here." He says, "We stress the value of quick decisions. Things are happening quickly in the marketplace, it's constantly changing and we can't dilly-dally around.

"Implicit in the idea of decision rights is that you have resources at your command," Daley adds. "As you develop your ability you will command more resources. Now when the market mechanism works, it doesn't mean it works perfectly all the time. You have to read the signals and adjust, directing your resources to areas that are going to be more valuable and away from bad positions."

Knowledge Processes Ensuring that valuable knowledge is constantly kept flowing through the organization is a major emphasis for Koch Industries. This effort has five major components:

- getting information on key industries, customers, competitors, and markets;
- constantly measuring progress on compliance and profitability, down to the smallest practical level (by project, product, plant, or customer, for example);
- teaching Market Based Management, focusing the firm's guiding principles and enhancing employees' economic thinking skills;
- the Koch Challenge Process, which is designed to ensure that projects and deals are constructively challenged from above and below, to apply the best knowledge in making decisions; and
- internal communication and knowledge sharing.

As new employees get hired or join the company through acquisitions, the Market Based Management team has the responsibility to help them understand and apply Market Based Management and the company's guiding principles. Koch's internal communications director produces a newsletter crammed with information about Koch's diverse businesses that goes out to Koch employees. In addition, he compiles detailed quarterly progress updates, which cover key compliance and profitability measures for each of the business groups and are presented to employees by each business leader. Breaking news from Koch's companies gets to employees via e-mails from Dave Robertson, Koch's president and COO, and all company leaders work to aggressively seek out and act upon employee input.

Incentives Each year many of Koch's nonhourly workers (who have their own benefits package) are evaluated and are eligible to receive bonuses based on how much economic value they've created for the firm during the previous twelve months. "The market sends clear signals about what people value and does a beautiful job of rewarding entrepreneurs for the value they create in the marketplace," says Koch. "If an entrepreneur creates a new widget and sells a million dollars' worth of them, consumers will let him keep a bit of the value he created, maybe five or ten percent after he pays his employees and other costs. Our compensation system is modeled after that and anchored in objective criteria, but it's still innately subjective. We measure everything we can and try to ascertain who contributed to the growth of Koch's value in a year. Let's say you created ten million dollars' worth of value for Koch and the market for that would permit you a five-percent return. We'd work toward bringing your total compensation in line with that five hundred thousand dollars, combining cash, deferred compensation, shadow stock, or other benefits that you value."

Market Based Management in Practice

Koch Industries even used Market Based Management to dramatically transform the revenue and profit performance of the company's 270,000-acre Beaverhead Ranch next to Yellowstone Park in Montana.

"Ray Marxer, our ranch manager," says Koch, "absorbed the spirit of Market Based Management, thought and acted like an owner and improved carrying capacity at the ranch by eight percent, increased the calf crop from ninety to ninety-five percent, increased weaning weights twenty percent, and at the same time cut operating costs by twenty-five percent. And he did it all with less than half as many full-time employees as the ranch had previously employed.

"First," says Koch, "Marxer had the vision to see that the ranch could be dramatically improved and that it required a much more stable, dedicated, and talented workforce. Next he looked at virtue, talents, and incentives and determined that people don't go into ranching for the money but because of the lifestyle, a good part of which is working with their families. So, he changed the rule that family members couldn't work on the ranch and built houses for families on the ranch with privacy and room for gardens. That immediately allowed him to recruit and retain a superior workforce.

"Then," says Koch, "he examined decision rights and knowledge processes and recognized there was no accountability, so he set up well-defined, measurable areas of responsibility and authority, and aligned the incentives.

"At the same time," says Koch, "the manager dramatically improved the ranch environmentally. He increased the seasonal population of deer and antelope to two thousand each and elk to more than four thousand, reintroduced cutthroat trout, won seven major environmental awards including one from the EPA and the Smithsonian, all because of innovative land use processes. Beaverhead became the first ranch in the country to be certified by the Wildlife Habitat Council."

Koch Industries' Secret Weapon

The phrase "creative destruction" was first used by Harvard professor Joseph Schumpeter in 1942, when he argued in his book *Capitalism, Socialism and Democracy* that "capitalism is a form of economic change that can never be stationary and that less effective firms, products, and methods must constantly be eliminated." When Charles Koch, chairman and CEO of Koch Industries, read those words he took them to heart. At Koch Industries the interpretation of creative destruction means that every business owned by the company could eventually be sold (on rare occasions shuttered) and replaced by others.

Currently the Koch Industries portfolio is composed of more than one hundred business units operating in nine different business groups.

The Current Koch Portfolio

Flint Hills Resources: Petroleum refining, chemicals, renewable fuels, lube stocks, and asphalt

Koch Mineral Services: Minerals trading and distribution, exploration, and production

Koch Pipeline: Crude oil and refined products pipelines

Koch Supply and Trading: Trades numerous commodities

Koch Nitrogen: Nitrogen fertilizer manufacture, distribution, and trading and other plant nutrients

Koch Chemical Technology Group: Mass transfer equipment, pollution control equipment, burners and flares, heat exchangers, membrane separations systems, and engineering systems

INVISTA: Nylon fiber polymer and intermediates, spandex fiber, specialty chemicals, and PTA licensing

Georgia Pacific: Consumer products, packaging, containerboard, bleach board, fluff and market pulp, structured panels, wood products, gypsum, and chemicals

Koch Farm and Ranch Holdings: Ranching

If you were a business owner and another company offered you more for your company than you thought it was worth, you'd probably sell the firm. Similarly, if the business was failing to meet your expectations, you'd consider selling it to another party or shutting it down. And that's exactly what happens at Koch Industries.

Each year every Koch business unit takes part in an exercise to assess its market value. The results of the exercise might mean the business unit will spend another year within the Koch family of companies, it occasionally means the business will be sold off, and in the rarest of instances, it might mean the beginning of a shut-down process.

"Each year," says Charles Koch, "we determine the present value and the market value of each business unit."

Hold Value The present or hold value of a business unit is determined by evaluating how much capital the business unit requires; measuring its cash flow and operating profits; and asking the most important question that can be asked at Koch: what is the business's rate of return on capital and equity? "The gist of the exercise," according to Koch, "is to determine what the business is really worth to us."

Market Value According to Koch, "The market value is simply what another company is willing to pay us for the business.

"We analyze the numbers and the future," says Koch, "and if the market value is greater than the hold value, we sell it, provided we wouldn't be giving up a core capability in the process." Following are the businesses that Koch has sold or exited in recent years:

Activated carbon	Grain milling
Air quality consulting	Grain trading
Animal feed	Image transmission
Broadband trading	International
Business aircraft	Meat processing
Canadian pipeline	Medical equipment
Carbon dioxide	Microelectronic chemicals
Ceramic products	Pizza dough
Chemical development	Power generation
Chromatography	Propane retailing
Coal mining	Refinery engineering
Commercial lending	Service stations
Cooling towers	Slag cement
Crude oil gathering	Specialty chemicals
Cryogenic systems	Sulfur plant design
Drilling rigs	Sulfuric acid
Exploration	Tankers
Feedlots	Telecommunications
Fiberglass products	Tennis court surfaces
Gas processing	Trucking

"Although it could seem otherwise, this is actually the most compassionate way to treat a business," he says. He explains his commitment to creative destruction by saying, "It goes right back to the original premise for this company. The only reason we exist is to create value and if we're not doing that better than another company can, they should have the opportunity. If a business can do better under different ownership, the employees will be better off."

Koch says there are many reasons why a business unit's market value is greater than its hold value. "Other companies might have greater capabilities than we do, they might have a different point of view regarding the future, a lower cost of capital than ours, there might be genuine synergy in their acquiring something we have, and perhaps we proved ourselves incapable of creating the value we thought we could add."

Units the company is most reluctant to sell are its trading, refining, and chemical-based businesses. Koch says, "Trading, refining, and chemicals are our laboratories where we've historically demonstrated we can invent, create, and develop other business for sale. So that factors in to the hold value of those three businesses. Generally, anytime the market value is greater than the hold value a deal gets done."

Koch bucks conventional wisdom, shuns traditional thinking, and says history has proven his belief that existing to create value and utilizing creative destruction are the surest ways to succeed in business in the long term. "Since the S&P 500 was created in 1957," he says, "fewer than ten companies have grown more than the market as a whole. What does that tell you about doing things the conventional way?"

A Common Finding

One finding that ties together all the companies we identified is that each company works hard to nurture cultures where everyone thinks and acts like an owner.

Brian Linneman, executive vice president and chief merchandising officer at Cabela's, says that financial rewards are only one part of getting people to think and act like owners. "First," he says, "you have to create an environment where people are encouraged to act like entrepreneurs," and cites one of his own experiences that took place while serving as the firm's corporate logistics manager. "I came up with an idea about changing the way we flow all the products out of our distribution centers," he says. "It was something that would have a monumental impact on our business."

When he completed his analysis, he went to his boss and told him he thought the company should do it. To his surprise, his boss said, "Go for it; do it." Linneman was shocked and said, "Wait a second, isn't there somebody or a committee I have to go in front of to get permission?" Linneman's boss said, "Nope, just go do it. What are you waiting for?"

When asked what would have happened if his idea hadn't worked out, Linneman says, "We have an attitude here that you can't make mistakes if you don't try things and if things don't work out or if you make a bad decision, you raise your hand and say, 'that one was mine.'

"Once people are thinking and making decisions like owners," says Linneman, "the next natural step is to financially reward them based on the value they add or create." We found it to be a fairly common practice that bonuses are granted not for the achievement of a specific set of numbers but instead for overall contribution as determined by people's managers. Linneman said, "Trust me, if you're doing the right job of managing people, you know exactly what they're doing and contributing and don't even need to use a piece of paper when it comes to bonus time. We always know who's contributing and who isn't."

In 1957 the auto parts company that employed seventy-two-year-old Charles F. O'Reilly and his son CH started a major reorganization that forced Charles to retire and his son to move to Kansas City.

Neither agreed with those plans and they decided to form their own company, O'Reilly Automotive. Charles and CH offered jobs to a number of people who'd worked for the previous company with one proviso: each had to become an owner.

Chairman David O'Reilly, grandson and son of the founders, says, "I was a very young boy at the time but remember Dad and Granddad insisting that if someone wanted to be involved in the new company they had to make an investment," he says. "Whether it was one hundred dollars or a thousand, they all had to become owners."

O'Reilly says fondly, "I worked at the stores in junior high and high school and knew every one of the people. Every one of them treated the company like their own because it was theirs. Working late, driving hours on a weekend to deliver a part, it didn't matter. They were owners." According to O'Reilly, "One of the big reasons for eventually going public was so we'd be able to extend the original formula of everybody being an owner to everyone."

Without question the most stable performer in the fast-food space has been Sonic Drive-In. And according to both Cliff Hudson, CEO, and former president Pattye Moore, "it's not because everyone thinks and acts like an owner, it's because they are owners!"

Hudson credits founder Troy Smith with the vision to build a company of owners. "You can own one store," he says, "and be an on-site owner-manager. Or you can own multiple locations but in each one of those stores you'll have a local manager—maybe a twenty-year-old kid—who's gone to the bank and borrowed some money in order to become a manager." And according to Hudson, "If you're a very large operator with fifty stores you'll also have a group of supervisors, each handling six to ten stores, and they'll be owners, too."

"Since you have franchisees who have borrowed the money to become Sonic managers," says Pattye Moore, "you obviously have people who are tuned in to revenues and profits, but more important, tuned in to customers. These are people who maybe started as a carhop or a cook and have worked their way up and have become upstanding business folks in the communities where they're located."

How much money can a Sonic manager make? According to President Scott McLain, "a typical store manager will borrow roughly ten thousand dollars in return for a fifteen to twenty percent share of a store's annual profits and a minimal twenty-four thousand dollar salary. If the store generates one hundred and fifty thousand dollars in annual profits, the manager can earn total annual compensation of around fifty-four thousand dollars." According to the company there's no cap on how much a manager can make and there are many who earn more than $100,000 annually.

"Even our carhops think and act like owners," says Moore. "At other fast-food restaurants all you've got is a minimum-wage hairy arm holding your bag of food out a window. But at Sonic even our carhops have the opportunity of thinking and acting like owners and making tips that can more than double their hourly wage."

Moore illustrates her point with a story. "Recently, I was at one of our stores in Georgia and saw something that happens all the time. I was sitting in my rental car waiting for my order and another car pulled up alongside me, and before they'd turned off their engine the carhop was there with their order playing a game we play at all our restaurants called beat the customer." Moore explains that beat the customer is Sonic's way of responding to regular customers who always drive in at the same time and order the same thing. "We love it," she says, "when we can deliver their order before they place it."

Barbie Stammer, president of a group that owns 150 locations, began as a carhop at a Sonic Drive-In thirty-one years ago. "I don't care what anybody tells you," she says. "When you own part of where you're working, you simply do better. Because I own part of this company," she says, "there isn't a moment I'm not thinking about it." She's known locally as the "Sonic lady" and that, she says, is great with her.

Rules for Getting Everyone to Think Like *the* Owner

Develop an Institutionalized Appetite for Knowledge Knowledge helps grow revenues. Charles Koch set out to learn the secrets of peace, prosperity, and progress and ended up uncovering a set of truths that allowed his company to turn in one of the world's best forty-year financial performances. When workers see other workers around them being rewarded for knowledge that creates value, they'll eventually join the club.

Have a Set of Rules Every game worth playing has a set of rules and business isn't any different. Have an inviolate set of rules centered on creating value that everyone in the organization— including managers and executives—can play by.

Build a Vision Based on Value Urge everyone to look through their marketplace lenses, always asking whether everything they do creates value in the mind of the customer and marketplace.

Provide Everyone with a Road Map Business owners know how they'll be measured. If workers are expected to think and act like owners, they must know and share the same definition of value, tacitly understand their role in creating it, and understand precisely how they'll be measured. Constantly guide, counsel, and redirect them to the creation of value.

Make the Right Decisions Business owners get to make decisions. Create a structure where decisions are made by the right people with the right information at the right time. Let team members earn the right to make increasingly larger decisions based on their track record of past winning decisions.

Loosen the Purse Strings and Reward People Based on the Value They Create Owners are compensated for the value they create. If workers and team members are expected to think and act like owners, they need to be compensated in the same way. Furnish team members a sufficient annual salary to attract them. Then define and quantify the value they're responsible for creating and pay them generously for the value they create. At Koch Industries it isn't unheard of for a worker with a $70,000 base salary to earn an additional $100,000 to $200,000 in bonuses.

Successful owners know that the value bar is constantly being raised and they won't continue to reap the same rewards by standing still. When a worker creates extraordinary value and is compensated for doing so, the results of her efforts should become the new standard within the organization. In this way everyone within the organization benefits from the value created by one person.

Know the Hold and Market Values of Everything Owners know what their holdings are worth both to them and the marketplace. Engage workers in a rigorous annual exercise to determine the value of the enterprise. Consistent implementation of this exercise will eventually result in all participants' being on the same value page.

Learn from Failure Effective owners don't take chances on things that could kill them and learn from those that don't. If workers are expected to think and act like owners, the lessons learned from failure must be shared with them and must become an acknowledged part of the company story.

Proving the Proposition of Think Big, Act Small

More than a decade ago, an interviewer asked David Koch, EVP of Koch Industries, about the big challenges facing the company during the coming decade. His response was, "As you get bigger, it's a challenge to maintain the same environment that existed when you were small. But with all the effort we're putting into maintaining a small company culture I believe we will be successful."

Think BIG, Act SMALL
THINK LIKE *THE* OWNER

- Maintain a voracious appetite for knowledge.
- Have a set of rules.
- Know that authentic success is achieved by creating value for others.
- Grant decision rights to the people with the best knowledge.
- Compensate people based on the value they create.
- Know the hold and market values of your business.
- Realize that attempts to eliminate all failure ensures overall failure.

Invent New Businesses
DOT FOODS

"Our company wouldn't be here today if we'd only stayed in our original business."

PAT TRACY, CEO of Dot Foods

In our book *It's Not the Big That Eat the Small . . . It's the Fast That Eat the Slow,* my coauthor and I quoted Charles Darwin: "It's the most adaptable of the species that survive." Following publication I received a number of e-mails informing me that we were in error and that the correct quote should read "It's the strongest of the species that survive."

It's worthy of mention here for three reasons:

- The e-mailers were partially correct. When I used that ubiquitous quote, "It is not the strongest of the species that survives, nor the most intelligent that survives. It is the one that is most adaptable to change," attributed to Darwin in scores of publications and etched in the marble floor at the California Academy of Sciences, I was sharing a paraphrase of Darwin's conclusions about evolution, not his actual words. ("If it vary . . . under the complex and sometimes varying conditions of life," Darwin wrote in *On the Origin of Species*, "[it] will have a better chance of surviving, and thus be *naturally selected*.")

- But the e-mailers were also partially incorrect. While Darwin did write, "One general law . . . let[s] the strongest live and the weakest die," he didn't intend "strongest" to be a measure of big-muscled, physical, brute strength. "Strongest and weakest" in evolution is measured in a species' fitness in changing environments. It's not the brawny that survives in biology. Nature selects those who can thrive following change.

- Many business types grew up believing that evolution theory proved being bigger and more powerful would protect them. They saw being the biggest as a virtue, pursued it, thought of themselves as strongest, and didn't want to deal with any evidence that contradicted that belief. But history shows a very different kind of organization—those who are quick, flexible

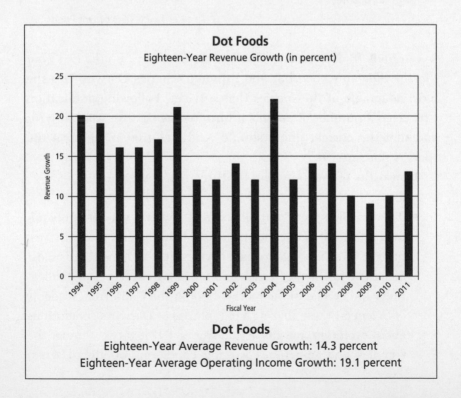

Dot Foods
Eighteen-Year Revenue Growth (in percent)

Dot Foods
Eighteen-Year Average Revenue Growth: 14.3 percent
Eighteen-Year Average Operating Income Growth: 19.1 percent

and able to reinvent—has been able to outperform with a dynamic and consistent track record.

Another trait of companies that consistently increase revenues is their ability to nimbly reinvent themselves as required. And no company has done a better job of reinvention than family-owned Dot Foods. At first blush the company appears to be the quintessential all-American rags-to-riches success story. Closer study reveals a company that owes its ability to consistently increase revenues to its mastery of the basics and the invention of a brand-new business that took a small company into the big leagues.

Dot Foods

Back in 1960, after years of working for other people, Robert Tracy (RT), the manager of a dairy plant in Mount Sterling, Illinois, decided to fulfill his dream and go into business. He took on as a partner someone with a factory that produced milk powder used by dairies in the manufacture of ice cream and dairy products. It was a gutsy decision. He and his wife, Dorothy, already had seven children; they had no money and had to mortgage their modest $20,000 home.

Borrowing Dorothy's nickname, RT called the company Dot Associated Dairy Products and set up shop in the family home. He sold and distributed the milk powder his partner produced. Dorothy handled the books, and deliveries were made from the back of the family station wagon and two leased delivery vans.

"The first few years were good ones," recalls Robert and Dorothy's son and current chairman, Pat Tracy. "During the 1960s, every small city had three or four dairy and ice cream plants and larger cities like Saint Louis had as many as thirty." Each represented a prospective client for Dot Foods and RT called on them all. He made the sales calls, Dorothy did the paperwork while keeping the home fires burning, and a couple of part-time drivers did the deliveries."

Within a few years there were more babies pressing for space at home and a business that required new premises and Dot Foods moved into the back of a farm tractor and implement dealership in

Mount Sterling. Tracy recalls the times fondly. "They'd be fixing tractors in one room, and you'd walk through that room into another and find yourself in a little warehouse full of milk solids."

When asked to describe his father's management style Tracy says he was a consummate salesman who wanted to run a business by treating people the way he'd want to be treated and respecting everyone as valued family members. Tracy's eyes get moist when he talks about his mother's contributions.

"Just imagine," Tracy says with a smile, "how you'd feel if you were a woman with seven kids running around the house with many more on the way and your husband came home and said, 'Hon, I'm leaving my well-paying job, mortgaging the house, going into partnership with someone you don't know and by the way, the office will be here in the house, you'll have to be the secretary and do the books, help make deliveries, and entertain the clients.'" One of Pat Tracy's vivid memories is of his mother cramming the children into the station wagon, loading the back with bags of milk powder, and making emergency deliveries around the state.

During the twenty-five years that followed, RT expanded the products the company distributed. Besides distributing dry-milk solids, Dot added corn-syrup solids used in the production of soft-serve ice cream and sherbets and chocolate products used to flavor milk and ice cream. The company became an almost indispensable partner for small independent dairies.

By 1980 the family had grown to twelve children, the company's offices had moved to a series of modest pole barns on the west side of Mount Sterling, and the dairy distribution business was doing $60 million a year and had a relatively small amount of debt. Pat Tracy says, "It was really a dream come true for Mom and Dad." But the dream wouldn't last long.

Consolidation Happens

After earning an MBA from the University of Illinois, Tracy joined the company full-time as a salesman and quickly recognized a dark cloud looming on the horizon, one he believed put the company's future in jeopardy. "Two of the states I covered were Alabama and Mississippi," Tracy says, "and it seemed that every time I traveled there I had one less account to call on. First, there were twenty-four customers and a few months later there were twenty-one and a year later only eighteen. Acting small instead of big, Tracy asked why and stared an uncomfortable truth in the face.

"In some cases," Tracy says, "cooperatives were buying the local dairies and either closing them or consolidating them into larger centralized operations. Other small plants were being forced to close because of increased government regulation and restrictive labeling laws. Much of what we sold was in small packages and once plants were consolidated they started buying their ingredients in tanker-sized quantities. It became pretty obvious," he says, "that we were running out of customers and had to find another business."

According to family members, Robert and Dorothy Tracy had everything tied up in the company. They lived (and Dorothy continues to live) in a very modest home and they'd never taken any cash out of the company, choosing instead to reinvest all their profits into the business. They had no outside assets and their entire net worth was in stock of a company whose customers were disappearing.

Pat Tracy credits his mother and father with allowing the children to search for other opportunities: ways to reinvent their business utilizing the capabilities and facilities they'd developed. "Mom and Dad were already in their midsixties," he says, "when we proposed that we get the company into the food service business in a big way. I believe," Tracy maintains, "that most people who'd founded their own businesses would have pounded their fist on the table and said, 'We're in the dairy and ice cream distribution business. That's all there is to it and that's where we're going to stay.'"

Pat Tracy's idea required borrowing $4 million for a new facility and if it didn't work out there would be difficult times ahead. "All we could tell Mom and Dad is that we'd make it work and that they'd never have to personally sign for another loan.

"We had a family meeting," Tracy recalls, "and following the discussion Dad looked at our mother and asked, 'Well, Mom, what do you want to do?'" According to Tracy, she met her husband's eyes and said, "Well, I've been following your lead all these years and it's done pretty well for us, so I'm with you on whatever you want to do." Tracy says his dad turned to the kids and said, "Well, let's go for it."

Thinking Big

The "it" that Pat Tracy and his siblings had in mind for the company was revolutionary. "For the prior ten years the company had been peripherally connected to the food service business and had a pretty good idea of how it worked and the problems within the business." It was in the problems inherent in the food service business that they spotted an opportunity.

"Historically," says Tracy, "you had thousands of food service distributors dealing directly with the food manufacturers and it was an inefficient process filled with problems.

"Food manufacturers," he says, "had all these minimum purchase amounts so that food service distributors were forced to purchase five or ten thousand pounds of product at a time. Because of the large minimum orders required, many of these distributors were forced to order product that might last them anywhere from six to twelve weeks at a time." Tracy says the system, while okay for manufacturers, didn't work for the customer for many reasons.

"Most food service distributors," he says, "weren't able to predict what their specific product needs would be that many weeks in advance and were constantly running out of specific products. But when they found themselves out of one particular item, they weren't able to quickly order more because they'd been bundling all kinds of stock keeping units [SKUs] in order to achieve the manufacturers' minimum order size, and they still had lots of inventory in stock, just not the item the customer needed."

Typical Scenario from the Food Services Industry before Dot Foods

XYZ Food Service Distributors—with restaurant, hotel, and hospital clients in a particular geographic area—receives an urgent call from a restaurant wanting three cases of a specific brand's low-fat mayonnaise.

Unfortunately, the food service distributor is out of the product and unable to order more from the manufacturer because it isn't prepared to place another ten-thousand-pound minimum order.

Meanwhile, they still have eight thousand pounds of various other products from their last order, which is unused and wasting space.

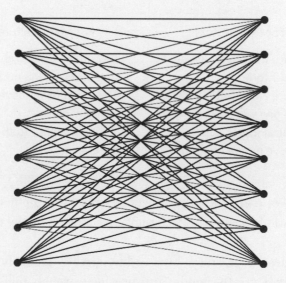

"Besides these distributors' having all their capital tied up in inventory," says Tracy, "there were big warehouses they had to build to store it in and tremendous logistical problems. Imagine what it was like with every manufacturer's trying to maintain a relationship and do business with every distributor?"

To illustrate his point Tracy takes a piece of paper and begins drawing dots and lines. "Imagine," he says, "that each of the eight dots on the left are food manufacturers and the dots on the right represent distributors and everybody is trying to do business with everyone else," suggesting the mental picture above.

"By the way, that example," says Tracy "is only with eight manufacturers and eight distributors. There are thousands of food manufacturers in the United States and more than ten thousand food service distributors. Imagine what it was like with each manufacturer trying to do business with each distributor. What you basically had was numerous individual inefficient supply chains."

Pat Tracy envisioned a business model that accomplished the following:

For Distributors	For Manufacturers
• Reduce the capital invested in inventories. • Reduce warehouse space. • Place one weekly order from a central source. • Improve product fill rates.	• Get out of the warehousing and order-taking business. • Deal with fewer buyers. • Simplify logistics. • Improve service to the customer.

Instead of many different inefficient product shipments (resembling a bowl of spaghetti), Pat Tracy envisioned a model that looked like this:

"Our idea," says Tracy, "was to buy directly from the manufacturers, warehouse the foods, and provide a weekly delivery to distributors that allowed them to place an order from a variety of manufacturers without a minimum order size. If they only wanted one case of a product, that would be fine and they'd never be more than four days from receiving an order instead of waiting for weeks to receive it from the manufacturers.

"For food service distributors," Tracy says, "it would dramati-

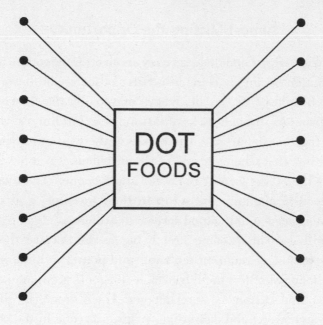

cally reduce the amount of capital they'd have tied up and reduce the space required for warehousing. We'd become a one-stop shopping service for them so they could actually go out and grow their businesses without growing their physical facilities."

Theoretically, Dot Foods would make money three ways.

- They would purchase full truckloads of goods from manufacturers and sell the products at slightly higher than truckload prices.
- The manufacturers would compensate Dot Foods for handling the transportation of their goods.
- Dot Foods would receive a sales and distribution allowance from the manufacturers for relieving them of, or assisting them with, those functions.

While it seems obvious today, as you'll learn in the next few pages it took years before the Dot Foods complete business model worked.

Almost Missing the Opportunity

Years earlier, Dot Foods had already inadvertently gotten into the redistribution business. "A manufacturer of ice cream flavors came to us in the mid-1970s," recalls Tracy, "and told us they had food service distributors throughout Iowa, Minnesota, and Illinois who were pooling together to purchase truckloads of their various syrups. The problem was that whenever one of the distributors wanted to place an order the others weren't ready for another one." Tracy says that Dot agreed to maintain the syrup in their inventory and sell and deliver it as needed to the food service distributors.

From that small act came a really big lesson. Because the manufacturer no longer required ten-thousand-pound minimum orders or the pooling of orders to fill trucks, its business grew, market share improved, and customers were happier. Tracy says that when Dot began warehousing and delivering syrups, everyone in the company was so enamored of and focused on the original ingredient businesses that they didn't pause to consider the future possibilities. "Later," says Tracy, "as we began reinventing the company the first question we asked was, 'What else could we be selling to these distributors?'" As Dot began moving into redistribution they started offering items like milk powder, peanut butter, salt, and packaged sugar.

A Cold Shoulder from Manufacturers

Their new idea looked good on paper and was warmly greeted by the food service distributors who would be able to purchase only the products they needed on a weekly basis. But the reception Dot Foods received from manufacturers was a frigid one.

"As soon as we told manufacturers that we wanted to buy their products and then sell them to their current customers they looked at us as if we were crazy," says Tracy. Wrinkling up his face and pursing his lips, Tracy imitates the typical response he received from manufacturers in the early days, "'Now, let me get this straight, you want to buy our products and sell them to people we're already selling to and why . . . if you can answer me and aren't just smoking something funny . . . would we ever want to do that?'"

Tracy was always ready with good answers and would start his pitch by explaining to the manufacturers that there were many valid reasons for selling to and redistributing through Dot Foods. First he'd tell them that by selling to Dot Foods they'd be improving their service to their customers, who would no longer have to purchase thousands of pounds at a time. Then he'd patiently explain that selling through Dot would also provide better customer service to the manufacturer's clients, which would insulate them against competitors who were constantly trying to take their business away. Finally Tracy would promise that Dot Foods would eventually have lots of other customers to whom they would sell the manufacturer's products so the manufacturer would ultimately have even more distribution.

"Most manufacturers simply couldn't get past the fact that we'd be selling their product to customers they already had," says Tracy, "and we were truly the Rodney Dangerfield of business. We couldn't get any respect!"

In many cases Dot Foods was initially forced to do unfavorable deals and even pay list price to manufacturers for their products. "We had to have some merchandise in stock so that potential customers would see we had a few things to offer and would give us the time of day. Finally, with a small amount of products in stock, the company started selling to its few nondairy customers, hoping to swell its customer ranks.

"Our customers started buying from us on a weekly basis," explains Tracy, "and within a short time they found they enjoyed the short lead time, and having no need to buy thousands of pounds of items at a time. They'd call us and say, 'This is nice. I like it but why don't you carry this or that product from such and such manufacturer?' We'd explain that we wanted to carry the manufacturer's products they were asking about but that we couldn't get the manufacturer's attention or even get a telephone call returned."

Eventually Dot's customers began putting some pressure on the manufacturers for them, two buying groups decided to experiment by allowing Dot to distribute their private-label products and the business slowly began to gain some traction. Within a few years the new business was generating about $15 million in annual revenues while revenues in the original milk solids business had flattened.

"We needed some real horsepower to make this thing happen," says Tracy. "People who could take the concept, go out and sell it, and make things happen."

A Cold Shoulder from Sales Pros

"We were struggling," explains Tracy. "We didn't have the money to recruit high-priced talent and being located in a bunch of Quonset huts in a rural town of two thousand people didn't help. People took one look and said to themselves, 'Whoa, what's this?'" Finally the company turned to a homegrown resource: the twelve brothers and sisters that RT and Dorothy had raised.

"Of the twelve children," he continued, "each completed an undergraduate degree and many went on for advanced degrees in law and business." As each of the brothers and sisters finished their educations, they returned home to Mount Sterling and went to work for the company. "On the one hand, we felt an obligation to provide everyone an opportunity and on the other hand, they were also coming back to the area because of family attachments. RT and Dorothy encouraged, but did not pressure sons or daughters to return to the business. They were, however, delighted each time one made a decision to do so."

All the brothers and all but one of the sisters eventually joined the company as sales reps, barely earning a living wage. "During the first part of the week," says Tracy, "we'd make our sales calls; then on Wednesdays head back to town and fuel the trucks, change tires and do whatever had to be done and then spend the weekends loading the trucks for the next week's deliveries."

Persistence Pays

"It took us at least ten to fifteen years," Tracy explains, "before we really began gaining momentum. We had many of the family members out there making sales calls and, as we added additional lines, more distributors were willing to do business with us. The more distributors we signed up, the more the manufacturers became interested in doing business with us. Finally the manufacturers began calling us and saying, 'We've heard from a lot of people that they'd distribute our products if they were able to buy it from you. We'd like to get into your program.'"

By 2005 Dot Foods had more than two thousand employees and generated annual sales of $2 billion. One third of the company's team members drove the trucks that delivered the goods to the company's 3,500 distribution customers; seven hundred worked inside the warehouses; and seven hundred worked in administrative, IT, accounting, and sales functions. Historically, the company had doubled its revenues every four to five years, and Tracy expected the company's growth to continue at a double-digit pace.

In 2006, younger brother John Tracy took over as CEO, and Pat continued as the chairman.

"Dollar sales were still growing double digits," John says of when he took the reins. "Except in 2008 we were up about 9.4 percent. But the other way we measure is in units—pounds or cases. Since the recession they've stayed positive between three percent and five percent per year. But this persistent high unemployment changed a lot of people. They began brown bagging or cooking at home instead of spending the out-of-home food dollar. That affected our customers, and that affected us." In the face of this difficult market and uncertainty, Dot Foods leadership again thought big instead of small.

"We recognized a mistake we'd made. We hadn't continued to invest as heavily in new stuff for about twenty-four months prior and had just been adding capacity to the existing business." So the executive team at Dot Foods got off their heels and prepared to pounce. "We didn't lay anyone off. We actually promoted a bunch of high-potential people. We threw some real resources at stuff that had been sitting on our horizon. We started chasing new opportunities." Dot Foods made fast progress in new areas like health and beauty products, imported and domestic specialty foods, and protein products (beef and pork). They have also added sophisticated supply-chain services to help their clients cover national accounts.

"We don't want a major hiccup [like so many companies go through]," John Tracy told me. "We are aware that we've been blessed in our lives and are a little paranoid. It definitely keeps me awake some nights. I think about how not to lose track of the things that helped us succeed and communicate the things that have driven Dot from day one to make sure every employee is aware. Our values and being trusted come first. Innovative solutions that provide answers to everybody we work for come second. And sharing our growth every day with everybody—employees, clients, suppliers, and our communities—comes third. That's our foundation. We continue to have high expectations."

Now, fifty years from that living-room and family-station-wagon beginning, Dot Foods has 3,500 employees, 70,000 products, and almost $4 billion in sales. Dot Foods is big in everything but the way it acts.

Acting Small

The Tracy family never stopped dreaming and thinking big; they wanted to be the biggest and best in the nation. Still, they achieved their objective by acting small:

1. Use Every Resource "Right Down to the Hooves" One of the lessons learned from Native Americans is their incredible stewardship with all their resources. They were thrifty and avoided any waste, learning, for example, to use every part of the animals they hunted, "right down to the hooves." It's a saying that illustrates an uncommon attitude of frugality and ingenuity. Dot Foods follows in that tradition.

2. Maintain Utilitarian Facilities The company moved from the family living room to a single room behind a truck and implement dealership to a string of Quonset huts and pole barns. It moved to a large modern facility only when it made financial sense. Every Dot Food facility is neat, clean, and functional and nothing else. There are no palaces and no monuments and the company has never built anything in order to indulge an executive's ego.

3. Put the People with the Most to Gain or Lose on Your Front Lines Dot Foods didn't have the money or desirable location required to recruit and hire expensive heavy-hitting salespeople. This may actually have been the company's luckiest break because when Dot's sales proposition failed to immediately hit home runs, chances are that most salespeople would have found it all too hard, started complaining, and either quit or tried to convince the family it had a bad idea.

Instead, the company turned to the people with the most to gain or lose. All but two of the twelve children became salespeople at one time or another and hit the streets, sold to clients, and helped build the company. The lesson for businesses that want to grow revenues is that a sales force composed of people with the most to gain or lose will work longer, harder, and more creatively and collaboratively than any outsiders they could hope to hire. In the process they'll prove that the math really does work.

4. Let Customers Drive the Need for Expansion, Not the Other Way Around When discussing expansion and growth, Former CEO and current chairman Pat Tracy frequently invokes one of his favorite expressions. "Volume is vanity and profit is sanity," he says, pointedly describing the company's views on growth. "Our expansion was driven by the manufacturers and our customers," says Pat Tracy. "We always kept our eyes on adjoining states and eventually manufacturers would tell us they had customers there who'd buy their products from us if we'd start doing business there. We'd go into the new state with only a few customers," he says, "assign a salesperson to the territory and build it from the ground up." The company never expanded for the sake of expansion or unless it would be profitable.

5. Never Forget Your Roots Mount Sterling isn't an easy place to get to. It's a five-hour drive southwest of Chicago and two hours north of St. Louis. The town's population is only two thousand and there are just eight thousand people in the entire county. And yet Dot Foods has remained headquartered in town and houses its largest distribution facility there. "Mom and Dad started the company here and we feel a responsibility to the town," maintains Tracy. "Our most important reason for staying is that we've been blessed with a wonderful workforce." Citing the work ethic of people in the Midwest, Tracy says, "Our truck drivers are the best in the world. While the turnover among truck drivers at most companies is about seventy percent a year, our turnover rate is frequently in single digits." Tracy says that the company's workforce has repaid the company's commitment to them with their fierce determination to do the right thing and take care of the customer at all costs.

6. Control Your Growth Some companies will do anything in order to grow revenues as fast as possible. Unscrupulous firms (do some mobile phone service providers ring a bell?) promise prospective customers everything and deliver nothing, hoping customers won't notice the horrible service they receive and even charge cancellation fees when customers want to get out of a bad deal.

Dot Foods could easily ramp things up and increase business at an even faster rate than the impressive double-digit revenue and profit growth numbers it has turned in each year. Instead, it has chosen to grow in a steady and controlled way. Each year the company accepts another 150 to 200 new distribution customers and adds only 25 to 30 new manufacturers. Such deliberate growth enables it to protect capital and ensure that the company's inside sales and customer service teams are able to support growth and maintain extraordinarily high levels of customer satisfaction. The company isn't so greedy as to need it all tomorrow.

7. Stay True to Your Principles and Values There's a large sign that greets visitors outside Dot Foods' home office informing everyone of the company's mission: TO POSITIVELY AND SIGNIFICANTLY CONTRIBUTE TO THE SUCCESS OF OUR BUSINESS PARTNERS. The company prides itself on having never varied from that founding belief.

Inventing New Businesses . . . Continued

Koch—A Creative Use for Leftovers

In Chapter 5 we noted that one of the business areas where Koch Industries has historically refused to sell is its refining interests because it uses these as labs to create other businesses. One such new business, invented by the company, is vintage Charles Koch.

When the in thing in the oil and gas industry was to build new refineries designed to process sweet Texas crude (the champagne of crude oils), Koch Industries had serious doubts. They reasoned that with enormous capacity for processing sweet Texas crude coming online there would be increased demand for the raw material that could theoretically increase prices. (The first rule of all markets is that the greater the demand the higher the price.) With so many new refineries processing the same crude oil in the same way with identical equipment, Koch couldn't see how it could gain a competitive advantage. It decided to zig while everyone else was zagging and invested heavily in expanding its Minnesota refinery, which was designed to process the least desirable of all crude oils—heavy, sour crude oil. This raw material is so thick and viscous that diluting agents have to be mixed into it just to keep it moving through pipelines.

Whether a company is processing sweet Texas crude or heavy, sour crude doesn't matter when it comes to the finished product. The processed output of both raw materials must meet the same rigid environmental standards. The big difference is in the vast amounts of by-products and gunk that processing heavy crudes creates—by-products that companies must dispose of or hope to sell.

One by-product is asphalt, and today the Koch Materials Group sells enough asphalt to pave more than 125,000 lane miles of roads each year. Instead of simply selling the asphalt it produces, the company began wondering how it could upgrade asphalt to give road builders a differentiated product. The answers they came up with became Koch Pavement Solutions, which develops, tests, and markets innovative paving solutions, and Koch Performance Roads, an engineering and pavement design firm that designs and oversees the construction of high-endurance roads, layer-to-layer for specific areas. Over the past few years, these two businesses, invented by Koch Industries, grew to where they have combined annual sales of more than $1 billion.

SAS—A New Pricing Model

Most software companies are actually sales companies built around a single software product or idea. Their business model is simple: sell as much stuff as possible for as much money as possible in order to hit the current monthly, quarterly, or yearly target. The problem with the model and what prevents companies that practice it from consistently growing their revenues is that they're always starting over. They work themselves out of breath selling to as many clients as possible and when the month or year is over, they take a deep breath and are forced to start all over again and repeat the process. After a while it all becomes what Yogi Berra referred to as "déjà vu *all over again*."

In Chapter 2 you read that SAS invents and provides software to their business and government clients worldwide. But SAS doesn't sell any software to anyone. Instead, it has adopted a licensing model and this is what has allowed it to become so formidable in terms of consistent financial performance.

Kelly Ross, vice president, U.S. commercial sales, the Americas, is responsible for 40 percent of SAS's annual revenues but began her career with another software company. "It was a start-up company and fun for a while," she says, "but after we'd made some sales and were trying to survive on maintenance revenue from them, the company started to dry up.

"One of the founders of the start-up was a mentor to me," she says, "and I told him that things weren't looking good for the company and I wondered whether I should be looking somewhere else. He said I should.

"When I interviewed with SAS," she says, "the two things I liked most about the company were the licensing model, which was different for the industry, and the second thing that was appealing to me was that in order to generate an annual renewal every year, you have to have very strong relationships with your customers.

"When the bulk of your revenues are based on renewing the same customers every year," Ross says, "genuine value is placed on the work you do and the long-term relationships you build. That's vastly different," she adds, "than going out and getting the big deal, the quick hit, and then moving on to the next one."

SAS renews an impressive 95 percent of its customer base each year. The revenues from those renewals account for 80 percent of the firm's total annual sales. Ross says, "It's easy to calculate what the new sales goal needs to be by looking at the renewal revenue base and retention rate, factoring in what we'll lose to consolidations and the few cancellations we receive and then determining how much new business we need to add in order to hit our target of fifteen percent revenue growth each year."

Ross says that an insight provided by Jim Goodnight greatly assisted the revenue generation process. "Jim told the sales organization to stop focusing on new sales but to focus on total revenue." That resulted in SAS's sales departments becoming equally focused on growing existing clients into larger customers. Ross says her sales staff devotes as much time to analyzing and diagnosing the needs of current customers as they do to pitching for new business. Ross adds, "The only way you can keep existing customers and grow them is by delivering superlative customer service and that occurs only by helping them grow *their* business."

Hypothetical Revenue Growth Model of Selling versus Licensing

COMPANY A	COMPANY B
A Company That Sells	**A Company That Licenses**
Set an annual target ($1 billion)	Set an annual target ($1 billion)
Maintenance fees ($150 million)	License renewals ($800 million)
New sales required ($900 million)	New sales required ($200 million)
	Existing customer growth ($100 million)
	Net new sales required ($100 million)

Compare the annual 15 percent maintenance fee charged by Company A and the 80 percent licensing renewal fee charged by Company B: which one stands a greater chance of achieving consistent revenue growth?

How would Company A generate nine times as much new business as Company B? Would its sales force be nine times the size, would it price its product at nine times as much or would it simply count on being nine times more aggressive? Along with nine times the effort would invariably come nine times the number of management challenges and headaches as well.

Almost by necessity, Company A would be forced to build a slamming, hitting, hard-closing sales machine while Company B would have more time and resources to analyze customers' needs and build long-term relationships.

By practicing an alternative way to price software Jim Goodnight assured SAS a consistent flow of revenue and an environment devoted to customer satisfaction.

Companies that think big and act small are constantly searching for innovative means to turn conventional wisdom upside down. They dream about new ways to add value while maximizing the use of every resource at hand.

Think BIG, Act SMALL
INVENT NEW BUSINESSES

- Figure out how to turn your business's asphalt into new roads (Koch).
- Instead of selling your product or service for cash, license it and have the client pay a renewal fee each year (SAS).
- Figure out how to make what you sell extraordinarily special to the buyer. People and companies pay a premium for prestige (Strayer).
- Examine the smallest revenue centers in your business and ask yourself the question, "With some reinvention can this become a brand-new business unit?" (Dot).
- List all the disorganized supply-chain processes that look like logistical "spaghetti" in your business and figure out how to bring simplicity and order to part of the marketplace. People and companies gladly outsource logistics that enhance their business opportunities (Dot).
- Pretend you know nothing and truly listen to your customers, vendors, suppliers, and the marketplace. They will lead you to new business opportunities ripe for invention or reinvention.

Create Win-Win Solutions
MEDLINE INDUSTRIES

"We go in, show our customers how we'll achieve their target savings on a line-by-line basis, agree to pay a penalty if we don't, and share any additional savings with them."

CHARLIE MILLS, CEO of Medline Industries

Sales and selling are tough work. And there's nothing harder than trying to sell the same stuff offered by other salespeople and companies. When there's no competitive advantage to distinguish a good, product, or service from the competition's, the only thing left to talk about is price. That discussion always ends up in the same place; the prospective buyer wants it cheaper.

To defuse the issue of price, some companies and salespeople resort to counting on friendships to get their deals done, piling on loads of freebies, making outlandish claims and promises or offering more added value (meaning lowering the price without admitting it). It's hard for most prospective buyers to relent and say yes. They don't know who to believe, might not get what they've been promised, and might even get ripped off.

At best, sales and selling have historically been an adversarial process.

Every company we identified in our research has succeeded in taking the adversarial sting out of sales. Each has institutionalized the art of authentically diagnosing the real needs of its customers and then crafting win-win solutions. Because they think big but act small they intrinsically understand that it's not about trying to master an adversarial process (which will never be mastered) but instead creating environments where everybody genuinely wins.

There's no better example of a company committed to the creation of win-win solutions for their customers than Medline Industries, Inc.

Medline Industries

Medline, with nearly $4 billion in annual revenues, manufactures and distributes more than 125,000 medical products, medical-surgical items, and textiles to hospitals, extended care facilities, surgical centers, home care providers, physicians' offices, and retail outlets. Medline has virtually eliminated the middleman by manufacturing more than 70 percent of the items it sells and then distributing them directly to customers from its thirty-two distribution centers. Unlike many of its competitors, Medline carries zero debt. And according to current CEO, Charlie Mills, an energetic and committed family man in his late forties, it was his great-grandfather the company has to thank for starting a business that foreshadowed the present Medline.

"In 1910," says Charlie Mills, "my great-grandfather A.L. started a small business in Chicago making uniforms for the people who worked in the city's meatpacking plants. It wasn't long before friends of my great-grandmother, who were hospital volunteers, suggested that the couple start sewing and selling medical garments as well."

The lifelong ambition of A. L. Mills was to return to his native Arkansas and as soon as his son (Charlie's grandfather Irv) was old enough to run the business he turned it over to him and went back to Arkansas. "When my grandfather was running the business," says Mills, "it became more and more medical garments and fewer other fabrics and uniforms." By the 1940s the company was doing several

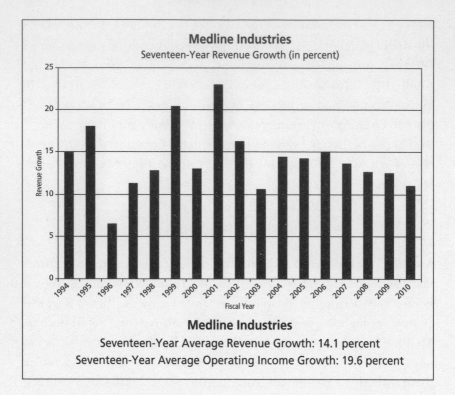

Medline Industries
Seventeen-Year Revenue Growth (in percent)

Fiscal Year

Medline Industries
Seventeen-Year Average Revenue Growth: 14.1 percent
Seventeen-Year Average Operating Income Growth: 19.6 percent

hundred thousand of dollars annually and employed thirty people. "When World War Two began," he says, "fabric was rationed and only available for medical purposes and the company switched exclusively to the production of hospital uniforms, surgical gowns, and bedding."

By the 1950s the company, known as Mills Hospital Supply Corporation, slowly began taking on other medical lines and opened up several warehouses around the nation. In 1961, with the company approaching $3 million in annual sales, Irv Mills decided to retire, pulled the plug, and sold the company to publicly traded Cenco Instruments. Mills's father, Jim Mills, and his uncle Jon Mills had just started working for the company when Mills's grandfather sold it and all of them, including Grandfather Irv, went to work for the new company and spent five years with it.

Eventually, Jim and Jon Mills found working for the company that had bought the family business frustrating. They felt stifled by the lack of innovation and commitment to customers and customer service that had been hallmarks of Mills Hospital Supply. In 1966 they left Cenco and founded Medline as a direct competitor with their previous employer.

"Medline started with ten people," says Mills, "and within two years we opened our first garment factory in Indiana, manufacturing scrubs and patient gowns." At the suggestion of Irv Mills the new company began innovating to set themselves apart in the marketplace. "Until Medline came into being," says Mills, "all hospital gowns and scrubs were white. Our company was the first to offer them in other colors and with printing on them. That might seem to be a small innovation, but it really helped differentiate us and grow the business."

From the very beginning Medline ran a fiscally conservative operation. While sales and profits grew, Jim and Jon Mills agreed to retain all the company's earnings for future growth. Medline continued adding salespeople, promised stock in the company to everyone who stayed for three years, and began growing steadily.

Charlie Mills recalls that Medline's one major misstep occurred in 1972 when the company went public. "The company believed," says Mills, "that by going public it would have access to capital with which to acquire other companies and that it would provide it with favorable publicity and press. Instead, all it ended up with were lots of additional time-consuming reporting requirements and limits as to how it could run itself." There'd be no more hoarding of retained earnings; shareholders in publicly traded companies want cash dividends. Medline's foray into the public markets lasted only five years.

"Our stock opened in 1972 at thirteen dollars a share," says Mills, "and quickly shot up to twenty-six dollars. But during the next five years as our earnings went up two hundred and fifty percent, the stock went down to as low as seven dollars a share." The family didn't sell any of their shares and finally, in 1977, bought them all back at thirteen dollars and became a privately owned sub chapter S company that essentially functions as a partnership. Today fifty-five nonfamily members and various members of the Mills family own the company. "We don't think of ourselves as being family owned," says Mills. "We're actually employee owned."

Medline does nearly $4 billion in annual sales, has six manufacturing facilities in North America, and twenty-five joint-venture manufacturing plants worldwide. The company manufactures many of the 125,000 products it sells and by maintaining thirty-two distribution centers, Medline is able to sell in every state and more than twenty countries.

We uncovered seven ways that Medline proves the proposition of thinking big and acting small:

1. Sell Directly

"The products we manufacture," says Charlie Mills, "make up more than seventy percent of our revenues. By manufacturing and selling directly we've been able to eliminate the distributor and take one level of cost out of the process." As a result, Mills says, "The prices we charge users are generally less than [those of] our competitors."

Prior to the late 1980s the government and most health insurance companies reimbursed hospitals on a cost-plus basis. That all changed with the introduction of a system that paid a fixed fee for medical procedures. For the first time, hospitals had to become extremely cost conscious and naturally gravitated toward the lowest-cost quality manufacturer. Mills says that the fixed fee reimbursement scheme provided and continues to give a boon to low-cost Medline.

2. Love Your Customers

"Our next competitive advantage," says Mills, "is that we're proud to be a great sales organization. We love calling on customers, working with and exceeding their expectations. My great-grandfather and grandfather were salesmen, so are my dad and uncle and so was every other key executive in the company. My cousins Andy and Jimmy are great salesmen and call on many of our best accounts. We've always viewed a large sales force as being vital to our long-term growth and never hesitated to hire salespeople and continually train them, believing that in the future, they'd be responsible for making us more profitable."

While Charlie Mills has the title of CEO, his cousin Andy serves as president, and Andy's brother-in-law Jimmy Abrams serves as COO, Mills says the titles are virtually interchangeable. "The three of us run like a partnership and only have the titles because the outside world expects there to be a CEO, COO, and president."

Something else the three men share is their love of sales. "We all worked as salespeople and even now," says Mills, "we're each on the road almost every week, taking care of customers and closely involved in the sales process." Mills even met his future wife while both were working as salespeople for the company, and his two cousins' wives have worked in sales for the company.

3. Stay Private

The third competitive advantage Mills cites is Medline's private ownership. "We have several major competitors," he says, "and we're probably hell on them because we're able to be so fast and flexible. Each of them is publicly traded and is forced to spend a lot of time managing analysts, earnings expectations, and share prices, and providing guidance, while we're able to focus exclusively on our core business." Mills maintains that publicly traded companies are almost required to be short-sighted thinkers, living quarter-to-quarter, while Medline can maintain a longer time horizon.

"I have a good friend," he says, "who just started a new sales management job with a publicly traded company. In January, this guy's first month on the job, the numbers were disastrous because the company had tried to jam everything it could into December. That's the kind of thing we'd never do because it's simply short-sighted."

While five of the nine companies profiled in this book are publicly traded, they all have similarly avoided thinking small—focusing on hitting quarterly numbers to please Wall Street's expectations.

4. Stay Debt Free

Medline is debt free. "If we need to purchase a new piece of equipment or build an additional warehouse that might not become profitable for a year," he says, "we have the ability to do it. We're truly a company committed to always having a better future." He explains his point further by saying, "If we had to spend a lot of money this year that might make our current year's performance look bad, but it guaranteed us a better next year . . . we'd do it in a second."

5. Don't Let Salespeople Say No

Most consumers would agree that it seems that the representatives of most companies are anxious to tell customers that "it can't be done." The fifth competitive advantage cited by Mills is extraordinary for a company with eight thousand workers.

"We have a rule," he says, "that only a member of the senior management team can ever say no to a customer. We were early adopters when customers told us they wanted to order by computer, we routinely make product changes as requested and we've even opened up new warehouses when customers have asked for them. Unless a salesperson's answer is yes," he says, "the customer or the salesperson has to escalate it."

6. Don't Let Extra Layers of Management Slow Things Down

Charlie Mills says that Medline's sixth competitive advantage is vital to the success of the company. "We make decisions quickly and act fast," he says. "Several months ago," he explained, "Johnson and Johnson announced they were leaving the gauze wound-care product business in hospitals. The moment they made the announcement, we roughly estimated the amount of sales we thought we could pick up, started running magazine and trade journal ads the next day, and immediately began running heavy production. When there's an opportunity we move quickly. There aren't any layers of management whose purpose is to slow down opportunities at Medline." Medline has doubled revenues in just the last five years—an incredible feat given the economy since 2008. Mills attributes this to fast decisions, flatter hierarchies, and no tolerance for bureau-cracy.

This finding echoes the best practices of companies I profiled in my last two books. Less bureaucracy plus speed equals the ability to seize opportunity.

7. Be a *Little* Entrepreneurial

The final competitive advantage that Mills says makes up the Med-line culture is the firm's entrepreneurial culture. "We're a *little* entrepreneurial," says Mills citing the following examples. "Several years ago, we went into the disposable gown business. It required an investment of five million dollars and has worked out very nicely for us. But things don't always work out so well. At the same time, we went into nonmedical uniforms for hospital and health-care institutions, and that one hasn't generated the sales we hoped for."

At various times during our research, Charles Koch, David O'Reilly, Pat Tracy, and the other CEOs we studied also used the words "little" or "small" to describe the entrepreneurial bent of their respective companies. Make lots of little bets and take small chances, but don't make a bet so big that it would upend the firm if it didn't work out.

Separate Sales Forces

Medline makes more than 125,000 SKUs available to their cus-tomers. Such a huge number of items would make it very difficult for a salesperson to even be aware of all the company's offerings much less have adequate product knowledge to represent them all. Medline's response to this potential dilemma is another example of how the company thinks big but acts small: they have four separate sales departments covering the nation.

"Up until 1985," says Mills, "the company had a single sales force that called on all prospects and customers. That year we came out with a sales force dedicated to nursing homes and long-term care facilities. Even though hospitals and nursing homes purchase some of the same products, the sales approach used on each is vastly different."

Reorganizing the company into two separate sales forces worked so well that, within a few years, Medline added another sales force dedicated to skin and wound care. "We acquired the right to represent the products of another skin-care company," says Mills, "and so we took over their sales force, added in our salespeople who'd been selling skin and wound care, and began growing a separate sales force. Our fourth sales force sells textiles: linens, sheets, pillowcases, mattresses, lab coats, and reusable gowns." Medline has 300 salespeople in their nursing home and long-term care markets, another 350 in the general hospital line, and approximately 50 each in the textile and skin- and wound-care sales forces. Recently, Medline has added sales forces for surgery centers, physicians' offices, original equipment manufacturers, and retail.

Making Internal Business Units Compete

Here's another example of how Medline thinks big and acts small. It has divided itself into eighteen separate product divisions responsible for the tens of thousands of items it manufactures. The managers responsible for running each product division are forced to run their own small business unit and serve real customers: the salespeople of the company, who can choose among the various offerings of all the product divisions. Mills provided the following example of how things work at Medline:

"Take Jim Piggott, for example. He's the president of our Dynacor Division, which manufactures plastic utensils, small procedure kits, and urologicals. He's in charge of about $150 million in annual sales and completely responsible for the products his division manufactures: their quality, cost, and the gross profit they generate. Because his division's products are primarily sold through our sales teams, he has to constantly figure out ways to compete against the other product divisions who are fighting for top-of-mind consciousness with the sales force.

"Product divisions compete for training time with new sales reps, and each would like as much time as possible with our new people. The better they perform, the more time they get. Each product division also competes for the amount of promotional attention they receive from the company. They also compete for promotion time with the sales force and for how much time each division's product specialists are allowed to spend in the field making sales calls with the salespeople."

By fostering internal competition, Medline harnesses the speed and competitiveness of smaller internal business units to drive the efficiency that is so vital in a business with thinning margins.

Share the Wealth

Many companies have made ongoing cost cutting standard operating procedure, placing the blame for such measures on everything from recessions (there were nineteen in the last century, an average of one every five years) to economic implosions (the dot-com debacle) and investors' demands for consistent profit growth. Unfortunately these companies seem oblivious to the fact that, at its best, cost cutting only accomplishes a temporary remission, and that increasing revenue is the ultimate cure. Nonetheless many companies continue to slash the size of their sales departments, cap the amount of commissions that salespeople can earn, and offload seasoned, high-priced sales talent. Such an operational philosophy is anathema to the executives who lead Medline.

"Most of our competitors," says Charlie Mills, "have cut back on the number of salespeople in the field, given the staff that remains larger territories, and tried to handle sales in-house or on the telephone. That's something," he says, "we'd never do. We do the opposite and believe in maintaining and generously compensating a large sales force. We see it as an investment in the future."

Mills believes it's faulty reasoning to think that cutting the size of or compensation of the sales force can help a company. "It's very easy to calculate that by cutting your sales expenses by fifteen percent in any given year you'd be able to momentarily increase profits and perhaps have very little effect on the current year's sales. It's the year after, the future, that you'd be damaging."

Each of Medline's more than eleven hundred salespeople has an annual quota that averages slightly less than $5 million for a starting salesperson. Instead of paying a commission on the gross revenues they generate, a system that encourages salespeople to constantly ask management for price reductions, Medline ties their salespeople's compensation to profitability by paying commissions based on gross margin. At the end of the year, if a salesperson fails to achieve his quota, he doesn't get a bonus, which can be 20 percent of his annual compensation.

The average sales representative at Medline earns between $100,000 and $150,000 annually; some make as much as $500,000; and the top salesperson in the company takes in more than $1,000,000. Although quotas are increased each year, the firm doesn't cap the commissions it pays its people. Mills says, "We have many salespeople in the company earning more money than the CEO and that's the way it should be. After all, the top executives also have stock that appreciates based on the work the salespeople perform in the field."

Providing Win-Win Solutions

Medline salespeople are trained to sell solutions to the customer's problems—not just products. The idea is to put everyone—the customers, the company, and the salespeople—in a win-win position.

One of Medline's unique selling propositions is its ability to essentially take over a portion of the cost reduction functions for health-care providers. "As an example," says Mills, "consider a hospital that's spending ten million dollars annually on supplies and would like to reduce that by five percent to nine-point-five million. We'll go in and show them how we'll achieve their target savings on a line-by-line basis, agree to pay a penalty if we don't, and share any savings above the five hundred thousand dollars with them."

Mills points out that the $500,000 cost savings described in the previous example drops straight to the health-care provider's bottom line and becomes operating profit for them. "Do you know how much a hospital or nursing home would have to increase their revenues in order to increase their profits by $500,000?" He answers by citing the example of St. Mary's Healthcare, which estimated it would have had to increase revenues by $28.5 million to achieve the $570,000 it saved using Medline's program.

The challenge, of course, is not just to dream up solutions, but to educate the customer about how he can directly benefit.

Medline's Future

Not a single CEO or company executive we studied, including Charlie Mills, ever made—on the record or off—a big, overwhelming announcement of where their company would be one day or how it would conquer the world. It's another example of their humility, but it's also as if each leader has learned that big aspirations are best kept quiet lest they be hexed by talking about them. Practically speaking, the greater the number of people whom one boastfully tells what one is going to do or make happen, the greater the number of people who'd be happy to see one not achieve it.

The only time Charlie Mills became less than forthcoming was when we asked about Medline's big goals and the future. He was just as hesitant to issue sweeping proclamations or share big dreams as all the other CEOs, and his tentativeness provides a fascinating insight into the minds of the people who lead all these companies.

"For a number of years," says CEO Mills, "we had a goal to hit one billion dollars in sales by 2000 and we achieved that number. Then we said we wanted to target two billion by 2006, which we achieved." Now they've doubled sales again to $4 billion.

When quizzed as to whether Medline will ever be a $10-billion company, Mills responds, "Whoa, that's too far out there. You need to be able to see a target to commit to it. We've had some discussions about being a eight-billion-dollar company some day," he says, "and I'm sure we'll get there. You need to take it one small step at a time." While Mills remained tight lipped about specific future dollar targets, he wasn't reluctant to discuss the need for growth.

Committed to Growth

"We've seen competitors get sold off, be acquired, or go bankrupt," says Mills, "because their sales stagnated and their costs didn't. That's scary and one good reason to be committed to growth. Additionally, we're in an industry that doesn't really have any inflation . . . if anything, we have deflation with constant pressure from health-care providers to lower the costs of what they buy from us. So if we have to lower our prices each year, that's another good case for constant sales increases."

Mills hit upon the same theme we'd heard from so many of the leaders of the companies we studied when he added, "We have eight thousand team members working with us, and each of them wants to do better and make more money next year than this year. In order to be able to afford to pay more and motivate them to do better each year, we have to grow as a company." The final reason that Medline is committed to growth involves an echo of the word "stewardship" we heard so many times during our research. "It's pretty sobering, isn't it?" a suddenly serious Mills asks. "Your parents put you in charge of a company that was growing when they gave it to you. It's your job to be a steward of the resources and continue the wonderful work they began."

More than one hundred years ago A. L. Mills accidentally stumbled into the solutions-providing business when he figured out that the meatpacking plants of Chicago needed a reliable source of inexpensive uniforms for their workers. His wife sensed opportunity when friends suggested the couple investigate the possibility of manufacturing uniforms for hospitals. Today Medline thinks big but Mills runs the company as though it were a small business by relentlessly searching for new ways to custom-tailor solutions for its clients and being aware of every opportunity that presents itself.

All the companies we quantifiably identified for inclusion in the book either sell their services and products based on providing solutions to their customers and partners (O'Reilly Automotive, Cabela's, Medline, Sonic Drive-In, PETCO), or their entire business model is predicated on the creation of solutions (Strayer, Dot Foods, SAS). Here are several other examples.

Solution Providing at Cabela's

We uncovered one of the most innovative uses of win-win solutions at Cabela's. When the company's second store, located in Minnesota, opened and quickly became that state's second largest tourist attraction, the firm knew it had landed on a winning formula: huge megastores designed as much as tourist attractions as retail outlets. Obviously the company wanted to open as many of them as quickly as they could absorb the growth, but a giant question arose: how would it come up with money to build them?

Going public was an option that might have provided the company with the capital needed to grow quickly, but the founders were fiercely private individuals not ready to make that move. There was also concern about what kind of reception Wall Street would give them. They'd built a mammoth and wildly successful catalog operation, but what kind of story would they have to tell with only two stores operational? Might the investment community dismiss them as two-trick ponies?

Borrowing lots of money from banks was an option, but the Cabela brothers didn't cotton to letting a bunch of bankers call the shots about how to run the company. The same was true for the issuance of bonds, which would have resulted in scores of performance covenants being placed on the company.

The ever-enterprising Dave Roehr, then serving as Cabela's CFO and a master at thinking big and acting small, hit on an idea. There must be a lot of states, he reasoned, that would welcome a major tourist attraction like Cabela's and be prepared to underwrite most, if not all, of the cost. "Why wouldn't state governments use STAR bonds [sales tax and revenue bonds] to help finance the retail stores?"

STAR bonds work like this: a government body issues bonds to finance the infrastructure improvements that will allow a new industrial and manufacturing park to open in a blighted section of its town or city. The bonds might pay for sewage, water, and electrical systems as well as a portion of a new freeway and exits. Then the sales taxes generated by the new industrial park are used to pay off the bonds. Theoretically, the developer wins by not having to pay for costly infrastructure improvements, and the government wins by having renovated an area designated for rehabilitation. The problem that almost stymied the use of STAR bonds to finance Cabela's stores was that while governments have money for manufacturing and tourism, there'd never been an instance of using economic development bonds to finance retail development.

The brilliance of the Cabela's use of STAR bonds is that they're used to create not only the infrastructure required for a mammoth store but also those parts of the store—the public spaces, museum, aquarium, mountains, and water features—that count as tourist amenities. When the bonds are issued, Cabela's buys them and then pays off the bonds from the sales taxes generated. The sponsoring government wins big time by having helped create a major tourist destination, and Cabela's wins by having most, if not all, the costs of the store underwritten by bonds, which allows it to conserve operating capital, especially if the bonds are marketable or can be converted to cash long before their maturity date.

Another win-win example at Cabela's is its in-house travel agency that arranges outdoor adventure ranging from white-water rafting trips in South America to photo safaris in the Serengeti. The department was started with just one employee and a secretary to assist Cabela's customers with their adventure travel plans. But according to current vice chairman Dennis Highby, it dramatically exceeded everyone's expectations and has become a stellar performer within the company. "It's fascinating the way it works," says Highby. "A customer calls, and after we determine where she wants to travel, how many people there'll be, and the things they want to do, we then supply her with a list of clothing and equipment we highly recommend. Even though the travel division makes money, we make more money supplying the travelers. It's a real win-win. By being properly outfitted, our customers get the trip of a lifetime and we do well in return for putting it together."

Solution Providing at PETCO

In recent years, most major retail organizations have done the math and figured out that it makes a lot more economic sense to keep existing customers than it does to constantly fight for new ones. As a result most retailers have implemented loyalty programs that provide customers with cards that record their shopping habits and which, in return, offer discounts or rewards for their loyalty. Most of these programs work well at improving customer loyalty and supplying the company with a wealth of useful data.

The purpose of most loyalty programs is to make customers faithful to a particular store. For example: a grocery store with a loyalty program wants its customers to remain loyal to it. The store doesn't really care what the customer purchases as long as he does his grocery shopping there. We've all seen the long series of low-price coupons printed on the back of each sales receipt. Given the amount of technology available today, many customers find themselves puzzled when they purchase a twelve-pack of Coke and find a coupon for two dollars off their next purchase of Pepsi. If a store was truly concerned about increasing its customers' loyalty, you'd imagine it would give them coupons for the things they actually buy. Of course, the little secret is that stores sell space on their coupons to whatever company is willing to pay for it. Most stores could care less what a customer buys, as long as she continues to shop in their store.

We discovered a loyalty program at PETCO (profiled in the next chapter) that speaks to the ethos of the company and is an authentic win-win for all parties concerned. Brian Devine, PETCO's chairman, says, "Our central philosophy here is to maximize the sales and profits that our vendors can generate in our stores. If we accomplish that, they'll be delighted with us, want to do more business, and give us a bigger part of the pie."

Nearly 80 percent of PETCO's sales are generated by customers using their loyalty cards. It's a card that company executives say is designed to allow everyone to win. "Our loyalty program," says Devine, "is built on loyalty to our customers and to our manufacturers, and that makes it unique.

"Occasionally," Devine says, "we'll run a buy-ten-get-one-free promotional event. When a customer buys ten bags of Science Diet dog food, we won't give them a free bag of another manufacturer's product that paid us a promotional fee. They'll get a free bag of the product they like to buy."

Devine says the loyalty programs of most retailers drive him crazy. "When you go into most stores and buy Minute Maid orange juice, they'll give you a coupon for Tropicana. They're allowing one manufacturer to cannibalize another company's customer. What we always want to do is protect our manufacturers and grow our relationships with them.

"For example," Devine says, "if you're a customer who buys Science Diet or IAMS or Nutro One, you'll only receive offers from us for that specific manufacturer. In fact, if someone has been a customer of one brand of dog food for several years and then suddenly stops buying it, we'll go into reactivation mode on behalf of that manufacturer and send a five-dollar offer trying to win them back."

One of the other ways PETCO works to garner the loyalty of both its customers and its vendors is by helping vendors grow the total volume of business they do with a customer. "If we notice that a customer buys a certain brand of dry dog food, but hasn't purchased that brand's biscuits or wet food, we might go so far as to send them a fifty-percent-off coupon for that company's other products."

Does PETCO's approach to loyalty work? "We generate double-digit response rates," Devine says, "which is like hitting the ball out of the park in direct-mail marketing. The objective is to grow the manufacturer's business, create loyal customers for it, and when that happens, we win, too."

Solution Providing at Koch Industries

In a previous chapter we detailed how Koch Industries had created two entirely new businesses out of asphalt, one of the by-products of processing heavy crude oil. One of those businesses, Koch Performance Roads, Inc., (KPRI), artfully demonstrates the value of genuine win-win solutions.

Several years ago, the state of New Mexico was faced with the challenge of upgrading Route 44 from San Ysidro to Four Corners. The highway had a notorious reputation as a two-way death trap, and government studies estimated it would take twenty-seven years to complete the widening of the road to four lanes, given capital constraints.

KPRI, a division of Koch Materials, came up with a proposal for New Mexico that bordered on genius. Koch entered into an agreement to provide innovative pavement design and construction management, backed by a long-term performance agreement or warranty. This agreement shifted the responsibility to KPRI for maintaining the pavement's performance for twenty years. The state paid Koch $62 million at final completion for the performance agreement, which Koch will use to maintain the pavement for twenty years, and make a profit.

Another key element of the deal was relieving the state's capital constraints. Koch helped New Mexico's Department of Transportation use a new form of bond financing: the state borrowed against future gas tax revenues, so it could afford to build the road all at once.

Through Koch's innovative approach, New Mexico's Route 44 was upgraded to four lanes in three years, saving more than $89 million for the taxpayers, who got a safer, more efficient road twenty-four years sooner.

Solutions Offer Genuine Value and Higher Margins

Imagine two fruit salesmen each trying to sell a bushel of apples that look exactly like the other guy's, and desperately fighting to convince a customer to buy his apples so he can hit his quarterly target.

Each salesman would probably promise that his apples were fresher than the other guy's. Each might conjure up tales of appellations and the orchards where his apples were grown. But to the buyer they might look exactly alike. Each could promise to sell his apples cheaper than his competitor's and be forced to wait while the prospective buyer checked to find out the commodity's current market price.

Meanwhile, while the first apple salesman was on the phone trying to get the home office to authorize lower prices and throw in a half bushel for free, a real solution provider would have swooped in, learned that what the buyer was really interested in doing with the fruit was making fruit salad, bundled the apple with complimentary goods, presented her with the most delicious fruit salad ever tasted, and closed a deal that allowed the buyer to pay the invoice the day after she'd received the shipment.

As simplistic as it is, the preceding example embodies most of what's wrong with the traditional adversarial sales process and what's correct about providing solutions. The traditional sales process relies on relationships, big claims and promises, and a constantly lowering of prices. Solution providing relies on identifying a prospect's real needs and then offering a customized plan that takes into consideration the requirement that all parties should have their needs profitably met. In industries that face increasing commoditization, solution providing becomes all the more essential.

Businesses hopeful of replicating the outstanding financial performance (increasing revenues by double digits every year for ten consecutive years without a miss) of these companies will have to become authentic providers of solutions.

Think BIG, Act SMALL
CREATE WIN-WIN SOLUTIONS

- Implement the Rule of No. No one's allowed to say no to a customer. Every answer that previously required a no will escalate to members of senior management who need to explain why to the customer.
- Create separate sales forces if necessary, so that salespeople have the time to become better solution providers.
- Don't cut or cap commissions or make across-the-board reductions in sales expenses to improve the short-term financial picture. It will bring you certain disaster the following year.
- Pay people for bringing in gross margin—not gross revenues. Get them invested in profitability—not revenue generation.
- Negotiate an annual revenue and gross profit quota for everyone and tie at least 20 percent of their annual compensation to their achievement.
- When making decisions, make certain to ask, "Is this a win-win approach?" If it is, go for it. If it isn't, make it one.
- Always search for other solutions you can offer your clients. Medline owes its existence to the wife of A. L. Mills, who followed up on a simple suggestion from friends to consider sewing hospital and surgical gowns.
- Share the big dreams for your business with very few people. The more people who know, the more there'll be expecting you to fall over or not make it.

Play Your Own Game
PETCO ANIMAL SUPPLIES

"I tell our buyers not to buy it if Wal-Mart has it, or we'll end up looking stupid."

BRIAN DEVINE, chairman of PETCO

It's almost impossible to name a business category that hasn't become crowded. Whether it's home improvement, airlines, fast food, discount and warehouse retail, entertainment, software, cell phones, travel and leisure, or almost any other category you can think of, the business universe is jammed with people and companies trying to find a unique competitive edge.

Companies that try being all things to all people find it impossible to stand for something that resonates with the marketplace. Witness the generally poor performance and raft of casualties in the troubled department-store, cell-phone, and fast-food industries during the past decade. On the other hand, if the selected niche is too narrow, it's often impossible to gain financial traction or build a real business.

All the firms we identified and studied who'd significantly grown their revenues for ten consecutive years or longer have carefully chosen the competitors they go up against.

Few leaders and companies have done as well at choosing and

defining a space and selecting their competitors while thinking big and acting small as Chairman Brian Devine, CEO Jim Myers, and PETCO, the $3-billion pet supplies and services company they lead.

PETCO

PETCO is the leading specialty retailer of premium pet food, supplies, and services. Averaging 15,000 square feet, each of the firm's nearly 1,100 super pet stores in the United States carries more than ten thousand high-quality pet-related items. PETCO is second to competitor PETsMART in total revenues, but dramatically outperforms it in terms of consistent revenue and operating profit growth. The company growth rate over the past five years is 25 percent and operating income has doubled.

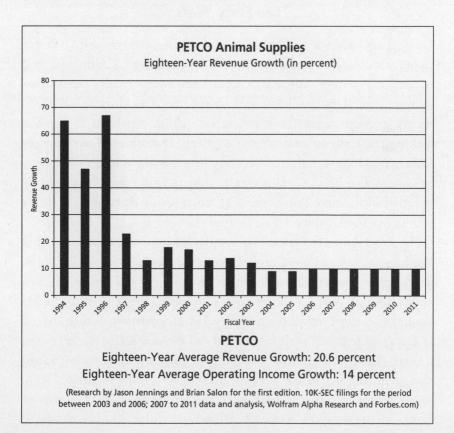

PETCO Animal Supplies
Eighteen-Year Revenue Growth (in percent)

Fiscal Year

PETCO
Eighteen-Year Average Revenue Growth: 20.6 percent
Eighteen-Year Average Operating Income Growth: 14 percent

(Research by Jason Jennings and Brian Salon for the first edition. 10K-SEC filings for the period between 2003 and 2006; 2007 to 2011 data and analysis, Wolfram Alpha Research and Forbes.com)

Former CFO Jim Myers was named CEO in 2004 and teamed with former CEO (now chairman) Brian Devine to continue the string of great successes at PETCO.

Most of the other companies we studied started modestly, held on to a big idea, and grew due to the perseverance of their founder(s) or founding families. The story of PETCO is filled with the same collection of challenges that confront many businesses during their lifespans, an entrepreneurial idea that got stuck and stumbled, a number of false starts, empty coffers and unpaid bills, and more than a few dark days. PETCO's story has a happy ending because of a buyout artist who saw a big potential payoff in the consolidation of an industry, and a specialty retailing genius who knew how to put all the pieces together.

The Early Years

Forty years ago, one of the owners of a Missouri-based distributor of pet supplies and products moved to San Diego, California, and opened a pet store called UPCO, an acronym of the parent company's name (United Pharmacal Company). Deciding that UPCO wasn't a great name for a pet store—think hairballs here—but lacking the cash to redo all the signage, they figured out that by adding two letters and dropping one, the name could inexpensively be changed to PETCO. During the next twenty years the company bumped along and slowly grew to encompass thirty small stores selling pet food, products, and supplies.

In 1988 Andrew Galef, a Los Angeles investor, reasoning that the business of pet food and supplies was ripe for consolidation, approached Boston-based leveraged buyout firm Thomas H. Lee about doing a deal. Together they purchased PETCO and quickly bought two more small chains: The Pet Department Stores, based in Los Angeles, and Well Pet, based in Oregon. First-year revenues totaled slightly less than $500,000 per store and the chain continued operating under three separate names. Well Pet outlets were small stores offering high-touch service; The Pet Department Stores were twice the size and offered twice the number of SKUs, and the PETCO stores were, in the words of a company spokesperson, "small, down and dirty stores with about twenty-five hundred SKUs," and extremely promotionally oriented.

By 1990 total annual spending on pet food and supplies had reached more than $12 billion but no single company—including PETCO—was doing more than $100 million: a paltry 1 percent market share. The executives at Thomas H. Lee began searching for someone capable of turning the company around, building it into a national firm and then taking it public. They called the head of International Operations for Toys "Я" Us to discuss the job, but he told them they were talking with the wrong person and suggested they speak with Brian Devine.

The New Leader

In the late 1960s an idealistic young Brian Devine was living in Washington, D.C., and working for the federal government on a program he designed to fight domestic hunger issues. He supplemented the government work he did for free by doing part-time budgeting and forecasting work for a company called Lash Distributors. At the time, toy manufacturers refused to sell directly to toy stores and would only deal with distributors. Lash Distributors was the name of the company an enterprising Charles Lazarus set up to supply his fledgling chain of nine stores.

On the same day that the government released funding for Devine's hunger program, he received a call from Lazarus telling him to come to the office and talk about a job. "I walked into the meeting," Devine says, "and Charles thrust a test at me and said that I had ten minutes to complete it. It turns out that I finished the test in less than ten minutes and my score was even better than his." Devine accepted Lazarus's job offer and joined the eight people who made up the home office of Toys "Я" Us.

Devine spent eighteen years working side-by-side with Charles Lazarus, growing Toys "Я" Us from nine stores in two cities doing $20 million in annual sales into a $4.5 billion powerhouse that dominated the American toy and game space in the 1970s and '80s.

After leaving Toys "Я" Us in the late '80s, he took the reins at Krause's Sofa Bed Warehouse, where he successfully generated enough cash to allow the founding family to buy the company back. When PETCO called, Devine was living on the East Coast, between CEO jobs, and ready for a new challenge.

"When the call came," Devine says, "I'd never heard of PETCO and called my son, who was living in Los Angeles, and asked him to check out the stores. He called me back and told me that it was the greatest store he'd ever seen, that it had a fountain for dogs to slurp water from and a bakery where they baked animal biscuits, and that he'd ended up buying two puppy toys. He didn't even have a dog.

"I flew out on a Thursday," says Devine, "and they asked me to stay over until the following Monday so I'd be able to meet some of the people from the company. During the weekend, I visited about thirty stores and they were all *very* bad. The only nice one was the store my son had visited. Some people would have become depressed visiting all those empty stores," says Devine, "but all I saw was a giant opportunity."

The following Monday Devine showed up at the company, and it turned out that meeting some of the people who worked for the company *actually* meant walking into a room filled with PETCO managers and executives and conducting an on-the-spot staff meeting/audition. Following the meeting, Devine spent a half hour alone with each of the people who'd been in the meeting asking them questions. "I wanted to know," he says, "what was good about the company, what was bad, who the good and bad people were, and what they viewed as the opportunities."

Devine was offered the job and received a bonus. "It turned out," he says, "that the previous team had cooked the books a bit and so the owners fired the president, CFO, and the VPs of operations and merchandising. The good news was that I was allowed to bring in my own people, the bad news is that the company was seriously underwater." Devine is also very careful to point out that some of the people who'd been with the company in human resources and information technology were very talented and are still with PETCO today as senior executives.

Our research uncovered no fewer than fourteen steps taken by Brian Devine that not only saved PETCO, but also provided the solid foundation used to achieve its remarkably consistent revenue and profit performance. His action plan is a worthy model for all managers, executives, and entrepreneurs committed to the achievement of dramatic and consistent revenue increases.

PETCO's Steps to Consistent Revenue Growth

- *Choose* your competitors
- Partner with your vendors
- Make honesty the only policy
- Get the right stuff in the right place at the right time
- Build a brand
- Always a wow! experience
- Differentiate, learn, then differentiate more
- Don't let headquarters screw things up
- Get the best information
- Lots of small bets
- Keep good people
- Be happy but never satisfied
- Play your own game, not Wall Street's
- Healthy pets, happier people, a better world

---

1. Choose Your Competitors Carefully

Devine's first move was to determine the space PETCO would occupy, and who it would compete against. "I looked at every store that sold pet food and supplies," he says. "I wanted to know how they were doing, how busy their stores were, and how the stores performed financially. I needed to figure out what we were going to be.

"There's one major competitor," says Devine, never mentioning it by name, "who has always used price as its sole driver. When I first shopped their stores, I saw concrete floors, merchandise stacked thirty feet high, and power equipment going up and down the aisles honking at you while you were trying to shop." Devine instinctively knew he couldn't afford, nor did he want, to compete in that low-margin space.

To thwart the nonstop barrage of unpredictable price promotions from this competitor, PETCO copied a tactic used by other retailers and prominently began displaying signs within their stores touting GUARANTEED LOWEST PRICES and offering to match its prices. Few people actually go to the trouble of bringing in an ad from a competing store, and Devine figured the promise of matching a competitor's price would blunt the price attack of other stores.

One of the lessons that's served Devine well at PETCO was remembering what happened to Toys 'Я' Us after he left. "Toys 'Я' Us was a specialty retailer," he says, "where customers would constantly walk in and exclaim 'Wow, look at this place.' Its undoing began when it began Wal-Mart-izing its stores and customers could find the same merchandise at Wal-Mart and at a lower price." Less than 1 percent of the ten thousand items carried in a PETCO store can be found in a Wal-Mart. "From the beginning," he says, "I told our buyers that if Wal-Mart has it, don't buy it or we'll end up looking stupid." Devine's guidance to his buyers is to find better items in the same category that the customer won't mind paying for because of the product's extra attributes and benefits.

After analyzing the percentage of grocery goods sold in PETCO's stores, Devine quickly decided he wouldn't compete with grocery stores or carry the pet food items they sell. "We actually threw them all out of our stores," he says. "Those big twenty- and forty-pound bags of pet food in grocery stores have as much as eighty-four percent waste and fill versus sixteen percent nutrients," he argues. "And while pets will eat a lot of it, it's because they aren't getting enough nutrients. We decided we would only sell the best things to our customers, and that allowed us to make a conscious decision not to compete with Wal-Mart or the other big chain discounters."

As Devine continued studying the marketplace, he discovered that competitors featuring aquariums and fish had significantly higher traffic than stores that didn't and in his first year he began experimenting. "During my first year," he says, "I got permission from the board to open two new stores and renovate three others.

We took out some slower moving merchandise and replaced it with aquariums and fish and increased our sales per square foot by five times. An area of floor space," he says, "that had previously accounted for three percent of sales was suddenly contributing fifteen percent."

Fifteen years ago, PETCO was the first to see the interest in organic, natural foods from pet owners. "I was on the board of Wild Oats [one of the first natural foods grocery chains acquired by Whole Foods in 2007] and saw the incredible momentum on the people food side," Devine said. "My retail savvy told me the same was going to happen on the dog and cat side. So we jumped on it. It's been growing twenty plus percent every year for over a decade and we can see the day when it will be the dominant category."

Devine and his team concluded that despite the trend toward big-box, self-serve discount retail, PETCO would become a value-added retailer of unique, healthy, and innovative products, offering a high level of service and convenience. PETCO decided not to compete with stores that relied only on price, grocery stores, or general-merchandise chain discounters. It made a bet that by playing its own game—offering a wow experience—it would build a loyal base of avid fans for its unique approach.

2. Truly Partner with Vendors

During the interview and dialogue process with PETCO, I realized something; when the people who lead PETCO use the word "partnering" to describe their relationships with the company's vendors and suppliers, they really *mean* it.

Brian Devine speaks frankly about manufacturers and buyers and relationships with vendors and suppliers. "During my Toys 'Я' Us days," he says, "I'd have buyers sit down with suppliers and someone would begin the meeting by saying, 'we're the biggest and this is the price we want from you.' My reaction was always the same," he says. "Fire that person. They don't get it. They don't understand that the only reason a manufacturer should give anybody anything or grant them any concessions is because of what you can do for them to help grow their business.

"When you try to run roughshod over your manufacturers," he

says, "you're going to become the company they're talking about, and if they believe you're trying to screw them, they're going to look for a way to pay you back and screw you first."

"Now we see more profit from our great relationships," Devine say. "Because of the way we've treated vendors, especially those with cool ideas and new products, the really innovative companies come to us first. We get two to ten years of exclusivity—and solid margins— before they get seduced to the dark side," that is, the Bentonville- and Phoenix-based superstore competitors whose names, like Harry Potter's nemesis, Lord Voldemort, are never to be spoken.

"Back when we were a private company," says Devine, "one of my partners used to say that I torture manufacturers." It's a characterization he wears with pride, but he also offers a modification to the description. "The truth is I do torture them but I do it with logic and I do it because I want to help them grow their businesses.

"We exist to drive the manufacturer's business," Devine says. "If we know how to help a supplier move more merchandise through our stores, we have a responsibility to convince them to do it." He offers the following example:

"If we have a supplier selling thirty million annually through the stores," Devine says, "but we believe they can do an additional five million dollars, we'll sell them hard on doing it. They all want the extra money," he says, "but some are afraid to step up to the pump and commit the resources to making it happen. We might suggest that they have to spend five hundred thousand dollars with us in advertising, marketing, placement, and demonstrations to achieve the sales increase, and that's where some of them get cold feet. That's when I'm occasionally called in," he says with a big grin, "to torture them with logic and convince them to do it. If they don't do it, they might end up saving the five hundred thousand dollars we're asking them to spend but they'll miss the extra five million in revenues next year and whatever that amount would be in future years."

Devine, Myers, and their team passionately believe they have the best collection of stores, most efficient information systems, best trained people, and most effective marketing and advertising programs in the industry. That fervent belief manifests itself in the shared belief that their job isn't to buy merchandise from vendors and resell it in their stores but instead to help lead manufacturers to the achievement of greater success. If that happens, they reason, they'll be more successful as well. "We're driving both engines—ours and our vendors'—at the same time," Devine concludes.

3. Make Honesty the Only Policy

"When I got here," says Devine, "the company was on workout with our bankers [meaning PETCO was unable to pay back its loans as agreed and the bank was *working* with them toward the objective of being paid off] and on COD with our vendors. We were seriously underwater."

Devine took the road less traveled in business. He began meeting with the company's vendors and had the same straight-from-the-heart message for each. "I told each of them that I wouldn't have joined the company if I didn't believe we'd succeed in turning it around, that we needed their support and that when we asked them for merchandise to please send it, and to trust me, that they would be paid.

"We ended up building some great relationships during that time," Devine recalls. "IAMS Corporation had a new president, and following our conversation, he picked up the phone and told his people to send us everything we needed and that we'd pay them when we were able. Another vendor partner is Aspen," says Devine. "A week before we were scheduled to send them $125,000, I called and told them we wouldn't be able to pay them next week as planned and that we needed another $175,000 worth of product." Devine finishes the story by saying, "The guy put the phone down, called the CEO on a speakerphone and explained what was happening and wanted to know what to do. I actually heard him say, 'Send him what he needs. If he was going to stiff us he wouldn't call. Ship it to them.'"

"Later," Devine says, "they told us the reason they didn't cut us off was because we were honest with them. I guess it goes back to my days at the old Toys 'Я' Us where I learned that when you're honest with everyone, they learn they can rely on you and they'll bet alongside you that disaster can be turned into victory."

According to Devine, the bankers at Security Pacific weren't as moved by his honesty as the vendors. "We worked out the business plan," he says, "and went to meet with the banker who'd been assigned to work with us. This guy was dressed in cowboy boots and suspenders that he kept snapping," recalls Devine. "He told us, 'I'm not interested in your plan, I don't want to look at your plan, and I don't want you as a customer.'"

Not to be deterred, Devine and his team pitched thirty banks and none of them would lend the company a penny. "Finally," says Devine, "two banks said yes. We went with the bank that wanted us to remain private instead of being rushed into a public offering." Using the proceeds from the new line of credit, PETCO was able to leave Security Pacific and begin plotting for growth. "I think a mainstay of this company is that we tell the truth," Devine says. "We have no hidden agendas; we're transparent to our associates and other stakeholders."

4. Get the Right Stuff in the Right Place at the Right Time

The formula for business success is pretty simple—get the right products in the right place at the right time for the right price. But simple is always difficult. "Systems and distribution ultimately win the game for you," says Devine, and he immediately moved to control inventories by installing a point-of-sale (POS) system. "We were scanning goods back in the 1960s at Toys 'Я' Us when hardly anyone else was doing it. We needed to get control of the inventories and figure out who had what and how many of them." An integral part of Devine's POS system was automated purchase orders and replenishment that promised that the inventory that was selling would be available in the stores.

On the distribution front, Devine immediately opened a distribution center on the East Coast to complement the West Coast facility. "Conventional wisdom dictates that if you're a regional business, you should grow outward," says Devine. "The problem with that is that as most regional companies grow outward, their systems start breaking down." Crediting Charles Lazarus with the idea, Devine says he adapted the strategic plan from Toys "Я" Us,

opening both an East and West Coast distribution facility, determined to fill in the rest of the country as capital permitted.

In 2011, systems to get the right stuff in the right place at the
right time are still a major preoccupation. "We're spending a lot of
money," Devine explains, "making sure we stay at the top of our
game [in communications, logistics, and distribution.] The advantage we have now [as a private company] is we can invest big dollars
on infrastructure without getting pressured for short-term earnings. Next year we're going to spend over sixty million dollars
upgrading systems and technology. We'll still grow our earnings,
but we want to facilitate our future our way."

5. Build a Brand, Not a Price Promotion
"The first thing I did was change the names of all the stores to
PETCO and put them under the same brand," says Devine. "It
made no sense to try to build three separate brands and try to
please three groups of customers because we would have had three
times as many challenges and, at the end of the day, would have
failed to build a recognizable national brand." Next, Devine decided
to stop all advertising. "People protested and told me that millions of
circulars and inserts had already been printed," he says. "I told them
to throw them in the trash and at least save the costs of distribution.

"The company's advertising had always been about price," explains
Devine. "The company spent all their advertising dollars during the
first week of the month offering discounted prices on all pet food.
They'd advertise a bag of food that regularly sold for $28.95 for a low-
ball price like $19.99, and they'd fill the stores, sell a lot of food and
not make any margin. Then all the stores would be dead for the next
three weeks. They were doing the same thing that department stores
had done with their sale, sale, sale promotions fifty-two weeks a year;
training people to buy only when products were on deep discount.

"The other problem with the company's advertising," says Devine,
"is that they were paying for it and the manufacturer wasn't contributing." In the year before Devine's arrival, PETCO had spent more
than $3 million on advertising but only collected $200,000 from
manufacturers. By the end of his second year, PETCO's advertising

spending was back up to more than $3 million but the company was collecting more than $2.5 million from manufacturers. "Between the manufacturers paying for their advertising and the offers they wanted to make, it represented a five million dollar swing," he says. "We were able to put those dollars straight to the bottom line."

Devine says his decision to momentarily stop all advertising wasn't as big a risk as it might appear. "I knew that customers weren't going to change the type of food their pets were used to eating, that eventually they'd run out and come back and pay the regular price. Within a few weeks, I got my first letter from a Nutro Food customer complaining about paying the regular price and I knew we were on our way. By not having those giant sales every month," he adds, "within a very short time we had the most predictable profit margins I'd ever seen."

6. Offer a Wow Experience

"From the beginning," says Devine, "we were determined that the customer-service experience at PETCO would be both fun and exciting. We fervently believe that if customers have a neutral to positive experience while shopping in our stores, they'll come back. But a negative shopping experience," he says, "will always fail to win a customer. If a store's prices are ten percent more than its competitors', but customers have a positive experience, they'll come back."

Within two years of his arrival, and with the previous steps already taken, the company opened its first ten-thousand-square-foot prototype store featuring the primary colors of red, yellow, and blue for which it has become well known, as well as the pet food, care items, grooming department, animal adoption services, birds, small animals, reptiles, and fish, and a constant parade of customers. It was ready to go on a tear and capture market share.

Most of PETCO's customers consider themselves to be parents to their pets and 70 percent are female. In an effort to provide a favorable shopping experience, wow their customers and truly become the place where the pets go, PETCO's stores have evolved significantly during the past decade. Rather than being located near destination shopping centers like Home Depot or Costco, where customers tended to shop once every several weeks, PETCO stores are likely to be located in a community-based shopping center frequented one to three times weekly by shoppers. Wanting stores that are easy to shop, the company limits store size to between twelve thousand and fifteen thousand square feet. They are open, bright, colorful, and odor free and have unique features such as dog bars, libraries, animal habitats, and theatrical displays.

Now PETCO is working on a new format, Unleashed by PETCO. "Unleashed is a four- to five-thousand-square-foot facility with everything but live animals for sale," Devine explains. Thirty stores are up and running and PETCO plans to add another hundred in 2012. "We're making Unleashed a place that is solely focused on giving great customer service. We have great service in our big stores and generate a seventy-five percent in our Loyalty Index. But Unleashed stores are getting eighty-five percent right out of the box. That's a really big number."

7. Differentiate, Learn, Then Differentiate More

It would tempt credulity to assert that once Devine and PETCO had taken the previously described steps, some kind of a magical journey to the achievement of consistent revenue growth suddenly materialized. Such is not the case. The business history books are full of stories of once great companies—including Devine's alma mater Toys "Я" Us—who lost the plot and ended up stuck in the mud.

PETCO owes its consistent financial performance to its ability to carefully choose its competitors, its mastery of the aforementioned basics, and its constant efforts to differentiate. Some of PETCO's innovations were described in earlier chapters and include: the company's willingness to scuttle a new design plan for its stores when a staffer came up with a better idea at the eleventh hour; ways for manufacturers to get their products inside PETCO stores even after the company's buyers decided not to stock them; and a unique program designed to reward customers for being loyal—not to PETCO—but to the manufacturer.

"Some people like the status quo and want to keep on doing the same thing," says Devine. "We believe that we have to be constantly changing and raising the bar. We work very hard not to react to our competitor [*again not acknowledging them by name*] but instead to react to ourselves. We are truly committed to constantly examining our execution and trying to figure out ways to improve it." Devine and an executive team headed by newly appointed CEO Jim Myers, who joined PETCO from KPMG before Devine took over, have spearheaded these and other initiatives—all designed to ensure continued long-term revenue growth.

"We have to stay one step ahead," Devine says. "We've created an 'Indulgent Aisle' and a 'Fashion' section. Also a PETCO Zoo where we put the animals together. So we're making it a better and better shopping experience and a bigger wow!" Devine adds, "Of course, the other guys will knock us off. In fact, when I show outsiders our operations I say, 'First I want you to see what we looked like two years ago.' And then I take them to the competition. Next I take them to our store and point out all the new things. It makes a great impression. They can see we have the vision, great store planning people, eleven hundred managers, and thousands of associates who offer great ideas. And we listen and act on them.

"There's still a lot to learn," Devine notes. "That's one of the great things about our life here. We're constantly getting better and getting every associate to think, 'How can I make the company more successful?'"

8. Don't Let Headquarters Screw Things Up

"We don't have a home office," says Devine. "Home offices are places filled with people who get in the way of innovation and always cause more trouble than they're worth. Instead, we have a national support center. The company is our collection of stores and we exist as a service to make certain they have everything they need to serve their customers.

"We empower our people," Devine states. "We're a customer service company and when the customer has a problem, we solve it with knowledgeable associates and the best technology for transferring expertise to each associate."

According to Devine, PETCO operates with a vision of "'health-ier pets, happier people, better world.' We stock the products and empower our people to provide healthier options. But if the cus-tomer has a problem with their pet, we want to help them solve it. When their pet is healthy again the customer is happier."

"The job of the national support center is to ensure that each of these 'companies' are provided with the merchandise they need, customers walking in the door, and the training to know what to do and how to sell to them once they're in the store. The stores are our customers and our job is to exceed their expectations.

"Some retail organizations who are forecasting a tough quarter are quick to reduce the number of employees in the stores. We would never injure our stores," he says emphatically, "so we'd never get rid of people at the store level or reduce advertising. Instead, we just don't hire anybody here at the national support center and everyone works a little harder until we're over the rough spot. The stores do it," he repeats. "They are the company. The stores are the company and must never be injured."

9. Get the Best Information

"Because we view ourselves as a collection of seven hundred sepa-rate companies," says Devine, "it requires that each store has its own assortment of merchandise." He credits the company's infor-mation systems as being responsible for the company's routinely achieving almost eight inventory turns annually in a business where half that number is considered successful.

Unless a company's information systems are proprietary, they're not a competitive advantage. The difference between the use of information systems at PETCO and most other companies is that it utilizes the data generated with the precision of a rifle instead of a shotgun's wide spray of buckshot.

"With the data we collect," says Devine, "we know each individ-ual customer, exactly what she buys and when, and we use our IS capabilities to keep and reactivate them if necessary. We're not only doing it for us," he says. "We're doing it for the manufacturer.

"The way we use our information systems has allowed us to

achieve higher inventory turns than Wal-Mart or Best Buy while maintaining high margins."

10. Lots of Small Bets

"Everyone here at the national support center," Devine says, "is always trying to come up with new products we should be carrying, innovative formats for the stores, and unusual twists to the way we do things. We're big testers, and if something works in the testing stage, then we'll roll it out across the nation." PETCO's institution-alized policy of testing first and then rolling out innovations is markedly different from the approach used by many companies who arbitrarily adopt new directions, change their entire chain, and end up saying, "Oops that didn't work out as planned."

11. Keep Your Good People

"Our number-one secret at PETCO," says Devine, "is that we never lose good people. When someone comes into my office to resign I simply tell them that I won't accept their resignation and then I go to work on them.

"I sit here and talk to them as long as it takes to have them rescind their decision." He adds that "sometimes it's taken as long as three days of talking to have them change their mind, but gener-ally things are worked out within one to two days."

What's Devine's magic for being able to have someone intent on leaving change their mind?

"I start by asking them if they like what they're doing," he says, "and then I ask them if they like the people they're working with and whether they're in a great industry with a successful company. Next I ask them if they're making as much money as they want to make, if they like where they live, and if their family is happy.

"Then we talk about the company they're considering joining. Is that as good a company, is that as nice a place to live and will your family be as happy? Finally," he says, "I simply ask them to stay, enjoy what they're doing, and be happy.

"We'll always find a way to keep great people," says Devine, "because it's people that make an enterprise successful."

It would be incorrect to conclude that the questions asked by Devine to retain the people he wants to keep are evidence of a domineering or manipulative personality. While all companies proclaim they don't want to lose good people, one of Devine's distinct competitive advantages is that he'll go to almost any length to keep them and make things right so that people want to stay.

It's working. Turnover is at historic lows—less than a single digit among PETCO store managers and overall (among store associates and others) half of where it was a decade ago. "We are able to recruit and keep people who worked for much larger companies, and people often turn down job offers from huge, prestigious organizations to come here," Devine explains. "We're growing, we've got a great story, we give out a tremendous amount of staff promotions every year, and we've made leadership training one of the most important priorities in our company."

12. Be Happy but Never Be Satisfied

One day when Brian Devine and Jim Myers had finished a business meeting with some people from outside the company, one of them asked Myers, "Brian's not happy, is he?" Myers deadpanned, "Brian's always happy, he's just never satisfied!"

Devine's indomitable will to constantly grow, innovate, move forward, and have fun provides everyone who works for PETCO with a sense that tomorrow will be even more filled with fun, achievement, and prosperity than the present. "We're only at seven hundred stores," says an ebullient Devine, "and we've already identified one thousand four hundred store sites. That means we're only halfway to the goalpost. We can reasonably open and absorb about fifty stores each year, which means there's lots of work to be done during the next twelve years."

One PETCO staffer summed up his feelings this way. "I've been here for ten years and can't imagine leaving because it's so challenging and there are so many things to do that I'll never get it done. As far as I'm concerned the key to life is having a full plate and lots of stuff to accomplish."

13. Play Your Own Game, Not Wall Street's

Devine says that back when PETCO was publicly traded some analysts complained to him about his not doing more to maximize the short-term earnings. Devine's response was always the same. "We've beaten every estimate for every quarter since we've been public. My job is not to maximize short-term earnings but to maximize the long-term success of the company.

"We try to grow our earnings twenty percent annually," says Devine. "If I were so inclined I could put the screws down, fundamentally change the company, have a few spectacular years, make a ton of money for myself, and then retire. Why would I want to do that?

"Our job," says Devine, "is to constantly search for new ways to *wow* customers and to grow the long-term value of the company. If we do that, everything else will take care of itself.

"Each year we build a budget," says Devine, "and take it to the board for approval. Then we tell the analysts what we plan on doing and they in turn set the expectation of investors. But one thing I always tell the analysts is that when we beat the Street's estimate, we're keeping half of the additional dollars inside the company whether they like it or not."

Just because Wall Street has more money in its pockets doesn't mean it has more brains in its head. Back when PETCO first went private in 2000, Wall Street was valuing the sock puppet at Pets .com more than all the people at PETCO. "We were making money and doing a billion dollars in sales," Devine remembers. "They did just forty million dollars and were losing one hundred million dollars." Brick and mortar was so 1990, according the Street's groupthink conclusion, so PETCO paid its investors a premium to go private. After the dot-com bubble imploded, PETCO went public again in 2002. Farsighted investors and scores of loyal employees (who were given shares as a bonus) made collectively more than a billion dollars.

PETCO went private again in 2006 when Wall Street lost the plot a second time. "Being private gives you more time to run your company. We're doing fine, growing our earnings at almost twenty-five percent compounded," Devine says. But it's clear that growth is the result of PETCO's playing its own game instead of Wall Street's.

"We use those monies the way we think is best," Devine says, "to add new systems, do more training, and to increase marketing and the number of people in the stores."

14. Healthy Pets, Happier People, a Better World

"In order to keep our people happy," he says, "we give them the unexpected. When people do a great job they rightfully expect a good raise and a good bonus. But that isn't enough. You've got to do more than that." Even Brian Devine's HR department approves of his version of hugs and kisses.

"Each year," he says, "we pick out ten people and give them a second bonus, something completely unexpected. Sometimes we give them gigantic raises. Other times we give blocks of stock to people who aren't even in a qualified plan. Whatever we give," he adds, "is significant and meaningful."

Few things excite Devine more than talking about the number of millionaires that PETCO has created. "When we went private," says Devine, "the board gave me a block of shares and told me to distribute them to the top five or six people. I rebelled," he says. "I told them that the list of people who'd be receiving wasn't four or five but fifty-five."

But it's not just about the money. PETCO raises money for favorite animal charities and causes. "We've grown our foundation [The PETCO Foundation] and invested around seventy-five million dollars." Executive director Paul Jolly and his team help almost seven thousand partners with the four Rs. They help rescue sheltered animals by finding loving homes, rehabilitate troubled pets by educating and counseling families and animals, rejoice in the life-affirming, life-enhancing bond between people and pets, and reduce the overpopulation of pets to stop the heartbreak of euthanizing animals.

PETCO empowers its people to put their hearts into the cause of animal welfare. "During Hurricane Katrina, we got a warehouse in Baton Rouge and flew in planeloads of food and essentials for the pets of New Orleans. Our people came in as others were leaving to rescue animals and see they had what they needed to make it through the disaster," Devine recalls. "Our New York store manager went to Ground Zero after 9/11 to find out what they needed for the rescue dogs. We ultimately gave over a million dollars to care for the animals. Just last month, when Hurricane Irene caused New Yorkers to evacuate, we convinced officials to let us stay open because people needed supplies to safely take their pets with them."

When a PETCO store in New Jersey was rocked by a gas explosion in March 2005, "our associates continued to go back in the store to save the animals, despite the risks. Some were injured when a second explosion hit," Devine said. "These are the kinds of things that make us all really proud to be here."

PETCO Thinks Big and Acts Small

When Brian Devine took the reins at PETCO, he and his team were required to begin a rebuilding process using little more than the fumes of an oily rag. There simply weren't any resources. They began opening twenty-five new stores annually out of internal cash flow, carefully testing every innovation because they couldn't afford a misstep. As they began growing, they continued doing business as merchants committed to the success of their vendors; they didn't begin beating them up nonstop rounds for price concessions. They fostered a corporate spirit based on valuing the contributions of their team members, generously rewarding them, and acknowledging their efforts. They take neither their market leadership nor superlative financial performance for granted, truly believing the big job lies ahead.

Play Your Own Game

It's the height of arrogance for any company to believe it can be all things to all people at all times and in all places. PETCO carefully studied the marketplace and determined what it wanted to be and what it didn't. It found its niche in the mid to high end and decided not to go head to head with PETsMART, Wal-Mart, or grocery stores. That decision allowed it to do its own thing and do it better than anyone else without the unnecessary burden of worrying about having to face off daily against cutthroat competition.

Each of the companies we studied—including SAS Institute and Dot Foods, who invented brand-new businesses—know it's foolhardy and often fatal to rush blindly into the marketplace trying to be all things to all people and attempting to compete against everyone.

Think Big, Act SMALL
PLAY YOUR OWN GAME

- Don't try to be all things to all people. You'll mean nothing to anyone.
- Shop around and study everyone doing business in the category you're considering. Answer the following questions: Who's doing the business, who has the customers, who's generating margin, who's making money, who's thrilling customers and what would it take to improve on what they're already doing?
- Don't go up against a company with a decided competitive advantage and the financial resources to squash you.
- Find a space you love and are prepared to make your life's work. (Brian Devine's disdain for hydraulic trucks beeping their way down store aisles precluded PETCO's entry into the warehouse arena.)
- There will always be competitors able to offer lower prices than yours. Figure out how you'll blunt a nonstop price attack without sacrificing margin.
- Figure out what will be required to own the space you're entering. Answer the question, "What barriers to entry will prevent someone from coming directly after me?"

Build Communities
STRAYER EDUCATION

"Never underestimate the challenge of execution because that's where a lot of organizations that seem to have everything on their side fall short!"

ROBERT SILBERMAN, chairman and CEO of Strayer Education

During the original research for this book, just as Facebook and Twitter were beginning to make a little noise, but long before they revolutionized the way we communicate, we made the observation that all the companies we'd included had already capitalized on the concept of social networking by making their customers members of very special communities. Based upon the conclusion of our original research in 2004 and 2005 and our follow-up research in 2010 and 2011, we've concluded that community building played a pivotal role in the success of each company.

If your business can harness the power of building and growing communities of workers, customers, and fans, you will have added an extremely potent arrow to your competitive quiver. In coming years, it may become a matter of life or death for your business.

The Strayer Story

For more than 115 years, Strayer Education has been in the business of providing training and education to working adults, helping propel them forward on their career paths and allowing them to become university graduates.

In 2005, when we first studied and wrote about Strayer, the company had twenty thousand students on thirty campuses in Maryland, North Carolina, Pennsylvania, South Carolina, Tennessee, Virginia, and Washington, D.C.

During the next five years (and despite the economic meltdown), the number of campuses and students nearly tripled to more than fifty-five thousand students and eighty-four campuses as far west as Texas and throughout the Southeast and upper Midwest. Students at the university are primarily working adults

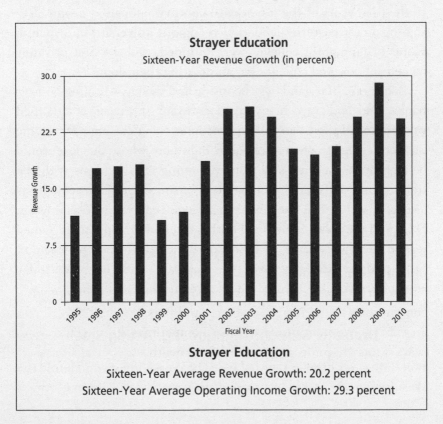

Strayer Education
Sixteen-Year Revenue Growth (in percent)

Strayer Education
Sixteen-Year Average Revenue Growth: 20.2 percent
Sixteen-Year Average Operating Income Growth: 29.3 percent

pursuing degrees in fields such as accounting, business administration, computer science, education, and health services administration. The company also offers courses online.

In contrast to the hundreds of continuing education companies that have sprouted up in the past few decades, Strayer stands out for its century-long history and prestigious accreditation by the Middle States Commission on Higher Education, which accredits schools like Princeton and Georgetown. Despite many other colleges and universities in the for-profit education sector having recently received black eyes, huge fines, and cease-and-desist orders from the federal government because of unscrupulous sales tactics and high default rates on student loans, Strayer has always been squeaky clean.

The Early Years: Thinking Small and Acting Small

In the final years of the nineteenth century, education began blossoming on the eastern seaboard. Prestigious universities prospered, scores of land-grant colleges were founded, and the first privately owned schools and colleges began opening their doors.

Baltimore, Maryland, was booming and the city's trading houses, banks, and brokerage firms faced constant shortages of qualified workers to fill their back-office positions. Schoolteacher Dr. Irving Strayer decided to open a school in Baltimore whose purpose would be to provide the men and women coming off the farms with the training and skills required to work in business. Strayer's school was a success and by 1904 he'd opened a second campus in Washington, D.C., and the college remained both successful and privately owned for the next eighty years. In 1986 Ron Bailey, the former president of Strayer University, purchased the company and the modern-day story of Strayer and its highly attractive business model began.

Dramatic Growth: Thinking Big, Acting Small

Ron Bailey was born in the coal fields of West Virginia and found the Washington, D.C., area by way of a stint at an army base in northern

Virginia. Upon completion of his military service, he attended a community college, received an associate's degree, and then enrolled at Strayer College, where he earned his bachelor's degree.

In 1974, having completed his graduate studies, Bailey was asked to join Strayer's adjunct faculty, teaching computer sciences. "My day job," Bailey says, "was making a lot of money running a computer center for a big trade association, but I loved teaching so much that in 1979, when Strayer asked me to join them full-time as a professor, I quit the other job, took a huge pay cut, and started doing what I loved."

Bailey's full-time teaching career lasted for only two years. "Because of my background with computers," he says, "before I knew it I was named VP of finance and then put in charge of computer systems." Bailey didn't enjoy being an administrator, and the first time he was offered the presidency he turned it down. "In 1986 they offered the presidency to me again, and I figured I'd better take it because I had no idea who I'd end up working for if I turned it down." Bailey says that when he took the helm there was one big thing he wanted to do—grow the company.

While Bailey wanted to grow the college, the owners wanted to sell it. "Doctor Charles Palmer lived in Charleston, South Carolina," says Bailey, "and he and his wife, Rebecca, were both getting old, didn't want to travel to Washington, wanted to sell, and kept pestering me to find a buyer.

"I traveled all over the world in search of a buyer," Bailey says, "and each time one materialized they wanted to pay for it with an IOU. Finally, I meekly raised my hand and told the Palmers that if they'd take an IOU from me I'd buy it.

"Doc Palmer told me that my IOU wasn't good because I didn't have any money, but I told him that I thought I could raise three hundred thousand in cash." The Palmers told Bailey they doubted he could raise that much cash, but if he could, they'd sell him the college for five million dollars with a down payment of $300,000.

In 1986, at age forty-five, Ron Bailey took the largest possible second mortgage on his house, cashed in his 401(k) and paid the tax penalties, emptied the family's savings accounts, sold personal possessions, and came up with the cash to close the deal. "Things were so tight at the closing," Bailey says," that my wife looked at me and asked what was going to happen to the car, and I told her we were going to sell it for the cash we could get.

"The day before the closing," says Bailey, "my accountant called and told me that'd I'd better go back and renegotiate the deal because there was no way I could make the numbers work. I told him that a deal is a deal and I had to make it work."

Once the closing had taken place, Bailey was greeted by an empty bank account. "Charlie Palmer had taken out so much cash right before the closing that I couldn't make the payroll. I didn't know what to do, so I asked the dean and some other instructors if they'd defer their payroll until the next month when I knew we'd have some cash from the international students coming in. Having to do that woke me up," he says, "and you can believe that I never had a problem with payroll again."

Between the accountants' telling him he was in big trouble and missing a payroll, Bailey says he was scared. "I was literally scared straight," he says, "and I began working eighty hours a week to make it work." He says that he tracked how much wax the janitors used on the floors and counted every sheet of paper. Bailey's perseverance paid off, and in less than five years, he'd paid the Palmer family their $5 million and owned Strayer free and clear.

"I'd figured out some things while serving as president," says Bailey. "First, I knew we had to have the highest-quality product and take the high road, which required gaining regional accreditation. We had to put the schools where students live and offer classes in the evening when our target student—the adult worker aged twenty-five and over—could take them.

"I started branching out as fast as I could and never forgot the accountant who'd told me I'd never make it. I just kept running and opening as fast as cash flow permitted while continuing to offer the highest-quality product possible."

In 1995 Bailey decided to take a breather and stopped opening additional locations for one year. He was amazed at what happened. "The cash kept rolling in," he says. "All the locations were profitable, and because we weren't facing the expenses associated with opening new campuses, the cash began piling up. The cash was like a train that kept running," he says, "and I didn't know what to do with it." One thing was certain. He wanted to repay those faculty members who'd deferred their payroll when he was unable to pay them and he wanted to share the wealth.

In 1996 Bailey took Strayer Education public and allocated a big block of stock for the school's employees. "Some of the deans who'd agreed to skip a paycheck ended up with more than a million dollars," he says, "and everyone received a prorated number of shares. I had janitors come up and thank me because they'd received enough shares to be able to buy a home." Strayer's public offering handsomely rewarded its employees, raised $30 million for school expansion, and meant that Bailey was worth $60 million.

By 2001 the school, which had grown from six hundred students to more than sixteen thousand under his leadership, had achieved a market capitalization of about $300 million, and a combination of factors caused Bailey to decide to sell his remaining 60 percent of the company. "I didn't like dealing with analysts and answering their stupid questions," he says. "And I didn't enjoy running the company for the benefit of a good quarterly report."

But it was a health scare gone from bad to worse that caused Bailey to decide to sell. Now fully recovered from the illness that led to partial paralysis, Bailey says, "When you're lying paralyzed in a hospital bed for months staring up at the ceiling, you realize how important family and friends are, and all the other things you want to do with your life."

Maintaining Momentum: Thinking Really Big and Continuing to Act Small

The people who purchased Bailey's stock are a group of private equity investors headed by president and COO Robert Silberman, whose previous positions include serving as the assistant secretary of the army in the George H. W. Bush administration and as CEO of CalEnergy, Inc.

"We studied the revenue and profitability growth of many industries," says Silberman, "and after carefully examining secular trends we decided that the education space is where we wanted to make an acquisition. Strayer was one of the few publicly traded companies that provided an opportunity for an acquisition."

Frequently when an outside group takes control of a company, the existing culture is abandoned in the interest of expediency, and the acquirers roar through the organization making wholesale changes in order to quickly boost the company's earnings. Silberman did the opposite.

"As a management team, the current administration has nothing but respect and gratitude for Ron Bailey and what he built," says Silberman. "He's one of the nation's great entrepreneurs. He recognized a vital need in the marketplace," says Silberman, "positioned Strayer to offer the finest education available, and then built a remarkable business model."

The following factors are largely responsible for the extraordinarily successful Strayer business model.

1. It's Not Capital Intensive

"The model that Ron Bailey perfected," Silberman says, "doesn't require outside capital to grow. We can expand indefinitely out of internally generated cash flow without ever going back to the capital markets." As each additional campus becomes profitable, the company is able to open another.

It costs Strayer as little as $1.5 million to open a new campus. Roughly half the money is used for rents, equipment, and supplies, while the other half covers the operating losses until the campus becomes profitable.

As each new campus becomes profitable, the company is able to open another. In 2010, Silberman repeated almost word for word what he'd told us five years earlier. "Frankly," he says, "we've been a little boring for the past five years. The strategy hasn't changed at all. We've just continued to execute the plan I outlined back then. The biggest challenge to growing faster," he says, "is the development of human capital and the time it takes to train our professors to be great assistant deans and then to become a campus dean."

According to Silberman, the biggest challenge facing Strayer is ensuring academic quality, which he says can only be accomplished by physical oversight. "Everyone from the president of the university down to the deans of the schools and the regional and area deans are involved in oversight and being physically present in classrooms to make certain that interactions between professors and students are going well."

2. More Demand Than Supply

In 2005, Silberman shared the opinion that for the foreseeable future there would be more demand than supply in the marketplace. "A person's lifetime earnings roughly double when they have a college degree instead of only a high school degree," says Silberman, "yet between sixty-five and seventy percent of working American adults in all zip codes don't have one. As the nation shifts from a manufacturing based economy to one that's knowledge based," says Silberman, "there's this huge burgeoning need for an advanced degree that's only accelerating." His opinion hasn't changed. When I spoke with Silberman recently, he said, "I don't see traditional universities all of a sudden waking up and deciding they're going to be ten times the size they are and start dealing with a group of students that they haven't normally wanted to deal with," that is, adult students coming back to complete bachelor's degrees. He added a resounding, "Yes, we think that demand will continue to outstrip the supply.

Eventually Strayer University expects to have campuses nationwide. "We expect Strayer to have a campus in every metropolitan area that's large enough to sustain one and where we see a need," says Silberman, adding, "every place that we've gone so far, there hasn't been a sufficient supply of first-rate university-level academics for working adults."

3. A Lack of Competition

There is a lack of competition in the space Strayer occupies. Silberman explained Strayer's niche. "Privately funded and state-run universities don't have the capacity or time to focus on working adults," he says. "Their focus is on eighteen-to-twenty-four-year-olds, graduate programs, and major research programs." Silberman also doesn't see community colleges or the extension programs offered by state universities as competitive threats. "Community colleges are a great entry point for people," says Silberman, "but they only offer associate degrees. What can anyone do with one of those degrees? Most traditional universities have some form of nighttime program," he says, "but it simply isn't their focus and many working adults aren't happy on their campuses."

4. A Highly Desirable Product
While a host of other privately owned colleges and universities compete with Strayer for available student dollars, most lack its prestigious academic accreditation and the respect that a degree from Strayer represents.

5. A Clear Mission and Focus
Strayer's other major advantage is its strong sense of mission. "Our mission is a simple one," says Silberman. "We're building a nationwide university system that makes it possible for working adults to get a high-quality college degree."

In order to ensure that it stays focused, Strayer is divided into two distinct entities. The business is run by VPs; the academic side is headed by the dean of the university, currently Dr. Sondra F. Stallard, president of the university. Each reports to Silberman.

"There are about a dozen people who work in this office with me on the business of the university," says Silberman. "But once you get outside this office all our resources are committed to delivering an excellent academic experience. We're not an enterprise willing to suffer any diminution in quality.

"Every interaction between a student and an admissions officer or professor has to be first-rate and exceed the student's expectations," says Silberman. "We're hyperfocused on making certain that every campus lives up to the quality that we believe is required of a prestigious degree-granting university."

6. Execution

"Once you have a good strategy," says Silberman, "what counts most is execution. And many companies underestimate the challenges associated with execution, and the business landscape is littered with great strategies that weren't properly executed. We believe," he says, "that the first thing we have to do is teach our students well and if we do that consistently, a lot of other good things will happen. For the most part," he adds, "what we've done for the past five years is exactly what we did for the five previous years, but it doesn't get any easier because in this business there's a diseconomy of scale."

The diseconomy of scale Silberman refers to is the fact that in an educational institution, every single interaction must be perfect, every one of them requires a human touch, and none of them can be automated. "In most businesses," he says, "there's a scale that comes from size, there's automation and productivity that can be garnered in large organizations, but our business runs the opposite way. It becomes harder and harder to ensure individual academic quality and the millions of interactions between professors and students. But we understand that," he adds, "and as a management team we're prepared to invest and do whatever is required to make each academic outcome a great one."

7. Build and Nurture Communities

During our study of Strayer we noticed there were a number of distinct communities within the organization.

The first community we observed is composed of the students of the university. They are for the most part working adults returning to school to complete a university degree. What makes them a community are their shared attributes, including a strong desire to advance themselves in their careers; their need to reconcile the demands of work, school, and home; a previous false start on the path to degree completion; and a sense of camaraderie as they help each other along toward the achievement of their degrees.

There's another community composed of faculty. Becoming a professor at Strayer is a plum position but not easily accomplished.

First, an applicant must have a graduate degree in a specific area and then successfully serve as an adjunct faculty member for five years before being considered for a professorship. Many full-time faculty members, who earn between $80,000 and $100,000 annually, maintain full-time academic positions or business careers elsewhere during the day (the school only conducts courses in the evening for the convenience of its students) and professorship is the only route to becoming a campus dean, regional dean, or provost. The shared attributes of this community's members are that they must fervently believe in the university's mission, be prepared to work without tenure, and come to terms with the for-profit nature of the enterprise.

Other communities at Strayer include the business area of the university, composed of people committed to deliver return on capital to Strayer's shareholders, and the alumni, whom Strayer counts on to return for advanced degrees and to be a significant source of referrals.

Sense of Belonging

In the course of our research, we found communities every place we looked. Besides the community of students at Strayer working to complete their degrees, there was the community of customers ready to pull out their wallets and proudly show off their Cabela's credit card as though announcing residency in an exclusive suburb. In Cary, North Carolina, it was the office campus of SAS, which is a functioning community with schools, soccer fields, restaurants, and medical services. PETCO's community is the millions of loyal card-carrying PALS member/animal parents and attendees of PETCOPark, and Sonic Drive-Ins become communities by virtue of being the gathering places in the small towns they serve.

Either intentionally or by luck, the leadership of these companies succeeded in filling one of its workers' and customers' most basic human needs: the need to belong.

Abraham Maslow's original hierarchy of needs argued that once people's requirements for sustenance and security have been met, their next biggest need is a sense of belonging. Many recent medical and psychological studies have proven his theory and contend that when people feel a sense of belonging, they're happier, healthier, and even live longer.

Predictably, when they feel a strong sense of belonging, customers are more likely to remain and spend more and employees are more likely to stay put and on task.

Maslow's Hierarchy of Needs

David Pitonyak, PhD, author of *The Importance of Belonging*, says, "People are hotwired to belong to groups and communities that acknowledge their existence, accept them, provide security and companionship and help them define their identity. That's why people belong to fan clubs; go to churches; wear sports memorabilia; and join associations, political parties, and even street gangs. People's need for an identity is so great they'll do almost anything to feel like they belong."

Communities are any group of people who come together to associate with others who share similar values or interests. By

becoming members of a community, people reduce their feelings of isolation, enhance their confidence, reinforce their beliefs, and gain access to others who are looking to have the same needs fulfilled.

It's hard to leave behind the communities where people have spent enjoyable times and shared gratifying experiences. In fact, the need to belong is so strong it calls people back thousands of miles to class reunions and hometown celebrations; causes rabid sports fans to travel for hours and wear silly Styrofoam head gear resembling giant pieces of cheese (Green Bay Packers); and is the glue that causes millions of military veterans to gather in club-houses around the country to reminisce. Few people willingly abandon communities that nurture and validate them.

Imagine how consistent a company's financial performance will become once its workers and customers view themselves not as workers and buyers of a product or service but as full-fledged members of a community that fills their need to belong.

Other Examples of Community

Cabela's

In some circles hunting and even fishing have become politically incorrect. "Hunting and fishing are sometimes called blood sports," says Mike Callahan of Cabela's, "and the people who practice them are known as the hook and bullet guys. Increasingly, it's become almost unacceptable to talk about. You probably wouldn't go to a cocktail party, and tell people you'd just been out duck or elk hunting and offer to show them pictures.

"We've built these great stores so that somebody who has an interest in and devotion to the outdoors and hunting can walk in and go, 'Ah, this is my kind of place; these are my kind of people; they know and understand how I think and feel.'"

Dot Foods

Mount Sterling, Illinois, home to Dot Foods, is a rare and welcome exception to the blighted conditions of many small midwestern towns. It's vibrant, healthy, and growing. The two thousand city residents and the eight thousand people who live in the county are rightfully proud of a downtown whose storefronts are occupied, where competing banks anchor all the street corners, the Irish House Hotel accepts guests, and the most popular menu item at The Station, the busiest restaurant, is the Horseshoe, a hamburger buried beneath a huge pile of french fries, smothered with melted cheese.

Rather than move the company to an urban area, where successful business owners gravitate, and despite the challenges associated with staffing needs of more than one thousand people at their main distribution facility, Dot Foods chose to remain in Mount Sterling. "Mount Sterling is where the company was founded," says CEO Pat Tracy, "and the biggest single thing we've been blessed with are wonderful employees. There's a strong work ethic here. People aren't afraid of hard work and they're committed to taking care of our customers."

Dot Foods works hard to repay the loyalty of its workers by generously donating time and money to the town. When a needs study for the community indicated that one of the area's greatest necessities was a recreational facility and community center, the Tracy family and Dot Foods provided both the leadership and funding to build a new YMCA. The company divides its banking between most of the banks downtown, makes certain its vendors and suppliers (and visiting authors) stay at the town's hotel, and even worked behind the scenes to ensure there'd be a community swimming pool, an airport, and a parochial school in town. Because Mount Sterling is geographically isolated, the company even built a learning center onsite where people can take university extension courses and earn college degrees.

Mount Sterling wouldn't exist in its present form without Dot Foods and Dot Foods wouldn't exist in its present form without the community where it was founded. In the case of Dot Foods and Mount Sterling, Illinois, we found two communities growing together in a symbiotic relationship.

SAS

SAS is consistently named one of the top companies to work for by every organization that conducts polls on the subject. A 2005 Price Waterhouse study of employee turnover among software designers and engineers revealed a 16–25 percent average annual rate of voluntary turnover (depending on the year), but at SAS it's less than 5 percent, or about four times better than the national average. Yet the average annual compensation is the same at SAS as the industry averages. Clearly people remain at SAS for something more than the money. We think it's the sense of fulfillment that comes with being part of the SAS community.

In an August 2004 article, the *Wall Street Journal* reported that an analysis of more than 150 studies on wealth and happiness (authored by Ed Diener and Martin Seligman, psychology professors at the universities of Illinois and Pennsylvania, for the journal *Psychological Science in the Public Interest*) concluded that happiness doesn't come from wealth or money but instead from social relationships, enjoyable work, a sense that life has meaning, and belonging to groups.

With its thirty-five-hour workweek, SAS provides employees plenty of extra time for social relationships and community involvement. Individual achievement at the company takes a distinct second place to group victories, and workers are lavished with benefits that include a cafeteria with a pianist, Montessori child-care centers (which costs an average of only $300 per month), an eighty-thousand-square-foot fitness center, and an onsite free medical center.

Community extends to company activities off the SAS campus as well. Each SAS office has the same feeling of community. Even the thousands of user conferences and new customer conferences it conducts each year around the world are designed to make people feel like valued community members. The unspoken message is distinct. SAS, its workers, and its customers are a special community of smart and enterprising people who quietly and humbly accomplish incredible things for one another.

Sonic Drive-In

In many small towns across America, the local Sonic Drive-In is one of the only restaurants, becoming the de facto community gathering place for everything from first dates to meetings of the local Little League. When people who grew up in small towns move to urban areas, it's only natural to continue making urban Sonic a big part of their life; memories were made there, tastes were developed, and good times were had. Sonic also has a loyalty program called Sonic Cruisers that provides e-mail updates, discount coupons, and events that nurture the concept of customers as a community.

Sonic has done a superb job of turning its vendors and suppliers into a community. According to CEO Cliff Hudson, "Our partners are always invited to company meetings and retreats. Their long-term interests are so allied with our own that it only makes sense to include them, make them full participants, and actively solicit their input." The vendors and suppliers we spoke with view their relationship with Sonic with near reverential awe, wondering why other companies don't get it and work with their vendors and suppliers the same way.

Sonic encourages each restaurant manager to also be an owner. As a result the towns and cities where the restaurants are located benefit from having someone actively involved in the community. Sonic franchisees pick their own local civic and charitable causes and are involved in activities including awards to encourage young kids to read, incentives to keep older kids in school, participation in blood drives to aid Red Cross chapters, highway trash pickups, and programs to promote railroad-crossing safety awareness.

One of the most important communities at Sonic is the more than sixty thousand people who work inside the restaurants. And there's nothing that excited former president Pattye Moore as much as talking about how the company has used an innovation known as Sonic Games to foster a sense of community among the company's team members.

"Our advertising partner Barkley Evergreen and Partners came up with a program that combined training, recognition, and motivation," says Moore. "It's our equivalent of the Olympics."

Each year Sonic's thirty-six hundred restaurants receive a huge box filled with instructions and training materials for each restaurant's seven work stations; Switchboard (where orders are taken), Swamp (fryer), Grill, Dresser, Fountain, Carhop, and Manager. Each local manager coordinates her own contest that includes written tests, time trials, and a Knowledge Bowl where interviewers call the stores and ask the staff on duty a series of questions. Each store's competition eventually identifies its most talented crew.

Simultaneously, mystery shoppers visit all the stores and evaluate and rank them based on their speed, service, and quality and reduce the number remaining in competition. Eventually, following regional and semifinal competitions, the twelve top-performing teams are notified of their status when a busload of people from headquarters shows up at the restaurant, tooting the horn and arms filled with prizes. The twelve best teams are sent to a city like Las Vegas where a drive-in is shut down for two days while the finals take place.

"The finals are the best," says Moore. "On the first day we judge team competition and there are judges dressed in referee uniforms and our regional people and vendor partners serve as customers and simulate a lunch rush for each team. The teams are scored for order accuracy, food quality and safety, and correcting orders. One of the things I love to do," says Moore, "is throw trash out my window and see if the carhops on skates pick it up and earn or lose points." The second day of the games features individual competition, with the event capped off by a huge awards ceremony where everyone is paraded on stage wearing their team jerseys.

"This is a once-in-a-lifetime experience for most of these kids," says Moore. "Most of them have never been on an airplane before, and they're being whisked off like the jet set to Vegas." And the Sonic community's bonds grow tighter.

Community Membership Trumps Mere Satisfaction

A decade ago, after studying hundreds of thousands of customer service relationships, Harvard professor Earl Sasser, the author of *Why Satisfied Customers Defect*, concluded that "two-thirds of customers who stop doing business with a company describe themselves as being satisfied." Sasser's research proved that mere satisfaction is an indication of neither an intention to remain a customer nor repurchase.

Sasser went on to provide insights as to what is required to ensure that customers continue doing business with a particular company. *"Complete* satisfaction," he says, "is the key to generating intense customer loyalty and superior long-term financial performance." Just as managers and business owners can no longer count on satisfied customers remaining loyal, there's no guarantee that workers who are merely satisfied will remain.

A few years ago, before my turn to speak to a gathering of the top executives of Verizon, one of America's largest telephone companies, a presentation was being made by Michael Fernandez, the firm's research director.

In his opening comments he introduced himself as a former Columbia University and MIT mathematician and the company's current head of research, but added that based on his findings, he now thought of himself as a born-again customer advocate. Then he proceeded to explain his transformation.

One of his findings was that nearly 46 percent of the company's customers—those who described themselves as being satisfied—would consider leaving the company if they received a switch pitch or slightly better offer from a competitor. In a quiet and unassuming manner, he pointed out that any firm where a significant percentage of the satisfied customers could be so easily convinced to leave was extremely vulnerable.

His next finding was the showstopper. His research consistently indicated that fewer than 5 percent of the company's customers who described themselves as completely satisfied would consider leaving.

"It's imperative," he said in conclusion, "that we must do whatever is required to move customers from the satisfied category into the completely satisfied category, or else our very existence is at risk."

To their credit, the executives of the company listened to what he said, implemented the action plan he recommended, and today Verizon enjoys less customer churn than all other phone companies and consistently records the highest levels of customer satisfaction as measured by outside research groups.

A major focus of any business's customer- and employee-satisfaction initiatives should be addressing the issue of whether it is fulfilling people's basic need to belong. The financial success of the companies we identified strongly suggests that companies whose employees and customers consider themselves to be members of a desirable community significantly outperform those who don't.

Think Big, Act SMALL
BUILD COMMUNITIES

- Recognize that people's needs for belonging and social fulfillment are two of the most powerful human needs.
- Identify groups of natural communities within your employee and customer bases.
- Figure out ways to acknowledge and validate these communities.
- Create loyalty programs that strengthen these ties.
- Determine other communities who could become your customers.
- Build plans to grow communities, not revenues.

Grow Future Leaders
O'REILLY AUTOMOTIVE

"Our future leaders are homegrown with experience and knowledge of the operation, a heavy dose of common sense, and a strong commitment to our culture."
DAVID O'REILLY, chairman and former CEO of O'Reilly Automotive

The companies we studied don't hire outside CEOs and allow them to tinker or play around with their culture. They haven't brought high-profile cost cutters aboard as COOs and CFOs to artificially inflate performance and briefly placate the bankers or Wall Street. And they've never hired outside sales wizards whose legions of cozy relationships promise to magically improve the next quarter's financial performance.

The companies that do the best job of consistently growing revenues grow their own leaders. Period!

Their performance proves that unless a company is upside down or about to drive off the edge of a cliff (and a desperate roll of the dice is the only remaining option), an enterprise is far more likely to achieve consistent revenue growth by relying on homegrown leadership than by casting about for sorcerers with magical answers.

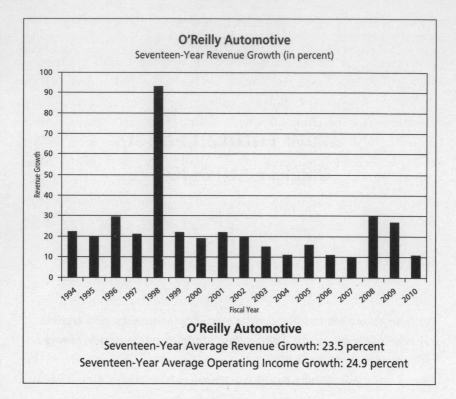

O'Reilly Automotive
Seventeen-Year Revenue Growth (in percent)

Fiscal Year

O'Reilly Automotive
Seventeen-Year Average Revenue Growth: 23.5 percent
Seventeen-Year Average Operating Income Growth: 24.9 percent

There's no better example of a company that's consistently grown its own leadership than O'Reilly Automotive.

A list of the company's top thirty leaders reveals that their average length of service exceeds twenty years, with none having been with the company fewer than five years, and many for more than thirty.

In 2004, when we identified and wrote about this Springfield, Missouri-based publicly traded company, it had twelve hundred auto parts stores in eighteen states and expected to come close to achieving a record $2 billion in revenues in 2005 with plenty of room for future growth and expansion. Wait until you learn how its consistent performance has blown away the competition.

The O'Reilly Story

Born in 1885, Charles Francis O'Reilly was the son of immigrant parents who'd escaped the potato famine in Ireland and settled in St. Louis, Missouri. Following college, he joined an auto supply company as a traveling salesman, selling auto parts to stores and automobile dealerships. Traversing his midwestern territory by train, he became enamored of the small city of Springfield, Missouri (population 57,000 at the time) and was convinced that it was destined to grow and prosper. He asked to be transferred to Springfield, eventually becoming the manager of the local automotive parts supply store where he was later joined by his son Chub O'Reilly.

Everything turned out the way Charles had hoped. Springfield's population doubled and subsequently tripled. The store that he ran prospered. The family's children and grandchildren were born, raised, and did well. In 1957, when Charles was seventy-two years old, the home office sent a consultant to Springfield to review the store's operations and made two surprise recommendations: get rid of the *old guy* and transfer the son to Kansas City.

Most seventy-two-year-old men would probably have tossed in the towel and retired, but Charles got his dander up and decided to open a competing store. Along the way he'd met an investor who agreed to put up most of the money in return for 49 percent ownership of the company. His son Chub joined him as a cofounder and the ten key employees of the store he was running asked to join him as well. Charles agreed to hire them all on one condition: anyone joining the new company had to make an investment and become an owner.

The Early Years

David O'Reilly, current chairman and CEO of the company until 2004, was only eight years old when the first store opened, but vividly recalls the effect of everyone's being an owner. "Whether they invested one hundred dollars or a thousand or had to take a loan against their houses, my grandfather required they make an investment in the firm. I didn't understand what I was witnessing at the time," he adds, "but everybody treated the company like it was their own. They worked late, did whatever had to be done to find a part for a customer, drove parts halfway across the state if they needed to, and delivered on Sunday and holidays if a customer needed something."

Fifty years ago the idea of requiring ownership of all employees was an almost unheard of practice, and we wondered what had led Charles O'Reilly to institute such a policy. "My grandfather truly appreciated and valued people," says O'Reilly, "and he genuinely wanted them to share in the success of the business." In fact, decades later, when the first ten employee/owners began retiring and the company started buying back their stock—those few hundred or a thousand dollars each had invested—their profits turned out to be sufficient to generously fund their retirements.

"For years," says O'Reilly, "our slogan was that the customer is king. We had it on our letterhead and signs everywhere, and we really do believe that. But when I'm with a group of new managers, I let them in on a secret. I tell them that what we really believe is that if we take care of our own people first and value them above everything else that superlative customer service happens naturally."

CEO David O'Reilly's grandfather Charles died in 1971, having seen the original store grow to a half dozen, generating several million dollars in revenues annually. O'Reilly's father, Chub, passed away at ninety-two, shortly after the hardcover edition of this book was published. David O'Reilly's brothers, Larry and Charlie, and sister, Rosalie, retired in their late fifties or early sixties and now serve on the board of directors. O'Reilly, youthful and fit in his mid-fifties, was the final family member to head the company and he steadfastly refuses to take credit for its success.

"There's absolutely zero room for egos when you're a family building a business together," says O'Reilly. "My brothers, sister, and I are competitive and very strongly driven," he says, "but we've never had room for heroes. Not one of us has ever claimed to be the key driver responsible for our success. In fact, we all take pride in our accomplishments *together*. Our rule has been," he says, echoing what we witnessed at Cabela's, Medline, and Dot Foods, "that we reach decisions together as a group, and whenever there was a family meeting it wouldn't end until there was unanimous agreement as to our course of action."

David O'Reilly worked in the stores throughout junior high and high school and then attended and graduated from Drury University, a small, four thousand–student liberal arts school in Springfield. Though a practicing Catholic, O'Reilly's years of study at an institution founded in 1873 by the Congregationalist Church to heal the wounds of the Civil War and offer a thoughtful liberal arts education to students, regardless of their gender, race, or creed, show through. Following graduation the prospect of big-city life lured O'Reilly to Kansas City, where he joined Southwestern Bell's management development program.

"Within a year," says O'Reilly, "I'd figured out that I didn't want to be part of a big, bumbling, bureaucratic bunch of red tape where I couldn't make a difference and decided to come back to Springfield and join the family business." At the time the company had four locations and O'Reilly's first job was working on the counter selling parts. His next stop was the telephone desk where he took customers' orders. This was followed by a stint developing the company's first computer system and eventually a job as sales manager for the company.

One of the ways that the company consistently grew its revenues in the early years was through its jobber business; it convinced other small auto parts stores in rural Missouri to purchase their inventories from O'Reilly.

Acting Small, Gaining New Customers, One at a Time

"I'd go out with the salespeople," O'Reilly says, "learn about the challenges these small businesspeople faced, their dilemmas and what made them either successful or unsuccessful." Given his grandfather and father's deeply rooted belief that the more successful their customers were, the more successful *they'd* become, it wasn't long before O'Reilly Automotive was performing value-added services unheard of at the time.

"Back in the mid-1970s," he says, "one of the biggest problems these small stores had was that local accountants knew nothing about inventory, cost of goods sold, and gross margin. As a result they'd end up with horrible-looking financial statements and the banks wouldn't loan them money for inventories."

O'Reilly addressed these needs by agreeing to do the accounting for these small stores and lend them money for inventories if required. "We charged them twenty-five dollars a month and actually did a profit and loss and financial statement for them and even cosigned loans at their local banks so they'd have inventory in their stores.

"As we slowly began expanding," says O'Reilly, "we stayed out of the areas where we had independent jobber customers, but when these stores owners decided to sell or retire, we were the natural buyers. We knew how much business they did, how profitable each was, the strengths of their people, their market presence, and what the business was worth." Eventually O'Reilly Automotive went on to purchase more than two hundred stores from owners whose original relationship with the company was as a buyer of parts from them.

O'Reilly credits the various jobs throughout the company that he, Larry, Charlie, and Rosalie had as teaching all of them an invaluable lesson that prepared each for their eventual role as CEO and/or COO.

"A big problem with many leaders," O'Reilly says, "is that they have unrealistic expectations because they lack the knowledge of-what's really going on in their organizations. A company can have a great business plan and strategy, but if its operations and infrastructure can't handle what it wants to do, it won't be successful."

By the late 1970s, David O'Reilly had become general manager of the company, Larry was heading sales, and Charlie was manager of store operations. With the lessons they'd learned and a new distribution facility completed, they decided they were ready for some serious growth.

Thinking Big and Getting Ready for Growth

"We all realized the company had some real potential," says David O'Reilly. "We'd been growing slowly and consistently but finally decided we could do more of what we'd been doing and faster." In 1978 the company made its first acquisition: a group of seventeen stores in the Lake of the Ozarks region of Missouri.

"One of our big customers decided to sell, and we bought them and converted them to O'Reilly stores." O'Reilly financed the acquisition by giving the seller a small down payment and having him agree to take a note for the balance.

O'Reilly Automotive has always been extremely financially conservative. "It wasn't long before the New York investor Grandfather had found wanted to start taking lots of cash out of the business," says O'Reilly, "which would have prevented us building a solid company. I still recall my grandfather and father going to the bank and borrowing the couple of hundred thousand dollars it took to get rid of him.

"Back then," says O'Reilly, "the family thought that debt represented something bad. It was as though you mustn't be doing things right if you have to borrow money." David O'Reilly earned $7,000 annually when he joined the firm in 1972 and well into the 1980s was only being paid $30,000 annually. "We knew," he says, "that the only way we could continue to grow was to be very conservative, pay ourselves a living wage based on our performance but never take out so much money that it would hurt the business or its profitability."

O'Reilly's strategy for acquiring stores was to pay the seller a fair price but always in the form of a down payment as small as possible and a note for the balance due that the company then worked feverishly to pay off in as few months as possible before taking another gulp and buying another store.

The same year that O'Reilly was completing its first major acquisition, it also made a bold decision that, had it been handled badly, might have upended the company. Instead, it worked out well and changed the direction of the company forever. They decided to pursue a dual marketing strategy and sell not only to their existing customers, but to the public as well.

"Until 1978 we never pursued retail business," says O'Reilly. "Our customers were garages, service stations, car dealerships, and businesses that installed parts and they didn't want us selling directly to the public. They thought that all car-owning customers belonged to them, not us. We knew the future meant selling directly to the public." Getting into retail required having two things happen: the stores would have to be merchandised for the public and their current wholesale customers placated.

"Our stores were clean," O'Reilly says, "but they were essentially drab wholesale part supply houses. We earnestly began a campaign to clean up the stores, make them brighter, remodel them as required, put in better lighting, and add consumer-oriented maintenance product lines and merchandise the windows." But dealing with its wholesale customers was a bigger job than renovating the stores.

"Getting into the retail business represented a huge learning curve for us," O'Reilly says. "Many retail customers would come in thinking they'd get a low price and then take it to one of our wholesale customers and ask them to install it. The first question the installer would ask them would be how much they'd paid for it. If the installer found out that the retail customer had paid the same or less than they'd pay, we risked losing their business."

O'Reilly performed a tough balancing act and resorted to asking retail customers if they were going to install the part themselves or take it somewhere else for professional installation. Salespeople were trained to set the price slightly higher than what the installer would pay for customers taking the part to an installer.

"Educating our installer customers was vital," says O'Reilly. "Our pitch to them was simple. We explained that we were getting into the retail business because we had to; that business was becoming more and more competitive and that we wouldn't be able to maintain all our locations, our vast inventories, our training, and thirty-minute delivery to them unless we were also involved in retail."

Begrudgingly at first, most wholesale customers eventually accepted O'Reilly's explanation and the company salved its wounds by promising them they'd always receive a better price in return for the installer's promise of continued volume.

In addition to buying existing stores, the company continued opening new locations, and finally in 1987 the competitive O'Reilly family, tired of being chided for running a chain of stores in small Missouri towns and never having faced a competitive environment, made their first venture into a competitive market and began opening stores in Kansas City.

"We opened two stores," says O'Reilly, "and from day one they were the best performing stores we'd ever opened. Their revenues skyrocketed and they made money out of the gate. We started opening stores in Kansas City like crazy, and within three years had fifteen stores doing extremely well. It was a huge accomplishment and it reinforced that we could compete anywhere."

It took more than thirty years, but in 1989 the company finally reached one hundred stores. "We never had a vision," O'Reilly says, "of how big this thing could become. We never had a certain number of stores we wanted to hit. We loved what we were doing, the company was profitable and we were becoming consistently better operators. We always agreed that we'd grow consistently, steadily, and profitably and see where it would take us."

Making Everyone an Owner . . . Again

By the early '90s the company had 127 stores but faced two new challenges. "You have to remember," O'Reilly recalls, "that the company had been founded on the principle of everyone's being an owner. Each year during our first thirty years, we tracked the book value of the company's stock, and as the original ten owners retired the company bought their stock back from them. When my grandfather died, my dad bought his shares and as a result ended up owning almost all the stock in the company." To avoid tax problems, Chub O'Reilly started giving his stock away to his children and grandchildren. "Dad was giving away his stock like crazy," O'Reilly says with a smile, "and said that all he wanted was to make enough money to get by.

"The problem his gifts to children and grandchildren posed," says O'Reilly "was that if any of those people wanted to sell their stock, the company would have been forced to buy it back from them. Because we were so busy expanding, we didn't want to have to use our cash reserves to buy back stock.

"The other problem," says O'Reilly, "was that because the book value of the company kept going up significantly each year, there were fewer and fewer people who could afford to buy shares. In order to make people feel like owners," he says, "we had a phantom stock appreciation program for key people, where their compensation reflected the growth in the value of the company. The problem with that program is it still wasn't actual ownership."

In April 1993, thirty-six years after the company had opened its doors for business, it went public. The joint concerns of a family member's wanting to cash-out and causing a liquidity problem and the desire to make ownership available for everyone were solved.

When some companies go public, everything changes, and in many instances, not for the better. Cultures are abandoned in the interest of saving money, analysts work over management to slash expenses in the interest of short-term profit growth, and CEOs frequently become more enamored of hanging out with self-important members of the investment community than running the business. O'Reilly argues persuasively and strongly that just the opposite occurred at O'Reilly Automotive.

"Going public was the best thing that ever happened to us," says

David O'Reilly. "We didn't change our culture at all," he says. "In fact, it just got stronger. Because we're so competitive we've always held ourselves accountable, but when we went public we wanted to outperform everyone else in our peer and industry groups. Our response," he says, "was a redoubling of our efforts to be accountable because we felt the whole world was watching us. That required our turning to our roots, our culture, and performing better than anyone else." Today, every team member at O'Reilly becomes a stockholder within six months of working for the company.

O'Reilly's original promise to Wall Street was that the company would grow 20 percent annually between same-store sales increases and new store growth—and it has kept its promise. In 1998 O'Reilly doubled the size of the company and added 189 stores when it completed its first major acquisition: the purchase of Texas-based Hi-Lo Auto Parts. Three years later it added another 85 stores when it purchased all the stock of Mid-States Automotive. By January 2003 the company had opened its one-thousandth store.

In 2004, copresident Greg Henslee was promoted to CEO. Henslee started on the parts counter for O'Reilly and soon was promoted to assistant manager, then to store manager and district manager. Henslee moved to O'Reilly Automotive headquarters in the early nineties where he spearheaded the change from manual to computerized inventory management. In 1999, he was promoted to copresident with Ted Wise (the current COO) and was named CEO in 2004. In July 2008, Henslee led the acquisition of CSK's thirteen hundred auto parts stores including Kragen, Schucks, Checker, and Murray's chain of auto parts throughout the Midwest, West, and Southwest.

Today, O'Reilly Auto Parts has thirty-six hundred stores and is on track to do $5.4 billion. It continues to build 150 new locations a year from the ground up providing opportunities for developing people, which means they've tripled the size of the company in six years.

Between the fact that there's still plenty of geographic room for growth (they run about 10 percent of the nation's thirty-five thousand parts stores) and the keen competitive spirit shared by the organization's leadership, one of the key areas of constant focus is growing future leaders.

O'Reilly's Steps for Growing New Leaders

O'Reilly Auto Parts heralds eight values and initiatives that deepen its bench by providing leadership development for its team members:

1. Lead by Example

Jim Batten was a fifteen-year-old schoolboy growing up in Bolivar, Missouri, when O'Reilly purchased a local parts store there. Hired to work part-time in the backroom sweeping up the floors and stocking parts, Batten vividly recalls a large delivery of parts arriving accompanied by then CEO Charlie O'Reilly. "I couldn't believe it," he says, "the man who owned the company took the time to come to the back of the store, introduce himself, shake my hand, and thank me for being part of Team O'Reilly."

Today Batten serves as the executive vice president of finance and CFO of the company and says that it's the authenticity, the utter lack of pretense, and the humility that make people want to stay with the company and become just like the leaders they see everyday.

"If someone wants a meeting with David O'Reilly," says Batten, "they get it. There's nothing in the culture that prevents anyone from meeting with the CEO or being forced to go through layers of hierarchy to arrange it." Batten believes that when team members consistently witness such humility and openness, they eventually aspire to make the style their own.

"It's about leadership by example," Batten says. "When David O'Reilly and I travel out of town together for a meeting or conference, we'll share a room to save money," he smiles and says, "and we see who'll be the first to make off with the extra bar of soap."

Current CEO Greg Henslee continues the tradition of accessibility. "It's not what you say, it's what you do that makes or breaks a company," says Henslee. "I was on the way to our little lake house for Labor Day," Henslee recalled, "and I stopped into one of our stores to pick up a few things. They were so busy; it was wall-to-wall customers." So Henslee rolled up his sleeves and helped out until the rush was over. "I don't know how any CEO could walk in and out of a store with customers needing help and feel like they are setting a good example."

Yet that's just what he's seen happen at many companies. "I've witnessed how people who run companies treat themselves versus the rest of the employees firsthand doing my due diligence when we are buying companies," Henslee revealed. "It's very different than our culture. At some point, the top executives appear to decide they deserve a better lifestyle and better benefits—more vacation, medical plans, work schedules, and things like that—and they just take it. Pretty soon the gap between the executives and the rest is miles apart instead of just inches. Those at the top develop a culture of entitlement and leisure. I see it as a sure sign of trouble to come.

"I have the same vacation time, the same benefits, and work the same schedule," Henslee emphasizes. "I think leading by example is one of the most important things about us."

2. Culture Is *the* Competitive Advantage

Every manager of an O'Reilly store spends a week at the home office in Springfield undergoing rigorous training, and the first thing he is taught is the O'Reilly culture. "We teach them our culture," says David O'Reilly, "but culture isn't something you can just go into a room and talk about. Everyone in the organization has to live it, eat it, and breathe it."

"I would define us," Henslee adds, "as a culture of completely applying high ethical standards—teamwork, honesty, trust, respect, all the words most companies use—treating suppliers, customers—both retail and wholesale—and each other fairly. But we focus on making sure we *do* all those things, especially the things that affect our customers."

3. Teamwork and Letting the Best Idea Win

One of David O'Reilly's fondest memories is the way the company selected locations for new stores. "We've always believed that two heads are better than one," says O'Reilly, "so when it was time to pick a new location, Ted Wise, Greg Henslee, my brothers, and I would all pile in a van together and drive hundreds of miles, jointly deciding where the new stores would be.

"Those trips were the most fun I've ever had," says O'Reilly. "We'd be on the road night after night, but besides picking new store locations, we'd talk about the people in the company, the roles people were in and the structure. By the end of one of those trips," he says, "we'd always figured out and agreed on everything that needed to be done."

And those trips led the O'Reilly leadership team to use collaboration systematically to make better big decisions.

When companies are acting big, big decisions are made by the big bosses. If those bosses need any input, they look to outside experts or bigger competitors. The best idea doesn't necessarily win in those companies; many times, the best idea isn't even discussed. Meanwhile, small companies listen to their team (including people on the front line and from other departments) with open minds, and they have the discipline to let the best ideas win regardless of the source.

"We still do the same today as we did back when we were eighty stores," Henslee said. "We make decisions by committee to a large degree. Take product decisions . . . we'll get a team of probably fifteen people including the installer side, the do-it-yourself side, finance, operations, and me, and we all get an equal vote. As the CEO I've only got one vote and I don't necessarily prevail. I've been on the wrong side of many debates."

Even in the biggest decisions, O'Reilly executives collaborate. They ran the company with a two-man committee (copresidents Henslee and Wise) for a critical period from 1999 to 2004. Conventional wisdom says that having two cooks in the kitchen is a sure recipe for disaster. Henslee and Wise's track record proves that's not necessarily true. "There were many times that I would have done something different than we ended up doing, but Wise influenced me," Henslee remembers. "And there've been just as many times that I influenced him. It seemed to work out pretty good."

4. Communicate, Acknowledge, and Keep Informed

Many companies publish an employee newsletter. O'Reilly publishes a monthly full-color glossy magazine titled *Team Spirit* that ranks among the best leadership training tools ever created.

Distributed to all 47,000 team members, the magazine has features about the community and civic activities that O'Reilly stores are involved in, as well as stories on the accomplishments of individual stores, and explanations of company benefits in easy-to-understand language. It contains important new product information, features pictures and biographies of team members; provides pictorial essays on the vacated, locked-up, and shut premises of the competition; acknowledges graduates of the company's leadership development program; provides updates on the company's financial performance and share price; announces winning suggestions by team members; lists the Gold, Bronze, and Silver Shamrock award winners; and announces marriages and births among the team.

"We now include a detailed letter from one of vice presidents specifying all the things that they have seen culturally that are good things going on," Henslee says. "It's a lot of work but we each take a turn."

It's almost impossible to read an issue and not want to be a member of Team O'Reilly.

5. Constantly Evaluate and Coach

The old saying "Good writers borrow and great writers steal" hasn't been lost on O'Reilly Automotive. "Since our earliest days," says David O'Reilly, "we've studied the good things that other companies do and then O'Reilly-ized them to fit our culture." One of those things is an O'Reilly variation of a performance-evaluation grid made well known to the business community by Jack Welch, former head of GE. Everyone on the O'Reilly team is ranked annually by the people they report to.

But there's a very important difference at O'Reilly. "The vertical axis has all our values on it and the horizontal axis is composed of the specific job's performance criteria," says O'Reilly, "and it works very simply. If someone's a great performer but has bad values, and finds themselves in box number two, we counsel and work with them to get them into box number four. Similarly, if someone has the values but doesn't produce, we coach them into box number four."

"Acting big" companies focus on performance and only give lip service to their values. But when you act small, you are every bit as diligent about the right character development as the sales and profits achievements. Doing the job right is just as important as hitting your financial goals.

Though primarily used as a coaching and development tool, David O'Reilly is quick to point out that only team members who

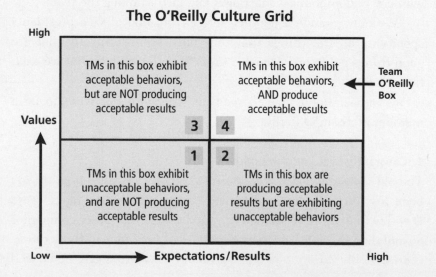

The O'Reilly Culture Grid

function in box four have a long-term future with the company.

"Although we use the O'Reilly culture grid as a coaching tool," says O'Reilly, "eventually some people have to be told that if they're not in box number four, they're with the wrong company and they simply don't belong here."

6. Make People Want to Stay

Anyone who's ever worked in retail knows that most of the industry deserves the bad reviews it receives regarding the treatment of its workers. Other than showing them how to swipe bar codes and credit cards, salespeople on the floor are often viewed as disposable nuisances by the home office. Store managers have traditionally been seen (and paid) as little more than irritations hired to unlock the doors and make sure people on the floor don't rob the joint blind.

One of the biggest tricks perpetuated by many retail organizations is to send a fax to a store manager the third week of the month announcing that the store's budget for hourly workers has been used up, and informing him that, as the manager, he'll fill in, resulting in sixty- to eighty-hour workweeks for the salaried manager.

When most companies say they value their workers, there's a big disconnect between what they say and what they do. Jim Batten, former CFO, says that when O'Reilly says it values people it means it. "Even our store managers have set schedules," he says, "and although they may be asked to work for a half day every other Saturday, we want our team members to enjoy quality nonworking time with their families and in their communities, as well as be productive when they are working."

Between the salary a store manager makes running an O'Reilly store, the generous health and dental benefits he receives, and his full participation in the company's 401(k) profit-sharing and stock options program, it's not inconceivable, if the stock continues its current rate of appreciation, that he could retire as a millionaire—a feat already achieved by some team members.

"We have so many team members who are enthused about our growth and their part in it. We've seen a lot of team members who have accumulated more than a million dollars with their equity," Hanslee says proudly. "There is opportunity for everyone here. It's one of the ways we keep everyone engaged."

7. Have Everyone Identify Their Successor

"Our leadership training is very broad based with no specific secret formula," says David O'Reilly. "We provide management and leadership training in assorted formats: written information, videos, and centralized personnel seminars, but the most important thing we do is challenge all senior management to target and develop successors for their jobs.

"The actual development of the successor certainly includes leadership training in the conceptual sense," says O'Reilly, "but the most important strategy is to challenge potential leaders with increased levels of responsibility and operational duties. In other words, we test the ability of leaders with real-world accountability.

"At O'Reilly," he concludes his thoughts on the subject, "our philosophy is that future leaders are mostly homegrown through experience and knowledge of the operation, with a heavy dose of common sense and a strong commitment to our culture."

8. Keep Doing It

One of the most striking things about O'Reilly Automotive is the length of service of their key executives, store managers, and team members. Besides the average key executive having been with the company for more than twenty years, each issue of *Team Spirit* lists page after page of people who have been with the company for ten, fifteen, twenty-five, and even thirty years.

The responses of everyone we spoke with, at all levels of the company, as to why they've stayed with the company so long, essentially echoed the words of David O'Reilly. "Part of it is the sense of accomplishment you receive from building something that positively impacts other people. It's also a way to channel my sense of competitiveness," he says, "and in my case I also feel responsible to continue the work that my family was fortunate enough to begin."

Continue to Offer New Opportunities

What does the future hold for O'Reilly Auto Parts? David O'Reilly says that adding stores at the prodigious rate of more than one hundred annually is a challenge. "Ours is a people business," he says, "and at the end of the day we have to have the right people managing the stores, the right people behind the counters, and the right locations.

"Each of those issues," he says, "poses a unique challenge and we have to stay on top of each of them. Our real estate department is pulling out its hair adding more than one hundred stores each year," he says, "but I remember when we were pulling out our hair when we were adding five or ten annually."

"We only run ten percent of the thirty-five thousand parts stores in the USA," explains Henslee. "We are in just thirty-eight of the fifty states. We're not in the Northeast, we're not in south Florida . . . there's a lot of geography for us. Plus there's a lot of opportunity to buy other operators in existing markets."

"We'll build ground-up stores, but we'll also continue to buy smaller chains," Henslee says. "We have the ability, the distribution centers, and the processes to turn stores into O'Reilly stores. We're set up to expand."

How Other Companies Grow Future Leaders

Dot Foods

"Our leadership development program," says John Tracy, CEO of Dot Foods, "begins by populating our business with great potential leaders both from within and outside the organization.

"We're always on the lookout," he says, "for the great all-around athlete, whether or not we have a specific position open at the time. When we find them we find a way to hire them and attach them to the organization in some way.

"By doing that," he says, "we always hope to have a stable of talented people to serve as our future leaders. Each of them," he says, "has a professional and personal development plan that's reviewed and updated annually. The professional side focuses on pursuing specific formal objectives and challenges in her area of responsibility. The personal focuses on specific things she is going to do to increase her own personal horsepower through training, development, and formal education.

"Our succession planning process," says Tracy, "which is conducted annually by our strategic planning group, assures that all our future leaders receive good visibility in front of the people responsible for running the business. Then," he says, "we cross-pollinate our emerging leaders by moving people around the company so they'll develop a broader experience base, improved teamwork approach, and greater knowledge of the business.

"While we also try to create environments where they have every opportunity to succeed," he says, "we also encourage them to take risks so their confidence is further enhanced and future risk taking more likely."

Medline Industries
Medline embraces several unique tactics to develop their future leaders.

At most companies, people are reluctant to give notice of their intention to leave for fear of being viewed as a short timer or traitor and quickly cast aside. In dramatic contrast Medline encourages people who are retiring or leaving to give them plenty of notice.

"In one instance," says Medline's president Andy Mills, "our director of sales gave us five years' notice, and our CFO, director of quality and regulatory affairs and our VP of marketing both gave us three years' notice. This allowed us to groom their successors," he says, adding that "in some instances, the successor was trained for as long as eighteen months. Occasionally, we've brought in the wrong replacement but still had the luxury of having more than a year to find the right person.

"Another thing we do," says Mills, "is cross-train people. We do this for several reasons, but most important, it makes people better managers and leaders.

"Another thing we do," Mills says, "is constantly search for new businesses to enter. By doing this we give people the opportunity to grow and take on different roles, and in many cases more responsibility and rewards.

"Finally," says Mills, "another thing we've done that has worked exceptionally well is our President's Award, given for the achievement of excellent results by our salespeople in each region. Instead of simply giving the winners a nice plaque to hang on the wall, we bring them in as a group, spend several days finding out from them what we need to do better as a company, and have them help us to map out our future. It's a great working session and way to get some of our award winners interested in future management positions in the company."

Sonic Drive-In

Cliff Hudson, CEO of Sonic Drive-In, says, "Few things grow managers and leaders as much as responsibility and empowerment, and we work to accomplish this on two parallel tracks.

"In our restaurants," he says, "our store-level managers are our partners. They share in the initial capital investment, and then share profits and losses along with us. They are empowered to take care of customers flexibly and are not capped on their financial upside for doing so.

"Vitally important," says Hudson, "is that every corporate employee has equity ownership in our company. We have a stock purchase plan in which the company subsidizes purchases of our common stock by employees. Our common stock is an option in our 401(k) plan and every employee receives stock options."

Hudson believes that Sonic's approach to business fosters commitment and loyalty that, in turn, invite a level of engagement in the business that most employers don't approach. "When we've lost senior management personnel," he says, "we've filled those positions almost completely from within our own ranks."

If the proof of the tasting is in the pudding (or at Sonic, in a banana cream pie shake) it appears to work. The company conducts an annual anonymous employee opinion survey. One conducted prior to the release of the hardcover edition of this book in 2005 demonstrates that 96 percent of its employees say they intend to be employed by Sonic Drive-In twelve months in the future.

Think BIG, Act SMALL
GROW FUTURE LEADERS

- Eliminate the disconnects between the company's proclamation of how important people are and its actual practices. Otherwise, the organization won't have any credibility with the *right* future leaders.
- Conduct an anonymous study of your team to learn how many people plan to be with the organization in the future. The results received will identify leadership needs.
- Leadership training must include learning the mission-critical operations. Otherwise, future leaders won't know what can be done and what's impossible.
- Aspiring leaders should spend at least half their time in direct contact with customers.
- Don't overcompensate yourself or suck the enterprise dry. Otherwise, that larcenous example will be set for future leaders.
- Make sure the prospective leaders fit the culture. If they don't, you don't want them, even if they're high producers.
- Allow people to give notice of their intention to leave far in advance. You'll have more time to replace them and further demonstrate the organization's commitment to people.
- Cross-pollinate, move people, constantly increase responsibility, and encourage risk taking.

SECTION THREE

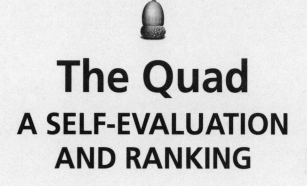

The Quad

A SELF-EVALUATION
AND RANKING

Faced with information saturation, most people seek out simple truths: maxims and symbols to make sense out of complexity. That's why nations have flags, products have logos, and companies have brands. These symbols are designed to serve as powerful mental triggers that call to mind collective prior experiences.

As we wrote this book we were literally overwhelmed by the inspirational stories and ideas we uncovered. We amassed a huge volume of operating statistics, terrific anecdotes, stories, and ideas and began wondering if we could take nearly two years of research, thousands of pages of interview transcriptions, and reams of financial data and compress them all down into *an easy symbol*.

In my past books I've avoided the use of charts, but this time my findings warrant a symbol worthy of inclusion. It breaks down the title of the book into four scenarios, each represented by a quadrant.

Four Possible Scenarios

TSAS	Think Small, Act Small
TSAB	Think Small, Act Big
TBAB	Think Big, Act Big
TBAS	Think Big, Act Small

The Quad serves as an easy reference point for each of the Building Blocks of leadership presented throughout the book.

In the following pages each of the Building Blocks is reintroduced with two short scenarios about the way your organization may think or act. From the scenarios offered, select the one that most closely describes the way your organization thinks and the one that best describes the way your organization acts.

The combination of your two choices will yield one of the four results above, which corresponds to a square of the quadrant. For each of your ten responses, place an × on the corresponding quadrant.

The Quad

TBAB *Think Big, Act Big*	**TBAS** *Think Big, Act Small*
TSAB *Think Small, Act Big*	**TSAS** *Think Small, Act Small*

Building Block 1   ■   Down to Earth

Select one of the following scenarios that best describes the way your organization thinks.

Think Small: People here lack an aspirational goal. They are content to punch the clock and do the day-to-day work, but lack a big cause to rally around.

Think Big: We maintain a balance between aspiring toward a big cause and still nailing the basics. We are not so obsessed with the big goal that we lose sight of being down-to-earth on a daily basis.

Select one of the following scenarios that best describes the way your organization acts.

Act Big: Different departments zealously withhold information from one another. People shift blame from themselves to others and deny accountability. It's almost impossible to schedule a meeting with anyone and there is no easy way of addressing grievances or proposing change.

Act Small: We work with each other on an informal, collegial basis that allows for greater information flow. This prevents bad news from remaining a secret, only to cause larger problems in the future. People receive encouragement and recognition from those around them. Like in a small community, the contributions of each individual member are recognized and appreciated.

Building Block 2   ■   Keep Your Hands Dirty

Select one of the following scenarios that best describes the way your organization thinks.

Think Small: People only feel responsible for their job description. They don't see the value in venturing outside of their own territory at work to understand what other departments are doing.

Think Big: We realize that the overall success of the organization is dependent on having everyone knowledgeable about how each department functions together. Workers and managers see themselves as part of a team that must cooperate to make the entire project succeed.

Select one of the following scenarios that best describes the way your organization acts.

Act Big: The leadership has little idea about what is going on at the front lines of customer contact. They're out of touch with the challenges faced by workers, delegate all customer service to a crisis control center, and attempt to stay above the fray.

Act Small: We promote a culture where people understand how one another's contributions play a role in the success of the overall company. We anticipate one another's needs and cross-train to cover multiple work functions, thus making us more adaptable to change. Our closeness with suppliers makes them valued business partners who have as much stake in our success as we do in theirs.

Building Block 3 ■ Short-Term Goals, Long-Term Horizons

Select one of the following scenarios that best describes the way your organization thinks.

Think Small: People are so focused on hitting quarterly numbers that they temporarily pump up sales at the expense of the medium- to long-term health of the company.

Think Big: We realize that our medium-term (two-year) plans provide aspirational guidance, but they will not be achieved without consistently executing numerous, simultaneous, sound strategies on a daily basis.

Select one of the following scenarios that best describes the way your organization acts.

Act Big: People are complacent that the future of the company will be stable and prosperous. Since they believe the battle is already won, they slack off today because they think they are part of a rising tide that will achieve success regardless of their individual effort.

Act Small: We realize that strategy is not a destination but a journey. Last year's strategy may be rendered useless based on geopolitical events or industry shakedowns. We are always honing the strategy based on new information and executing the small steps every day that will take us there.

Building Block 4 ■ Letting Go

Select one of the following scenarios that best describes the way your organization thinks.

Think Small: People in our organization stubbornly advocate the status quo as opposed to trying anything new. They don't want to give new ideas a chance because they have a personal stake in the old way, their ego is on the line, or they don't want to lose face.

Think Big: We realize that over the long term there will be changes in the types of goods and services we provide, and that letting go of the past is sometimes necessary in order to move forward.

Select one of the following scenarios that best describes the way your organization acts.

Act Big: One of our products or services has been dead for years, but we continue to prop it up for the sake of holding on to its glorious past. So many people are involved that it's difficult to come to a consensus about a major decision because there's always a vocal minority who stands to lose.

Act Small: We constantly review our products and services to make sure they are compelling and moving forward. We keep track of product life cycles and don't waste time defending old ideas if time would be better spent pursuing new ones. We preserve the benefit of a small organization in which the performance of the overall group is better understood by each team member, and people are less inclined to cling to bad ideas because they can closely observe the real impact of their misguided notions.

Building Block 5 ■ Have Everyone Think Like *the* Owner

Select one of the following scenarios that best describes the way your organization thinks.

Think Small: People don't feel like their contributions are recognized or rewarded. They lack motivation to improve the way they work or find ways of being more productive because there is a poor alignment of incentives.

Think Big: We realize that optimizing everyone's performance leads to value creation, which in turn drives the success of both ourselves and those around us. We hold ourselves to world-class performance metrics and regularly self-evaluate to discover areas for improvement.

Select one of the following scenarios that best describes the way your organization acts.

Act Big: Our organization has become overly hierarchical and people are separated into functional silos. People are only concerned with the success of their own team or department, at the expense of the goals of the total organization. People are influenced by the opinions with the loudest voice, rather than the soundest logic.

Act Small: We have incentives for people to create value and they receive due recognition for their achievements. We promote cross-functionality so that everyone can help each other do their job better. We take small failures in stride and realize that they are a necessary part of the experimental discovery process.

Building Block 6 ■ Invent New Businesses

Select one of the following scenarios that best describes the way your organization thinks.

Think Small: People are overconfident that our business model is robust for the foreseeable future and don't see any need to critically evaluate it or modify it to adapt to changing conditions. They think that as long as we keep doing what we do best and fly under the radar, we'll be fine.

Think Big: We realize that today's cash cows could become tomorrow's hamburgers. The long-term success of our group is reliant on us always seeking ways to improve what we do and innovate. We acknowledge that some of our smallest revenue centers of today could be reinvented to become brand-new leading business units of the future.

Select one of the following scenarios that best describes the way your organization acts.

Act Big: Since we have large market share and decent margins, people focus all their energy pitching today's cash cows and don't allocate any time and investment in R&D to find the next cash calf.

Act Small: We have implemented systems to constantly evaluate our capabilities and see how they could be expanded to enter new realms. We pay close attention to customer needs to find ways of expanding to better serve them. We aren't afraid to refocus our efforts when circumstances change.

Building Block 7 ■ Create Win-Win Solutions

Select one of the following scenarios that best describes the way your organization thinks.

Think Small: People view vendors and suppliers as costs to be squeezed. They don't care about their success so long as they continue to offer discounts and perks. People want to structure deals the same way they've always been done. "If it ain't broke, don't fix it."

Think Big: We realize that people work harder, create more value, and are more loyal when they've been dealt with fairly, and keep that in mind when structuring deals that benefit both our company and theirs. Giving a supplier a bigger piece of the pie on one deal may lower our short-term profits, but will generate many times that value in long-term goodwill.

Select one of the following scenarios that best describes the way your organization acts.

Act Big: We hardball our vendors and suppliers to get them to lower their prices, threatening to abandon them if they don't give in to our demands.

Act Small: We treat our business relationships as strategic partnerships that benefit both sides. We maintain strong long-term relationships by helping one another realize profit-able growth. We fight commoditization through differentiation, learning true customer needs, and tailoring solutions to make a higher value-added offering.

Building Block 8 ▪ Play Your Own Game

Select one of the following scenarios that best describes the way your organization thinks.

Think Small: People think that many other companies besides ours offer basically the same thing that we do, but they cling to the hope that our customers will be loyal to us, even though our larger competitors can undercut us.

Think Big: We realize that there are always new niche categories in the market to seek out and enter. We know the challenges of competing solely on price with competitors who can always undercut us. Occupying a niche gives our brand an identity that customers can identify with, which allows customers to develop deeper appreciation and loyalty. Through our creative differentiation, we earn the right to charge a premium, since we indeed offer a better, more unique product and/or experience.

Select one of the following scenarios that best describes the way your organization acts.

Act Big: Our company tries to please everyone and has strayed from our core capabilities into activities that stretch us too thin. We are competing in fields in which we don't have a competitive advantage, forcing us to work that much harder to keep up with our more focused competitors.

Act Small: We frequently reevaluate our capabilities and discuss ways in which we can develop unique offerings that set us apart from our competition and place us in a category of our own. We don't fight battles we cannot win and instead look for barriers to entry that will protect our niche.

Building Block 9 ■ Build Communities

Select one of the following scenarios that best describes the way your organization thinks.

Think Small: People who work here don't feel a strong sense of affiliation with the company. They assume that our brand identity is fixed and can't be changed. Customers view us as a generic provider, without a personality, and while satisfied, they show little loyalty to us in the face of a better offer.

Think Big: We realize that team members and customers are happier and more loyal when we make a genuine effort to give them a sense of community. This goodwill may not produce immediate returns, but over the long term we know it will be a formidable competitive advantage.

Select one of the following scenarios that best describes the way your organization acts.

Act Big: Attempts by management to bring workers or customers together are trite and halfhearted. People feel too timid to question the initiatives, so they are presented with one bad idea after another. Customers feel less and less affinity for us as we've become a bland, impersonal, corporate behemoth.

Act Small: We bring people together—workers *and* customers—under common banners that unite them and give them solidarity. People are proud to call themselves part of our group and our company logo is proudly worn as a badge of affiliation. We evangelize and actively follow through on the positive aspects of our brand identity, which we view as a sacrosanct promise.

Building Block 10 ■ Grow Future Leaders

Select one of the following scenarios that best describes the way your organization thinks.

Think Small: The leaders of the company are in it for themselves and can't wait to jump ship and leave the company behind without a succession plan in place.

Think Big: We feel a responsibility to develop a deep bench so that the company can continue its successful trajectory. We delegate big decisions to managers coming up the ranks to test their leadership skills and prepare them for larger responsibilities.

Select one of the following scenarios that best describes the way your organization acts.

Act Big: The leaders of the company pay no attention to grooming a new generation of leaders, causing the workers, suppliers, customers, and investors to lose faith in the ability of the company to self-perpetuate. People are promoted to leadership positions without a proven track record. The leadership vacuum makes us vulnerable to a hostile takeover.

Act Small: The leaders of the company spend ample time identifying potential future leaders, meeting with them, showing them the ropes, and passing knowledge from one generation to the next.

Evaluation

Once you've completed the exercise you should have ten ×'s marked within the various quadrants.

If eight to ten ×'s are in the upper right quadrant marked TBAS, your organization rocks! It doesn't mean you can't improve, but with that many ×'s in the desired quadrant, you already know that and are relentlessly working for constant improvement. Chances are good that your financial performance is on par with those companies in the book. Congratulations!

If six to seven ×'s are in the upper right quadrant marked TBAS, your organization is far better off than most. Even though your company may be faring well financially and achieving annual double-digit growth in revenues and profits, there are weaknesses that will affect your long-term performance. Significant amounts of work are required in those areas where you failed to achieve TBAS status. Good job!

If four to five ×'s are in the upper right quadrant marked TBAS, your organization is probably not achieving the same long-term financial performance as the companies in the book. There are serious issues that threaten your long-term performance.

If you're an employee of a company with fewer than four ×'s in the upper right hand quadrant marked TBAS, we feel sorry for you. If you're the owner or person in charge, you need to make a serious assessment of why your organization has tumbled into disarray—the answers are in this book's chapters—and immediately build and implement a plan designed to *save* the business.

How Will You Respond to Your Organization's Score?

At some point we all experience results that don't please us. It might be a medical exam that discloses high blood pressure, too many pounds revealed on the scale, a bad test grade, or an embarrassingly high golf score.

Some people choose to respond to bad news by burying their

head in the sand like an ancient dodo bird, hopeful that what's threatening them will magically go away. Unfortunately, other creatures ate all the dodo birds—while their heads were in the sand—and they became extinct.

Others resort to churlish remarks directed toward the bearer of the bad result. "The doctor's a quack. That scale doesn't work. The professor's out to get me. These golf clubs stink!"

A smaller group of people acknowledges the bad result, becomes determined to do better, makes an assessment of what's required to achieve the desired result, and commits to following a course of action that gets it to where it wants to be.

Here's hoping you'll use the results of this test as a starting point to achieve the full economic and human potential of your organization.

The Research
EATING AN ELEPHANT

The Research: Eating an Elephant

The initial assignment was to identify the companies that do the world's best job of consistently growing revenues. How does someone go about identifying the best anything in the world—let alone figure out how they do it? Here's the story of our two-year journey to find the best of the best.

A search at the Web site of the U.S. Census Bureau's Statistical Abstract of the United States confirmed my fears. "There are," according to the site, "more than 27 million businesses in the nation and that doesn't include millions of businesses who file their tax returns as 'individuals.'" A quick e-mail inquiry to the World Bank was promptly and politely answered with, "There are an estimated 100 million businesses worldwide, but because of poor reporting in some nations, that number might actually be higher." Thank you Census Bureau and World Bank: how could anyone find the best of *anything* out of 100 million?

I had two years to identify the greatest sales organizations on the planet, figure out what they do differently and better than anyone else and commit those findings to the printed page. The clock

was ticking and finally, after a few weeks of delaying and staring blankly at a computer screen, I decided to get the show on the
road.

Years ago a friend asked, "Do you know how to eat an elephant?" I shook my head, admitted I didn't, and waited for the
punch line. He said, "It's easy: one bite at a time." It wasn't very
funny, but he'd unerringly provided me a bit of advice that I've frequently called on when a project or deadline looms large ahead of
me. I began by breaking this elephant into bite-sized pieces.

The Research Program

Below is the bite-sized pieces research list assembled in March
2003. It ended up serving as the step-by-step instruction manual
for the book. It's included here because the discoveries and findings presented in this book will be offered not as spineless maybes
and theories, but as a new set of truths, so it's important you
understand the steps taken to arrive at those truths.

- Assemble a research team.
- Define and quantify what "best" means.
- Define the universe to be studied.
- Gain access to the financial data of all the companies.
- Get inside the companies and figure out what they do.
- Ruthlessly evaluate and select the findings for the book.

The Research Team

For *Less Is More* I'd been fortunate to assemble a great research
team. Unfortunately, the women from the previous team weren't
available. One was working as a financial analyst in New York and
the other was attending Harvard Law. While awaiting the start of
business school at UCLA, Greg Powell, who had led the previous
team, agreed to serve on the new team and head the effort to interview prospective lead researchers.

More than eight hundred résumés were received and eventually we hired a new lead researcher. Brian Solon received a bachelor's and MBA from UC Berkeley, a law degree from Santa Clara University, had several years of work experience in law and finance with stints in Europe and Asia, and produces music when he isn't doing business. He was our kind of person.

With Powell's dogged determination and uncanny ability to totally focus, Solon's classic training, and my willingness to be challenged by guys two decades my junior, we had the makings of a team. In many books the author's point of view takes center stage and the researchers, acknowledged in the back of the book, skulk off into the background, their work completed. The work of Solon and Powell is so central to this book that you'll frequently be exposed to their questioning and points of view.

Define and Quantify "Best"

We knew that the integrity and success of the book would rest on our getting the following question answered correctly.

> **What constitutes a great sales organization?**

There were lots of spirited discussion and differing points of view, and eventually hundreds of e-mails were dispatched to publishers, clients, colleagues, readers, and companies I'd previously written about, asking for input and advice. Clearly we'd struck a nerve because the responses poured in. Defining "best" wasn't going to be as hard as we'd originally thought because every response and conversation on the subject eventually got around to one of the following three points of view.

- "Great sales organizations grow every year during good times and bad," responded almost everyone. They explained their responses further by arguing that "Any company can have great sales growth when there's lots of demand, but great companies have figured out how to create demand and grow revenues even when the economy isn't great."

- Others had a different perspective and said, "Great sales organizations grow organically not only through acquisition. Don't be fooled by companies with great numbers who grow their numbers only by buying other businesses."

- And a surprisingly large number of respondents argued for a component of the definition that we'd not originally discussed. "Great sales organizations grow their revenues *profitably*. Some companies cut prices to increase revenues and gain market share but don't have any profit left over to show for their efforts."

Finally, we arrived at a working definition.

The best sales organizations grow organically and profitably every year despite economic conditions.

The problem with our working definition was that it didn't have any numbers attached to it and we wouldn't be able to examine thousands of databases in order to identify potentially great sales organizations until we knew how much revenue and profit growth we were seeking.

We decided we'd begin searching for companies that had grown their revenues by 10 percent or more annually, reasoning that any enterprise that demonstrated the ability to consistently grow revenues by that amount might potentially become a target for further study. But we still needed another number.

How many years of 10 percent or more annual revenue growth would constitute great? Instinctively we liked the resonance of the number ten and agreed that if a company had grown revenues

10 percent or more each year for ten years without missing a single year, they'd probably make up a small and elite list of performers. That would mean they'd survived the recession of the early 1990s, enjoyed the robust years of the late '90s, and survived and prospered during the 2001–2002 recession and slowdown. We agreed that any company that had managed to grow by double digits every year throughout those turbulent times must have great stories to tell.

Defining the Universe

There's no way to study the world's estimated 100 million businesses, and if a way did exist, the task would be so enormous that the findings would be so out of date by the time the research was complete as to be rendered useless. Our next task was to determine which businesses would constitute the universe we'd study, and eventually we agreed to study every publicly traded company in the world (about twenty thousand of them) and the thirty thousand largest privately held companies—a total of about fifty thousand businesses.

Our reasoning was that the financial statements of all publicly traded companies are available and accessible and that many of the largest privately held companies would use bank loans or debt (bonds) as financing vehicles. Their covenants with banks and underwriters would mean that sufficient financial information would or could be available if we dug deep and hard enough.

We knew we might miss a few companies by limiting our study to the above mentioned group, but didn't think we'd miss many. Any company that routinely achieves double-digit revenue growth— even if they aren't publicly traded or one of the thirty thousand largest private firms—would generate sufficient publicity that either we'd learn about them or they and/or their business model would have been acquired or copied by the companies we were researching. Ten years of consistent 10 percent revenue growth doesn't go unnoticed.

Gaining Access to Financial Data

To evaluate publicly traded companies, we enlisted the assistance of Factset Research Systems in Greenwich, Connecticut, a leading provider of financial and economic information to the investment community. Their more than two hundred databases contain the historical financial statements of every publicly traded company in the world.

Our objective was to generate a list of all publicly traded companies that had grown their revenues by 10 percent (or greater) for ten consecutive years without having missed a year. Factset performed more than 121,000 calculations and returned the names of 110 publicly traded companies that had achieved our target revenue numbers. (See Chart 1 on page 245.)

Evaluating privately owned companies was more difficult. We used the *Fortune* 1000 database as well as their Global 500 database, the *Forbes* list of America's largest privately held companies, and the resources of Dun and Bradstreet's Hoover's Online Unit, which tracks and provides data on more than fifty thousand privately held companies. Eventually we came up with an additional 159 companies we thought might pass the revenue test and become prospective targets. (See Chart 4 on page 249.)

Work was painstakingly slow. It took several months to determine that out of the 50,000 businesses we began studying, only 269 (about .05 percent) had possibly grown revenues by 10 percent for ten consecutive years.

We began sending out hundreds of e-mails attempting to confirm the revenue performance of the companies and decided it was time to simultaneously begin conducting our profit test as well. Because the number ten had served us well on the revenue analysis, we used it again for our evaluation of operating profits. It was back to Factset and back to endless online searches, but this time with another question: of the 269 companies, how many had also grown operating profits or earnings per share by 10 percent or more for ten years? (See Charts 2 and 3 on pages 247 and 248.)

Weeks and months were whizzing by. In many instances scores of e-mails were flying back and forth with just a single company as we tried every possible tactic to garner responses and confirmations. Privately held companies are notoriously (and rightfully) stingy about releasing revenue and profit numbers. We kept at it. There were days when a single response from a CFO either counting their company in or out was sufficient reason for celebration, and we slowly continued adding single companies to the final list.

There were humorous incidents as well. One day while on the phone with Brian, he said, "You won't believe an e-mail I just received from a CEO." He read it to me, "Yes, we hit your numbers, but we'll pass on being part of your book." At that exact moment an e-mail arrived on my laptop from the company's CFO, whose message was, "We'd love to be in your book, but, unfortunately, our past financial performance doesn't even come close to your criteria." We howled, deciding if the CEO would lie to us he'd probably lie to anyone and guessed it would only be a matter of time until he'd end up jailed cooking the books.

We knew we were getting close when we finally winnowed our list down to twenty-seven companies. The companies that remained were either publicly traded (so the financial information was supposedly accurate), or in some cases the company's financial performance had been confirmed by their CFO, and in a few instances, we were still digging and fighting to get confirmation. The list included privately owned universities, a number of retailers, service and entertainment companies, technology firms, a health-care provider, a chain of coffee shops, a chain of gyms, distribution businesses, companies involved in diversified businesses, a chewing gum company, and even a circus.

A Revelation but Not a Detour!

By the time our list had been narrowed to twenty-seven prospective companies, a growing realization, long simmering, had to be addressed.

Because of the stringent financial criteria employed, we'd ended up with a short list of companies that'd mastered the art of consistently generating revenue and doing it better than all other companies. But because one of the qualifiers required the companies to also grow profits every year, we'd ended up with more than a list of great sales organizations; we had in our hands a very short list of the very best companies. This raised an important question.

Are these companies great because they know how to sell, or do they deliver consistent and robust revenue growth because they're essentially great companies? Is it the leadership of the sales effort that makes the organization's overall financial performance stellar, or is it the leadership of the overall company that allows for outstanding revenue growth? Our answers would determine the book's focus.

We opted to place our bet on the belief that it was the leadership of the organizations that allowed these companies to generate such outstanding performances. Although we believe that the companies included in the book are the best contemporary business models in existence, our focus would remain unchanged. *Think Big, Act Small* would be about how the companies that made the cut do a better job of consistently growing revenues than all other companies.

The Qualitative Search Got Under Way

While we continued aggressively pursuing final confirmation of financial performance from several companies, we began building extensive research dossiers on every company in the event they made the final cut. These dossiers were hundreds of pages in length and contained financial information, analyst reports, newspaper and magazine stories, reports of lawsuits, and company press releases. If something had been written or published about a company, we found it and it became part of our central files. As we began reviewing the thousands of pages, we were confronted with another issue I hadn't expected.

As a research meeting got under way, Greg Powell, who was reviewing a list of qualifying companies, rolled his eyes and exclaimed, "You can't write about a company that sells cigarettes in one of your books," he said. "It'd be completely irresponsible and unconscionable. Social responsibility," Greg continued, "is about achieving commercial success while pursuing responsible actions. Those are the kind of companies you need to write about."

For the duration of the meeting I tried to view the business world through eyes two decades younger than my own. Both Greg and Brian see their life's work in the business space and neither could be called *tree huggers*, but by the end of the day, they'd convinced me that social responsibility would be a consideration during our qualitative deliberations. So off the list came companies that sold cigarettes, performed lab testing on live animals, companies accused of shoddy construction in massive class action lawsuits, and companies operating under consent decrees with the government because of racial discrimination. Simultaneously, and to their credit, a few other companies came forward and acknowledged they'd failed to meet our financial targets and finally we had a manageable list.

Top 17 Finalists

1. **The Apollo Group**—A for-profit education company
2. **Automatic Data Processing**—The largest payroll and tax-filing processor in the world
3. **Bed Bath & Beyond**—A domestics retailer in the United States
4. **Cabela's**—A multichannel retailer of hunting, fishing, and outdoor gear
5. **DeVry University**—A for-profit education company that provides programs for working adults and underemployed young people
6. **Dot Foods**—The largest privately held food service redistributor in the United States

7. **Flying J**—A leading truck-stop operator in the United States

8. **Infosys Technologies**—Based in India, the company offers a range of customized software services

9. **Koch Industries**—The second-largest private company in the United States

10. **Kohl's Corporation**—Operator of discount department stores

11. **Medline Industries**—A private medical supply distributor and manufacturer

12. **O'Reilly Automotive**—Operates about 1,200 O'Reilly Auto Parts stores

13. **PETCO Animal Supplies**—A pet supply specialty retailer

14. **SAS**—The world's largest privately held software company

15. **Sonic Drive-In**—The largest chain of quick-service drive-ins in the United States

16. **Starbucks**—A specialty coffee retailer

17. **Strayer Education**—A for-profit private university

Building the Final List

Once we'd finished identifying the final list of companies we were going to write about, it was our intention to begin an extremely rigorous field research program that would include visiting company headquarters, becoming consumers of the companies, doing in-depth meetings and interviews with the CEOs and other company executives, as well as interviewing vendors, suppliers, workers, customers, and franchisees.

There was no way we'd be able to adequately research and report on seventeen companies (it would take too long and make for a confusing book), so again, because the number ten had served us well so far, we decided to focus our energies on ten companies. But which ten should we select?

Again, we dispatched hundreds of e-mails to our community of readers, clients, and associates asking them which companies they'd like to read about and determined we'd provide the same weight to their responses as we did to the following criteria:

Industry Category The list of seventeen finalists reveals a heavy concentration in retail (Bed Bath & Beyond, Cabela's, Kohl's, O'Reilly's, and PETCO) and education (Apollo Group, DeVry, and Strayer). Not wanting an undue concentration in any single category, we eliminated two retailers and two educational companies, reasoning we didn't want a finished work that was overly concentrated on a single industry type.

Ownership Our goal was to create a final list whose composition would be roughly half publicly owned and the other half privately held.

Overexposed We wanted to tread on ground that hadn't been trampled by stampedes of journalists and authors, and dropped Starbucks from our list.

Geography We were surprised that only one company on our list of finalists was from outside the United States. In my previous two books, half the companies had been from the United States and half from other nations. Possibly there's a zeal for privacy on the part of privately held businesses in Europe, Asia, and South America that we didn't succeed in breaking through. Maybe the databases *were* accurate and there simply aren't any other companies that met our stringent criteria. Perhaps our search in dollar terms masked some double-digit performances in foreign currencies. However, given the thoroughness of the Factset database, we are certain that no publicly traded company in the world was missed.

Originally we decided to include Infosys on our final list of ten firms, given its outstanding financial performance over the past ten years. We compiled a massive dossier of information about the firm and scheduled an interview with CEO Nandan Nilekani.

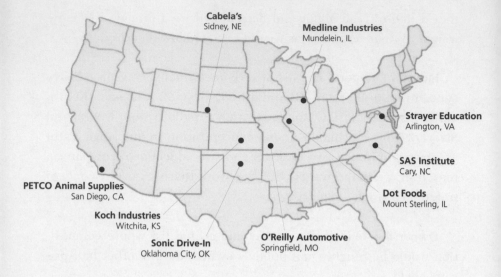

However, we ultimately realized that a book with nine U.S. companies and only one firm based elsewhere would appear odd, so at the last minute we decided to omit Infosys and limit our study to nine U.S. firms.

Having decided to focus on U.S. firms, we attempted to have roughly half of the companies on our final list east of the Mississippi and the other half to the west.

Getting Inside the Companies

We began with a blitz of personalized letters and autographed copies of my previous books to the CEOs and executives at the companies, congratulating them on their performance and informing them that based on their companies' outstanding performances, they'd been selected for inclusion in the book.

Not a single response!

I started making calls to the companies, encountered one stone wall after another, and was growing more frustrated every day. It seemed that nobody wanted to speak with us.

One day I recalled the words of my first full-time boss, an

overbearing, tough-guy type who'd ended up throwing a temper tantrum at me. "Jennings," he yelled, "there are *reasons* and *results* and I want the results!" It was a hard lesson at the time but one that's served me well. There'd be no giving up. We were going to get inside every single company.

In fairness to the companies an important fact should be noted, one that didn't occur to us for many months. The heads of all these companies probably have as many journalists knocking on their doors as they do salespeople trying to sell them stuff, and each could probably make a full-time occupation out of agreeing to meet with everyone who comes along wanting their time and resources.

In retrospect I look back at our fight to gain entrance not as a matter of being stonewalled, but as having been put to a test. "Demonstrate your worthiness," they seemed to be saying. "Show us what you're really made of, make us understand why you're different from everyone else, explain the benefit that will accrue to us if we work with you, and then we'll let you in the door."

There was also the issue of secrecy. The companies we'd identified have intentionally and beneficially flown beneath the radar and have gone largely uncovered by the business press. Each has proprietary systems and methods of operation they'd prefer remain secret.

We addressed this objection with the following response: during a time where business and its leaders are being bashed on a daily basis in newspapers, magazines, and television, this would be a book about *great companies doing things right*. We reasoned that each had a social obligation to cooperate with us and share their knowledge with other aspiring businesspeople committed to doing business the right way.

We cajoled, jumped through hoops, were persistent pains in the you-know-what, and on one occasion resorted to a bit of intimidation by promising to write about them based on information from anonymous sources. Eventually, over a period of many months, we gained access to every company we wanted to write about.

The Research

We began our fieldwork by conducting wide-ranging, free-for-all, no-rule interviews with the CEOs of every company. There's no person better equipped to tell the story of a company than the person who founded or leads it. During these meetings we were able to learn the history, values, and culture of the company, and in almost every instance it was during this first meeting that we began unearthing the magic that had allowed these companies to achieve what few others have.

Following our CEO interviews were scores of follow-up interviews with other company leaders, managers, and workers, followed by dialogues with customers, vendors, and suppliers.

The Findings

By the time our research was complete we'd landed on scores of findings worthy of inclusion. The book would be too long and muddled if each finding was allocated its own chapter, so we began the difficult task of combining, eliminating, and editing with the objective of ending up with the ten most important and actionable findings. For the benefit of those readers with insatiable appetites for information, we've posted interview transcripts and documents associated with the project at www.jennings-solutions.com.

At first glimpse, a few of the truths we discovered may appear to be simply common sense. However, as the old saying goes, "The most common thing about common sense is how uncommon common sense is," and each is worthy of review in light of the new perspectives offered. Most of the truths we unearthed are counter-intuitive and buck conventional wisdom.

We strived for thoroughness and accuracy in every aspect of our research but realized that the achievement of perfection is impossible. If we missed a company or if a potentially big finding flew over our heads unrecognized, it wasn't by intention, design, or exclusion but purely by accident. We hope our imperfection will provide an opportunity for spirited dialogue.

Research for the Revised Edition in 2011

When it became obvious that I'd not only be researching and writing a new book on the subject of reinvention but revising this book as well, I turned to my trusted colleague Larry Haughton and asked for help. During the past twenty years he and I have worked together consulting and transforming many companies. We coauthored *It's Not the Big That Eat the Small . . . It's the Fast That Eat the Slow*, and he's served as the head of research on my past two books.

We reached out to the heads of communication and the CEOs of all the companies we'd written about in the original hardcover and asked for their cooperation again. Everyone felt their company had been honestly and accurately portrayed in the original hardcover version and were very helpful and cooperative on the revised edition.

We scheduled interviews—sometimes a number of them—with each of the companies, built a list of questions based on our original findings, recorded our interviews and, as usual, generated thousands of pages of transcripts. Then, we verified the financial performance of each company and began the challenging and time-consuming process of including updated and new information into the original text.

It was extremely gratifying to see that all the companies we profiled had maintained their extraordinary status. I hope that five years from now there's sufficient interest in these remarkable leaders and companies that I get to do it all over again.

If your company meets our financial growth criteria—10 percent or greater growth in revenue, profits, and/or earnings per share for ten years in a row—we want to know who you are. Contact us and we'll acknowledge your performance through our Web site, future editions of the book, and in our speeches done around the world.

SECTION FIVE

Charts

The following charts are those originally used to identify the companies chosen to be profiled in the original hardcover edition of this book published in 2005. They are included in the interest of transparency so the reader can see why these particular companies were selected.

CHART 1
Factset Results

Publicly Traded Companies Achieving 10 Percent Growth in Revenues for Ten Consecutive Years

1 Abercrombie & Fitch
2 Ace Cash Express
3 Administaff
4 Advanced Environmental Recycling Technologies
5 Affymetrix
6 American Retirement
7 Amsurg
8 AOL Time Warner
9 Apollo Group
10 Bed Bath & Beyond
11 Bio Reference Labs
12 Biosite
13 Bisys Group
14 Brinker International
15 Calpine
16 Carmax
17 Central European Distribution
18 Cheesecake Factory
19 Chelsea Property Group
20 Coinstar
21 Colt Telecom Group
22 Concord EFS
23 Cost Plus
24 CSG Systems International
25 Digital Recorders
26 Dollar General
27 Dollar Tree Stores
28 Duane Reade
29 Equity Office Properties
30 Exactech

31 Express Scripts
32 Factset Research Systems
33 Fiserv
34 Florida Banks
35 FTI Consulting
36 Genesis Microchip
37 Guitar Center
38 Harley-Davidson
39 Health Management Association
40 Hibbett Sporting Goods
41 Home Properties New York
42 Horizon Organic Holdings
43 Hot Topic
44 ICT Group
45 ICU Medical
46 IDT Corp
47 Impath
48 Infosys Technologies
49 Intercept
50 Kendle International
51 Knight Transportation
52 Kohl's
53 Lifecell
54 Lifeway Food
55 Linens 'N Things
56 Lowes
57 Madden Steven
58 Manhattan Associates
59 Masco
60 Medicis Pharmaceuticals

61 MedImmune
62 Mercury Interactive
63 Merit Medical Systems
64 Metro One Telecomm
65 Microsoft
66 MTR Gaming Group
67 Nektar Therapeutics
68 Charleys
69 O'Reilly Automotive
70 Orthodontic Center of America
71 Outback Steakhouse
72 P F Changs China Bistro
73 Pacific Sunwear California
74 Performance Food Group
75 Philadelphia Consolidated Holdings
76 Prepaid Legal Services
77 Priority Healthcare
78 Probusiness Services
79 Progressive Corporation of Ohio
80 Qiagen
81 Quiksilver
82 R&G Financial
83 Radian Group
84 Rare Hospitality International
85 Regis
86 Renal Care Group
87 Rent-a-Center
88 Resmed
89 Retalix
90 RF Micro Devices
91 RMH Teleservices
92 SCP Pool
93 Simpson Manufacturing
94 Starbucks
95 Steiner Leisure
96 Stericycle
97 Strayer Education
98 Sungard Data Systems
99 Techne
100 Tractor Supply
101 Triad Guaranty
102 Tweeter Home Entertainment Group
103 U S Physical Therapy
104 Vodafone Group
105 Wal-Mart Stores
106 Walgreens
107 Wellpoint Health Network
108 Western Wireless
109 Whole Foods Market
110 Williams-Sonoma

CHART 2
Factset Results

Publicly Traded Companies Achieving 10 Percent
Growth in Operating Income for Ten Consecutive Years

1 Amsurg
2 Apollo Group
3 Automatic Data Processing
4 Ballard Power Systems
5 Bed Bath & Beyond
6 Brown & Brown
7 CBL & Associates Properties
8 Colt Telecom Group
9 DeVry
10 Engineered Support Systems
11 Expeditors International Washington
12 Express Scripts

13 Financial Federal
14 Harley-Davidson
15 Home Depot
16 Infosys Technologies
17 Knight Transportation
18 O'Reilly Automotive
19 Omnicom Group
20 Patterson Dental
21 Radian Group Inc
22 SCP Pool
23 Starbucks
24 Walgreens
25 Young Innovations

CHART 3
Factset Results

Publicly Traded Companies Achieving 10 Percent Growth in Earnings Per Share for Ten Consecutive Years

1 Apollo Group

2 Autozone

3 Bed Bath & Beyond

4 Cathay Bancorp

5 Concord EFS

6 DeVry

7 Donaldson Company

8 Engineered Support Systems

9 Expeditors International Washington

10 Financial Federal

11 Harley-Davidson

12 Infosys Technologies

13 Kohl's

14 99 Cents Only Stores

15 Omnicom Group

16 Patterson Dental

17 PMI Group

18 Radian Group

19 SEI Investments

20 Sonic Drive-In

21 Starbucks

22 Sterling Bancorp New York

23 Strayer Education

24 S Y Bancorp

25 Total System Services

26 Walgreens

CHART 4

Private Companies
Contacted to Verify 10 Percent Growth in Revenue and Operating Income for Ten Consecutive Years

1 24 Hour Fitness Worldwide	32 Conair
2 Academy Sports & Outdoors	33 Concentra
3 Aecom Technology	34 Core-Mark International
4 Alberici	35 Cox Enterprises
5 Alex Lee	36 Crown Equipment
6 A-Mark Financial	37 Cumberland Farms
7 American Century Investments	38 David Weekly Homes
8 AppleOne Employment Services	39 DeBruce Grain
9 Arctic Slope International	40 Deseret Management
10 Ashley Furniture Industries	41 Devcon Construction
11 Asplundh Tree Expert	42 DHL Airways
12 Austin Industries	43 Dick Corp
13 Barnes & Noble College Book-stores	44 Discount Tire
14 Barton Malow	45 Doane Pet Care
15 BDO International	46 Dot Foods
16 Beck Group	47 Dreamworks SKG
17 Ben E Keith	48 Dunn Industries
18 Big V Supermarkets	49 DynCorp
19 Bloomberg	50 Eby-Brown
20 Borden	51 Edward Jones
21 Bose	52 Enterprise Rent a Car
22 Boston Consulting Group	53 Epix Holdings
23 Brasfield & Gorrie	54 Ergon
24 C&S Wholesale Groceries	55 Express Services
25 Cabela's	56 Feld Entertainment (Ringling Bros)
26 Central National—Gottesman	57 Fidelity Investments
27 CH2M Hill Cos	58 Fisher Development
28 Cigarettes Cheaper	59 Flint Ink
29 Cinemark USA	60 Flying J
30 Clark Enterprises	61 Follett
31 Clark Retail Enterprises	62 Frank Consolidated Enterprises

63 Freedom Communications
64 Genmar Holdings
65 Glazer's Wholesale Drug
66 Golden Rule Financial
67 Gordon Food Service
68 Graybar Electric
69 Green Bay Packaging
70 HB Zachary
71 He Butt Grocery
72 Heafner Tire Group
73 Hearst
74 Heico Companies
75 Hewitt Associates
76 Hobby Lobby Stores
77 Hoffman
78 Horseshoe Gaming Holdings
79 Houchens Industries
80 HR Logic
81 HT Hackney
82 Hunt Consolidated / Hunt Oil
83 ICC Industries
84 Icon Health & Fitness
85 J Crew Group
86 JM Huber
87 JR Simplot
88 Kingston Technology
89 Knoll
90 Koch Industries
91 Longberger
92 Love's Travel Stops & Country Stores
93 MA Mortenson
94 Manasha
95 Marc Glassman
96 Mary Kay
97 MBM

98 McCarthy Building Cos
99 McKinsey & Co
100 Medline Industries
101 Micro Electronics
102 Modern Continental Cos
103 MSX International
104 National Distributing
105 National Envelope
106 New Age Electronics
107 New Balance Athletic Shoes
108 Parsons
109 Parsons Brinckerhoff
110 PC Richard & Son
111 Pepper Construction Group
112 PETCO Animal Supplies
113 Peter Kiewit Sons'
114 Pilot
115 Platinum Equity
116 Premcor
117 Primus
118 PrintPack
119 Publix Super Markets
120 Purity Wholesale Grocers
121 Quad/Graphics
122 QuikTrip
123 RaceTrac Petroleum
124 Republic Technologies Intl
125 Ritz Camera Centers
126 Roll International
127 Rooms to Go
128 Rudolph and Sletten
129 Sealy
130 Services Group of America
131 Sheetz
132 Simmons

CHART 5
Publicly Traded Companies*
RECENT PERFORMANCE VERSUS MARKET INDICES

For the five years 1998 through 2003			
	Total Return	Annualized Return	Growth of $10,000
O'Reilly Automotive	193.79%	19.68%	$29,379
Sonic Drive-In	268.66%	24.29%	$36,866
Strayer Education	243.72%	22.85%	$34,372
Russell 2000	37.77%	5.49%	$13,777
Russell 1000	26.32%	3.97%	$12,632
S&P 500	25.27%	3.83%	$12,527
Dow Jones Industrials	47.66%	6.71%	$14,766

For the two years March 11, 2002, through February 9, 2004			
	Total Return	Annualized Return	Growth of $10,000
O'Reilly Automotive	22.93%	10.88%	$12,293
Sonic Drive-In	27.02%	12.70%	$12,702
Strayer Education	128.25%	51.08%	$22,825
PETCO Animal Supplies**	60.64%	26.74%	$16,064
Russell 2000	28.09%	13.17%	$12,809
Russell 1000	8.70%	4.26%	$10,870
S&P 500	7.19%	3.53%	$10,719
Dow Jones Industrials	9.57%	4.68%	$10,957

*Cabela's, not included, began public trading on June 25, 2004.

**PETCO began public trading (for the second time) on February 26, 2002.

Conclusion
by Brian Solon
Lead Researcher

In the course of working on this book I had the opportunity to travel throughout the country, to places many Californians consider unfamiliar (and vice versa). Spending time in Colorado, Illinois, Kansas, Missouri, Nebraska, North Carolina, Oklahoma, Texas, Virginia, and Wyoming was a long overdue awakening. As an added bonus, the trip revealed exotic new cuisines seldom found in vegan-friendly Marin County, including: hush puppies, deep-fried jalapeño cheese poppers, Mount Sterling Horseshoes, and shit on a shingle (creamed chipped beef on toast).

All too often people speak of two Americas. However, working on this book uncovered a valuable insight. Great business ideas can originate and thrive anywhere. It isn't vital to have a midtown corner office or adhere to a particular political persuasion to succeed.

Scary Times

The beginning of the twenty-first century has been downright scary for business. In a few short years we've witnessed stock market collapses, massive corporate bankruptcies, terrorist threats, and CEOs toppled and/or imprisoned for fraud—either for their own deeds or because Sarbanes-Oxley (and Eliot Spitzer) held them personally liable for the failures of their employees. In this environment, who in their right mind would aspire to the awesome pressures and responsibilities faced by today's business leaders?

The past few years have been uncertain times, wreaking havoc on many businesses. Uncertainty discourages investment, causing a vicious downward spiral of undercapitalization. Uncertain futures cause paralysis and inaction at a time when consumers are demanding more action, better products, and increasingly personalized services. In the face of such widespread chaos, it's natural to return to the fundamentals.

After spending time with the well-run companies in this book, one almost forgets about the past several years of management debacles. These companies are built on solid fundamentals and have been getting it right for years. They are examples of how to foster a culture of success that is based on treating people well and giving everyone opportunities to prosper. They have built communities, invented new businesses, and created innovative solutions for customers and suppliers. The leaders pay close attention to, and intimately understand, the core functions of their companies.

It's striking to hear these companies' stories, meet the people who work for them, and see their business models in action; it's wonderfully refreshing to see things being done the right way. These great companies deserve recognition for their performances, which in turn give credence to the underlying philosophies that guide them.

Le Quick Fix

As a society we're becoming more and more accustomed to receiving new and exciting ways of achieving the quick fix. From low-carb diets to Viagra, the public is showered with precious pills and radical solutions that will make problems go away—*now*.

In contrast this book is not a tactical guide or a bully pulpit for experimental philosophies. We give credit for the proven guiding principles and business fundamentals described herein to the people who run the organizations profiled.

By focusing on the guiding principles of organizations that have *proven* their ability to sustain success over the long term, we dispel the quick-fix myth. These guiding principles are admittedly not academic jargon, nor were they developed in the mountaintop lab of a thought leader. Actually, they're relatively simple ideas; the genius behind them lies in how they have been applied by these companies, despite differences in location, industry, political persuasion, or ownership model.

Keep It Simple

We live in interesting times. Complexity causes people to yearn for simple, profound ideas that can be readily related to diverse situations. People gravitate to confidence, decisiveness, and clear, powerful messages, searching for the ultimate metaphysical reference point. So we end as we began, with this message: to build an organization with balanced focus, camaraderie, and the ability to prosper over the long term . . . think big, act small

ACKNOWLEDGMENTS

A research and writing effort this immense required the cooperation and assistance of more than one hundred people. I am grateful to everyone who agreed to participate.

There's nobody better in the world of business publishing than Adrian Zackheim; this was my third book with him. The team he's assembled at Portfolio/Penguin, the imprint he founded at Penguin Group (USA), is the best in publishing. I offer my sincere gratitude to Megan Casey, editor of the original hardcover edition, and to Natalie Horbachevsky, who did a tremendous job of guiding me through the revisions for the trade paperback edition of the book. Thanks also to Will Weisser, vice president, associate publisher, and marketing director, and to Allison McLean, director of publicity. Special thanks to my agent Alan Nevins with Renaissance Literary Agency in Beverly Hills, California.

The Companies

The people at the companies written about in the book went beyond the call of duty in being available to us, hosting us in their cities, and always providing us with accurate information and access to company personnel. We'll always hold many fond memories of each of them.

Cabela's: Tommy Millner, CEO; Dennis Highby, former CEO; David Roehr, retired executive vice president, Cabela's and CEO of Cabela's World's Foremost Bank; Mike Callahan, senior vice president of retail and marketing; Brian Linneman, chief operating officer; Sean Baker, director of accounting; Joe Arterburn, corporate communications manager; Kellie Mowery, corporate communications assistant; Karen Kennedy, executive administrative assistant; Attorney Lyneth Rhoten, Koley Jessen P.C., Omaha, Nebraska; Greg Talamanatez, manager of Cabela's Sidney, Nebraska, store.

Dot Foods: Pat Tracy, chairman; John Tracy, CEO; Bill Metzinger, chief financial officer; Ryan Tracy, son of Pat Tracy.

Koch Industries: Charles G. Koch, CEO; David Koch, EVP; Melissa Cohlmia, director of corporate communications; Mary Beth Jarvis, communications director; Dick Anderson, director, Market Based Management; Rod Learned, internal communication director; John Pittenger, senior vice president, corporate strategy; Patti Parker, communications coordinator; Kay Spence, Charles Koch's assistant.

Medline Industries: Charlie Mills, CEO; Andy Mills, CFO; John Marks, director of corporate communications.

O'Reilly Automotive: David O'Reilly, Chairman; Greg Henslee, CEO; Tricia Headley, VP of corporate services and corporate secretary; Michele Richardson, investor relations coordinator; Jim Batten, former chief financial officer.

PETCO: Brian Devine, executive chairman; James (Jim) Myers, CEO; Bruce Hall, former president and COO; Brian Shaw, director of strategic development; Fran Lilyea and Carole Prewett, Brian Devine's assistants.

SAS Institute: Jim Goodnight, CEO; Kelly L. Ross, VP, U.S. commercial sales; Keith V. Collins, senior VP and chief technology officer; Desiree Adkins, SAS External communications; Diane Lennox, manager, third-party validation, corporate communications; Marti S. Dominick, corporate affairs program manager; Mette Bak Scheel, SAS Denmark; Pamela Meek, director of public relations.

Sonic Drive-In: Cliff Hudson, CEO; Nancy Robertson, director of corporate communications; Pattye Moore, board member, internal consultant and former president; Scott McLain, president, former CFO; Andy Ernsting, account supervisor, Barkley Evergreen Partners, Kansas City, Missouri; Terry Harryman, controller (franchisees); Buddy McClain, reigning operator of the year, Jackson, Mississippi; Chuck Harrison, largest Sonic franchisee; Karen Toepfer, Chuck Harrison's assistant; Bobby Merritt, longtime franchisee, Las Cruces, New Mexico; Barbie Stammer, former carhop and now president of Merritt's operations; Gus Morris, franchisee; Joe Zacher, multistate franchisee and former carhop for founders Troy Smith and Charlie Pappe; Ronnie Solberg, franchisee; John Winterringer, second-generation operator based in Shawnee, Oklahoma.

Strayer Education: Robert Silberman, CEO; Ron Bailey, former CEO; Michelle Wooten, training coordinator; Holly Yocum, Robert Silberman's assistant; Sonya Ulder, VP corporate communications.

The Researchers

Greg Powell and Brian Solon joined me for the initial research; when Greg left to complete his MBA, Brian stayed on board for the full two years of the project. When it came time to revise the book for the paperback edition, I turned to my colleague Laurence Haughton, who was indispensable in seeing the book through to its completion.

Our Readers

When we started the project we identified a group of eleven people with very diverse backgrounds whom we asked to serve as evaluators and readers as we made our way through the project. Their insightful thoughts and comments were exceedingly helpful and kept us on track. This group included men and women from across the country in a range of occupations: Chris Fadeff, Boston College student; Mark Thompson, former Charles Schwab VP, and currently host of *Leaders of the New Century* for Network Public Broadcasting International; David Donahue, associate dean of library and information sciences, Middlebury College; Jane Hennessy, senior vice president of Wells Fargo Bank; Chuck Adams, business consultant and former CFO, Omni Hotels; Mike Flaherty, business consultant; Mark Glickman, CPA, San Anselmo, California; Patrick Regan, retired portfolio manager who now grows grapes in Sonoma; Michael Regan, New York–based equity analyst; Joseph Hudelson, author and educator, Archbishop Mitty High School; Patrick Weston, attorney, Bingham McCutchen LLP.

But Not Least!

Special thanks to Ashley Bryan, president, Safety Organization for Schools, for aesthetic expertise and boundless patience; David Pitonyak, PhD, author of *The Importance of Belonging*; Irene Walters of the Houston Genealogy Library; George Staubli (the "there-will-be-no-excuses" guy on the project); Mark Powell of Casto Travel for coordinating all our travel arrangements; trainer Jeff Marth at the Bay Club Marin for keeping me healthy and fit; Bill Deane for keeping the laptops, computers, and handheld devices working; Lisa Knoll of Factset Research Systems; our friends at KGWN television in Cheyenne, Wyoming, for the studio tour and unexpected interview; Karen DeLise and Kat Sovyak of the Word Gallery for their exemplary work on thousands of pages of transcription. As usual, Bruce Ritter, investment counselor in San Rafael, California, was always available to help us ferret out financial information, find whatever we needed at a moment's notice, and serve as general skeptic, questioner, and helpmate.

OTHER BOOKS BY JASON JENNINGS

THE REINVENTORS

HOW EXTRAORDINARY COMPANIES PURSUE RADICAL, CONTINUOUS CHANGE

by Jason Jennings

Published by Portfolio/Penguin, an imprint of Penguin Group (USA), in 2012, *The Reinventors* answers the biggest worry for 97 percent of all CEOs and top executives—"We see the clock is ticking. . . . How do we reinvent our business model before time runs out?"

But *The Reinventors* is more than a road map for taking a company from A to B. The book changes the game, showing you how to create a new culture that reimagines, rethinks, and reinvents, so you jump past A to B and on to C, D, E and F.

Featuring scores of terrific stories that make every point easy to understand and share with others, *The Reinventors* offers new insights and strategies to help you drive change and maintain momentum:

THE EIGHT BIG DISCOVERIES
- Constant change and growth
- Letting go
- Picking the destination
- Who stays, who leads, and who goes
- Keeping everyone on the same page
- Forever frugal
- Systematizing everything
- Don't hesitate

The Reinventors is available in hardcover and e-book.

HIT THE GROUND RUNNING
THE MANUAL FOR NEW LEADERS
by Jason Jennings

This bestseller was published by Portfolio, an imprint of Penguin Group (USA), in 2009.

Hit the Ground Running identified the nine top performing *new* CEOs of the Fortune 1,000 class of 2001–2008 and created a front-row seat for you to learn as they quickly pulled together their teams, implemented the strategies, doubled revenues, and tripled earnings, making everyone proud that *they* were chosen to lead.

These gripping case studies include: The Goodrich Corporation (CEO Marshall Larsen), Allegheny Technologies (CEO L. Patrick Hassey), Mohawk Industries (CEO Jeff Lorberbaum), Questar Corporation (CEO Keith Rattie), The Hanover Group (CEO Frederick Eppinger), The J.M. Smucker Company (co-CEOs Tim and Richard Smucker), Staples (CEO Ron Sargent), Humana (CEO Michael McCallister), and Harris Corporation (CEO Howard Lance).

THE TEN RULES IN *HIT THE GROUND RUNNING*
- You will reap what you sow
- Gain belief
- Ask for help
- Find, keep, and grow the right people
- See through the fog
- Drive a stake in the ground
- Simplify everything
- Be accountable
- Cultivate a fierce sense of urgency
- Be a fish out of water

Hit the Ground Running is available in hardcover and e-book

LESS IS MORE

HOW GREAT COMPANIES USE PRODUCTIVITY
AS A COMPETITIVE TOOL IN BUSINESS

by Jason Jennings

This bestseller was the first book published by Portfolio, an imprint of Penguin Group (USA), in December 2002.

The book identifies the most productive companies on the planet based on the criteria of revenue, cash flow, return on invested capital, and return on equity per employee per year.

The companies written about in the book include: Nucor Steel, World Savings, Yellow Transportation, IKEA, Lantec (a manufacturing company in Louisville, Kentucky), SRC Holdings in Springfield, Missouri, The Warehouse (a New Zealand and Australian chain of discount stores), and Ryanair, Europe's largest discount airline.

Key Findings

FOCUS

- Productive companies all have a big objective.
- The culture is the strategy.

STREAMLINE

- Tell the truth.
- Simplify everything.
- Get rid of the wrong managers and execs fast.
- Forget mass layoffs.
- WTGBRFDT?
- Know the real financial drivers.
- Systematize everything.
- Seek continuous improvement.
- Rationalize compensation.

DIGITIZE
- The plug-in myth.
- Technology does not create a competitive advantage.

MOTIVATE
- Keep everyone on the same page.
- People are naturally motivated, so remove barriers of frustration.

EMBODY
- A lean spirit
- Leadership traits:
  - long-term focus
  - embrace simplicity
  - high moral fiber
  - humility
  - coach leadership
  - reject bureaucracy
  - believe in others; trust
  - institutionalize leadership

Less Is More is available in both hardcover and paperback editions and e-book.

IT'S NOT THE BIG THAT EAT THE SMALL . . .

IT'S THE FAST THAT EAT THE SLOW

by Jason Jennings and Laurence Haughton

Published in 2001 by HarperCollins, this bestseller identifies the fastest companies on the planet. The book's surprising big finding is that speed has nothing to do with physical speed but instead with fast thinking, fast decisions, fast to market, and the ability to maintain momentum.

The companies profiled in the book include: AOL, European fashion retailer H&M, Spanish fast-food giant TelePizza, Charles Schwab, Clear Channel Communications, Australia's Lend Lease, and Hotmail.

Key Findings

FAST THINKING

- Anticipate the future.
- Spot trends before others.
- Challenge assumptions.
- Put every idea through the grinder.
- Create an environment where the best idea wins.

FAST DECISIONS

- Create rules/principles that guide the company.
- Get rid of bureaucracy.
- Understand the value of shuffling portfolios.
- Always reassess everything.
- Measure and calculate risk.

GET TO MARKET FAST

- Launch a crusade.
- Own your competitive advantage.
- Get vendors and suppliers to operate on your timetable.
- Stay below the radar.
- Simplicity.
- Institutionalize innovation.
- Hire other fast people.

SUSTAINING SPEED

- Use narratives and stories.
- Be ruthless with resources.
- Build a scoreboard to measure activity.
- Stay financially flexible.
- Prove the math.
- Institutionalize everything.
- Stay close to the customer.

INDEX